PLANES, TRAINS, & BROKEN STRINGS

THE LAUGHABLE BUT TRUE STORY OF AN IMPOVERISHED INDIE—MUSICIAN TRAVELING THE WORLD

TOM EDWARDS

Planes, Trains, & Broken Strings

TOM EDWARDS

First edition published 2014

Cover illustrations by John K. Victor
www.johnkvictor.com

Cover deign by Vanessa Mendozzi
www.vanessamendozzidesign.com

HOWARD-HILL PUBLISHING GROUP
ISBN: 0692342389
ISBN-13: 978-0692342381

For my parents, Andy and Tracey.

DISCLAIMER

Everything you're about to read is true. I kept a journal during my travels, albeit out of sheer boredom more than forethought. Therefore, I had thorough records to consult when I pondered—*what was the name of that town where we stole plastic lawn chairs from the sex workers for our pirate campsite?* etc. That being said, some names and certain aspects of events in this book have been changed to protect involved individuals from criminal prosecution, angry girlfriends, legal liability, bears, or whatever other dangers are lying out there in wait.

A wise woman who was traveling in the mountains found a precious stone in a stream. The next day she met a fellow traveler who was hungry, and the wise woman opened her bag to share her food. The hungry traveler saw the precious stone and asked the woman to give it to him. She did so without hesitation. The traveler left, rejoicing in his good fortune. He knew the stone was worth enough to give him security for a lifetime. But a few days later he came back to return the stone to the wise woman.

"I've been thinking," he said, "I know how valuable the stone is, but I give it back in the hope that you can give me something even more precious ... Give me what you have within you that enabled you to give me the stone."

-Origin Unknown

1

ON THE ORIGINS OF MY ESCAPE
CHILLICOTHE, OHIO, USA

In the summer of 2013, I left my rural Ohio hometown for a year-long backpacking trip around the world. Two friends, Corey and Aaron, joined me. We sold most of our worldly possessions to pay for our plane tickets in advance. After purchasing the tickets, insurance, and gear we had about $4,000 to last us a year. We had all the hubris of your average twenty-something year olds, believing we'd make money on the road one way or another. I embarked on this misadventure for a couple reasons.

First, let's talk about Samantha. That's not her real name, but it's a lot more neutral than other pseudonyms I gave her during the salty year following our breakup. She and I dated for about a year. She had two kids, a son and a daughter, whose fathers weren't in the picture. I was as immature as they come when we met and the thought of such a serious commitment terrified me. But I was so quickly smitten by her charm, sense of humor, and beauty that I figured I'd give it the old college try. As time passed I fell in love with the kids too and became a stand-in dad to some degree. For the first time in my life I felt the real prospect of settling down and building a future with someone. I felt an earthy sense of purpose, enchanted by the mysterious existential wonder of watching miniature human beings experience life's comedies and tragedies for the first time. So when Samantha cheated on me, it was kind of a stick in the metaphorical bicycle spokes.

I took a month off work and traveled the American West in a van and pop-up camper with a few friends (one of whom you'll get to know well throughout the pages of this book). When I returned home, there was a newfound pep in my step. I finished projects around the house that had lain dormant for months or years. I exercised. I started the process of taking on an ownership role at the third-party Verizon Wireless franchise where I worked, potentially opening a store of my own with financial backing from the owner. Then Samantha called.

Within a couple of weeks, we were back together. There were the usual apologies and resentments that come with patching up an unfaithful relationship, but we really hit a stride in the months that followed. We began building our life together and I explored the idea of moving out of the small house I'd built so I could move into a larger home with her and the kids.

Then, a few months later, she cheated on me again. I know, I know. My friends and family said the same thing. But something I've learned in the years since is that you can't talk someone out of such a situationship. The only prescription is for the patient to step on the rake a few more times until it smarts enough to take a step back and consider a different approach.

Smarting well enough this time, I sunk into something I wouldn't quite call a depression—because if you would have asked me at the time, I would have told you I was having a blast. I drank, I slept around, I chain-smoked cigarettes.

So to recap, one reason for leaving was recover from a breakup. Another reason was my career. "Work" is a generous term for the three years I spent in sales at the cell phone store. I'd meandered through a number of vocations since entering the workforce: slinging drinks and plates at Golden Corral, rough framing houses as a carpenter, tech support at a call center, cart tech at a golf course, and even a stint during high school as a "ceiling maintenance specialist." That last one was sort of a Subway Sandwich Artist title, by the way. Ceiling Maintenance Specialist *really* meant I earned seven fifty an hour to scrub acoustical tile ceilings with a sponge attached to a long pole. My boss was a gentle backwoods fellow named Bill. Bill wore white coveralls over his camouflage and sprayed the ceilings with a heinous chemical concoction that bleached the collars of all my shirts. I followed behind him with my specialist sponge-stick in a set of my own coveralls. One time, after my daily bout of wheezing and hacking, I asked if we should be wearing masks. Bill scoffed, then shouldered his Ghostbusters-style blaster pack and spewed another fine mist of carcinogens into the air.

In contrast, much of my time at the cell phone store was spent goofing off with coworkers, browsing the Internet, or trying to convince customers that Android phones were better than the iPhone (Verizon couldn't sell iPhones at the time).

One such snoozy afternoon I found a website called The Runaway Guide by Lief Haerem which showed all kinds of cooky travel tips: How to illegally cross a border. How to hitchhike. How to hop trains. How to find food in dumpsters. It planted a seed in my brain: Maybe I could go on a *real* adventure. I didn't need a bunch of money saved. I didn't need an itinerary. I could make it up as I go, scrounging food and skipping around on trains and cargo ships. I would answer to no one.

On the other hand, did I mention how cushy my day job was? And that I was on the cusp of inheriting my own store? For a twenty-three year old with no college degree and no other realistic prospects, it was a hard opportunity to shrug off. I had made it a mere two years in my only learned trade, carpentry, before swearing it off. (I'd discovered the seventy-something-year-old guy I roofed with was only in his early fifties.) I was a decent enough musician that I made some cash gigging at local bars and restaurants on the odd weekend, but I harbored no illusions that I was going to be the next Paul Simon. Art Garfunkel maybe, but even that was a stretch. After a few months of vacillating, I decided I'd be a fool to pass up the opportunity in front of me. I shut out my daydreams and focused on the task in front of me.

A career at a cell phone store had its challenges though, even despite the lack of physical labor. I learned a lot of things working for "the man." The most glaring of which was the cancerous futility of boardroom-borne strategies in the real world. Once per quarter our regional sales rep Trey would come in for a visit to grace us with the latest wisdom from up-top. One visit in particular was a watershed moment that led to the crumbling ruin of the entire franchise—and my aspirations as a humble cell phone shopkeeper.

We had a colorful cast of regulars in our store. One of my favorites was a grumpy old farmer named Herschel who came in to pay his bill with a hand-written check each month. At the time, Verizon allowed customers to renew their contract every two years in exchange for a discount toward a new phone. This man had been sitting on a phone upgrade since people were communicating through telegraph lines. We brought up the upgrade every so often and he would unholster his trusty old flip phone from a hip-mounted leather pouch and tell me it would outlive us all.

Trey had just said to me and my boss Lubo, "There's no reason you can't sell a smartphone to every single person who walks through this door," when Herschel sauntered through the door and pulled the checkbook and a Bic pen out of his dust-powdered denim overalls. I pulled up his account from memory to process the payment and was met with the usual red banner signifying the phone upgrade. Trey noticed the banner and zipped across the room like moth to flame. He pointed to it. I nodded and shrugged. He frowned and then turned to Herschel. "You know, you could get a new phone today."

He kept writing the check without looking up. "I know it. They tell me ever' time I come in here. I ain't interested."

Trey pulled out his phone. "Have you seen the new Droid?"

"The what now?"

"It's a smartphone. It has all kinds of cool apps."

Herschel stared at him.

"Look," Trey said, pulling up the Zippo lighter app. He tapped the screen and the lighter flipped open, showing the flame.

"The hell am I supposed to do with that?"

"Well there're all kinds of apps on here. You can do your banking, you can get weather forecasts ..." he gestured toward me, "hasn't he told you about any of these?"

Herschel turned to me. "Who the fuck is this asshole?"

I shrugged. "Oh, that's Trey. He's from corporate."

Trey lost the battle, but was determined to win the war. He left unperturbed by all the evidence before his eyes, convinced Droids would one day achieve ubiquity among the rural population of Chillicothe, Ohio.

Trey's unreasonable directive was a tinderbox, and the match that lit the whole thing aflame was my boss Lubo's insatiable search for a good scam. Trey's perfectly ironed slacks had just swished through the exit when Lubo began to craft his *magnum opus*.

Here's how a typical third-party cell phone store operated: the store would buy cell phones at a cost near full retail. When they sold the phone and signed a customer to a two-year contract they received a commission which covered the cost of the phone plus enough to make a profit. The commission was based on whether the customer signed up with a smartphone or a dumbphone.

"Here's what you're going to do moving forward," Lubo told me and my coworker. "Every time a customer buys a dumbphone, you come in the back and write down the serial number from a smartphone. Take that in the front and process the phone upgrade with it. Then after it goes through, just swap it to the dumb phone." This would trick the system into issuing a smartphone commission of seven or eight hundred dollars on a dumbphone he probably paid thirty bucks for.

"You want us to do that with every single dumbphone?" I asked.

"Yes. I'll give you twenty bucks extra commission for it."

My coworker Matt chuckled. "You goddamn greasy motherfucker. First of all, that's brilliant. I'll give you that. But don't you think someone is going to get suspicious that all the sudden every single phone we cell is a smartphone?"

"No, it'll be fine," he said. "You heard Travis. That's exactly what he wants."

We stood in silence for a moment.

"All right fine," Lubo said. "Let's call it twenty-five bucks extra commission."

A few months later I received a call from the franchise owner. He didn't get into specifics, other than to say my new store wasn't going to happen. I sped into work to talk to Lubo. When I walked in the back door he was seated at our break table. In front of him were several leather bank slips bursting with cash. Matt was pacing around the opposite side of the room. "Goddamn greasy motherfucker..."

"I think I can weather this," Lubo said. "I think I've saved back enough to cover the fines."

"Well that's something," I said.

"I can only afford to keep one of you though."

I could still hear the profanity from Matt as I stepped out the back door.

Sitting in my car a moment later I felt a strange euphoria. In a few short months, I'd lost my girlfriend and my job. But I'd gained a whole world of possibilities. I had nothing left to lose.

• • •

Corey and I had been close friends for years. He's one of the most easygoing, friendly people I know, and we'd traveled well together on the trip out west in the pop-up camper. When I played music at restaurants and bars, he often accompanied on the cajon—a small box-shaped drum that produced a kick and snare type of sound—and other various percussion. I approached him about joining me on some kind of international backpacking trip and he expressed immediate interest despite one hiccup: he was in a relationship with a woman named Katie, and things had gotten pretty serious. Similar to my own recent entanglement, she had two children and despite his initial hesitation (if there was anyone more immature than me at the time, maybe it was him) he'd stepped in as a father figure to them. Stepping away for an entire year was a huge deal to all involved and he needed to feel out the situation and see what could be possible.

While Corey was wrestling with his decision, I began obsessing over the trip. It was March and I knew I would have to leave as quickly as possible or I'd find a way to chicken out. June or July seemed long enough of a runway to work out as many details as possible, gather gear, and save some cash without waiting so long that life would find a way to derail the whole thing. Instead of looking for a new job, I called as many venues as I could to book gigs. After a couple weeks of frantic phone calls, I ended up with two to four shows per week making enough income to keep the bills paid and start setting some back for the trip. All the while, I became that annoying friend who wouldn't shut up about their upcoming trip.

As a young man fresh off a breakup, the world spun around my circle of friends. Almost every Sunday groups of us would take our kayaks out to the local creek and spend most of the day floating, drinking, and finally congregating on a small island to burn through the last bit of daylight. Aaron was a constant fixture on the creek. His childhood home was along the shoreline, and we all took out our kayaks and stored them there for the next Sunday-Funday. He was generally viewed as our resident guide. He was always there to start a fire and grill some food, fish someone's tipped kayak out of a tough spot, or provide extra tackle to fish for smallmouth bass. His yellow lab Fisher was always at his side, panting in good humor in his canoe or kayak. It was on one such Sunday afternoon, as I was drifting-off a hangover from the night before, that Aaron expressed interest in joining me and Corey.

"I've been thinking about it a bit," he said before flicking the ash from his cigarette into the muddy water. "If you guys have room for one more, I'd like to join."

I was taken aback. Aaron was a friendly enough guy, but he was more of an acquaintance than a close friend. That said, I knew he was a self-reliant and capable traveler. He'd spent weeks traveling with Fisher around the west, camping most of the way.

"We have all the room in the world," I said. "No pun intended. But you know what we're planning, right? Kind of making money as we go, figuring it out along the way?"

"Yeah, Corey's told me some. I figure I ain't got much to offer as far as making money along the way, but I've got a bit saved back. Maybe it'll all come out in the wash."

Aaron's family owned a landscaping company and he helped manage and work it. He explained he could pick up some additional landscaping work on the side and bank it all for the trip.

That's about all the negotiation it took. We spent the rest of the float talking about all of the possibilities, the what-ifs, and the potential barriers. By the time we were pulling our kayaks out of the creek that night, under the sing-song of bullfrogs and crickets, he was in one-hundred percent.

Corey secured his position shortly after. He and Katie came to an agreement. This was a once in a lifetime opportunity of course, and she saw the value in Corey sewing his wild oats (*sans* any wild mares) before settling down. Her only stipulation was that he return within a few months. Aaron and I expected to spend about a year traveling; Corey would return after five or six months.

We sold everything that wasn't nailed down. My prized Taylor guitar, the pop-up camper we'd taken out west, countless bits and bobs. We added destinations to our itinerary like ordering sushi for the table. Spain, because a friend at a bar told me how beautiful the women were. Germany because I always wanted to go to Germany. France and Switzerland were natural choices, being situated between the two. *What if we headed down to Italy after that?* Then to Thailand, *that would be wild.* Island-hop through Malaysia and Indonesia and then catch a boat to Australia, where a friend of Corey and mine lived. *Wonder if the travel agency would let us take a two-week layover in New Zealand on the way back to the U.S.?* They did. We booked tickets from New York to Barcelona, from Rome to Bangkok, from Perth to Auckland, and from Auckland to Los Angeles. The trails between each city were to be trekked at our whim and fancy.

We purchased these tickets with a huge chunk of the money we'd saved. Afterward we began buying and assembling gear: backpacks, hammocks, sleeping bags, water carriers, cooking equipment and utensils, cameras and audio recording equipment, computers. We purchased traveler's insurance and made arrangements for a long absence. A pair of friends would look after the house I'd built on my parents' property. My dad took "rented" my truck in exchange for taking over payments and insurance while I was away. We threw a "fundraiser" party with local bands and gathered some last-minute cash for the coffers. And then we met at Aaron's house to organize our packs and pool all of our money together.

The three of us sipped crispy Budweisers as we measured our net worth. There was about $4,000 total to last us a year of traveling. Now, I know what you're thinking. We were a touch naive, to put it politely. But, we had a plan! The brilliant scheme was as follows.

I would create a website where we would catalog our journeys. This website would be called "Artists Abroad," and it would bring untold riches. Who had thought of blogging their travels on the Internet before? No one, that's who. We would get cash sponsorships or free hotel stays using the inevitable clout that would come from sharing our adventures with the world. I had invented something completely original and groundbreaking. Maybe I would call it, "travel blogging." *Yes*, the website I'd managed to paste together with untold hours of clacking and cursing at my computer looked like it was designed with a Crayola calculator. But no matter. Our premise was so unique that people would shrug off the ratty exterior and blast wads of cash in our general direction with t-shirt cannons.

Second, Corey and I would play music along the way. Either through busking (playing on the street for tips) or booking shows at bars and restaurants.

Third, Aaron would take pictures. Question mark, question mark, profit.

Thus the groundwork was laid for a yearlong jaunt of merry adventures. I dreamed of heady midnights in European cities, whisking off with fair French maidens and glugging Italian wine. Zipping in speedboats across Pacific Island chains. Motoring over the Australian outback in Land Rovers and doing—I don't know—something or other in New Zealand (I knew fuck all about New Zealand).

In late July we bade goodbye to friends and family with teary eyes. We were finally on the road, Kerouac's three dim-witted godchildren, bursting free into the great blue yonder.

2

FROM NYC TO THE INOUT HOSTEL
NEW YORK CITY, USA & BARCELONA, SPAIN

June 23rd

Our first flight departed JFK airport in New York. To catch it, my cousin Blake and his girlfriend Ali volunteered to drive us in their minivan and spend a week in New York City with us before we headed across the Atlantic.

Like the three of us, Blake and Ali were partiers. The drive to New York concluded with beer cans rattling out of the van as we jumped from seedy motel to seedy motel. Eventually we lucked out on an apartment rental (basically an AirBnB before AirBnB was a thing) and had a wonderful time exploring the Natural History Museum, hiking Central Park, and gorging ourselves on Brooklyn pizza.

This short stopover was my first taste of humble pie. I tried carrying my backpack and guitar during our hikes around Central Park to start getting in shape. Better late than never, right? I was soon heaving and gasping. I watched cash slip through the cracks of Manhattan parking garages, fare counters in taxis, and one or two g-strings at a grungy strip joint we landed in one night. Fortunately my cousin refused to let us pay for anything during the whole week, but by the time we were hugging goodbye in front of the terminal, I began to wonder if we'd gotten in over our heads. It was too late to turn back, though. Thinking of the shame and embarrassment I'd feel sauntering back into my hometown with my tail tucked was too much to bear.

• • •

Hours later we were standing outside of a train station, staring up at a steep hill. According to notes scribbled in my small journal, its path wound to our first hostel in Barcelona, Spain. None of us had slept on the flight and our first go at navigating foreign public transportation with heavy backpacks had wicked away what little energy we had remaining.

"Jesus, look at this thing," I said.

"Yeah," Corey said. "But there are beds and a shower at the top."

"And a cold cerveza," Aaron said.

We heaved and grunted our way up the long slope.

INOUT Hostel was perched at the end of the road on the mountaintop. There weren't any other buildings or residences, save one small cafe next door. We walked inside to the check-in and I approached the counter.

"Hello, I made a reservation online."

"Que?"

Goddamn it. That's right.

"Umm, habla Englais?"

"Mmm, no."

"Ummm …" I pointed to the computer: "*Reserva … tioné?*" I guessed.

The receptionist seemed to understand, handing me a form to fill out and asking for our "*pass-a-portas.*"

After I handed it back to her, she said "*Dos*," and pointed to the clock on the wall. It was eleven.

"We can't check in until two?"

Goddamn it.

One of the other guests directed us to the cafe we'd seen, which, as it turned out, was also a twenty-four-hour bar, owned by the hostel. We were all famished, so we decided to wait for our room there and get some food. We also hadn't filled up any water bottles since we'd stepped off the plane. We made the short walk to the cafe with our packs and I approached the counter.

"Agua and ... *el* ... *pizza* ... *tioné?*"

We were really going to have to work on our Spanish.

Aaron and I attempted to take a nap on a nearby bench, but were awoken by a group of schoolchildren who filed into the cafe patio for lunch. I was annoyed until I heard the toddlers all talking in Spanish, which was utterly adorable.

The Spanish spoken in Spain is different from the Latin American Spanish that North Americans are used to hearing. To my uncultured ears it sounded like the group was speaking Italian until Aaron corrected me. The two languages are so similar that in many cases an Italian person and a Spanish person can converse in their native tongues and understand one another.

I got out my guitar and played a song for the children. I was surprised to see a five- or six-year-old girl act as translator for the group. The teacher herself spoke little English, but this kid could speak fluently in English and Spanish. I felt like the six-year-old me must have been a useless moron in comparison.

I played a few more songs and then rejoined Aaron and Corey at a table in the cafe.

At two in the afternoon we made our way back down to the lobby. There was a man behind the counter this time who spoke some English:

"Sorry, still no clean. Come back at four o'clock."

We felt we couldn't go any longer without sleep, so we trotted off into the woods to pitch our hammocks. Once there we decided we'd only pay for one bed and just take turns rotating between it and the woods. The main benefit of having a room in the hostel would be access to the showers. Once nestled in our nylon hammocks, we quickly fell asleep.

We didn't wake until around seven in the evening. That nap was absolute bliss. Waking up to the cool evening breeze and the sounds of Spanish birds chattering away to each other through the trees … this was when it dawned on me that I was in a different country. I'd been too sleep-deprived to recognize the novelty until that moment.

I could hear children laughing and playing, scooters and small diesel-powered cars puttering on the far-off roadway. I was an absolute stranger to everything and everyone in the most perfect way. There were no bills to worry about, no bosses, and no responsibilities. I'd never felt more alive.

• • •

Later in the evening we wandered back to the bar and cafe. After two or three *cervezas*, I pulled out my guitar and started to play.

A group of hostel guests were partying at a nearby table and upon seeing the guitar, invited us over. There was Roddy, the tattooed Scotsman, Braveheart accent included, drinking gin and shouting curse words. Then there was Lisa, a young Scottish woman with brown hair and aviator sunglasses, which I seem to remember her wearing even at night. Arnej (or "Slovenia" as we called him, an obvious ode to his country of origin) had a thick accent similar to a Bond movie villain. He was bald and probably in his thirties. There were two artsy Canadian sisters, Karen and Christina, Will from California, Charles from the UK, the easygoing US Marine named Stone, and Carlos, who was a native Barcelonian. Last but not least was the Australian, Damian, or "Damo." At well over six feet tall with a voice that carried across the property, Damo was larger than life. He was the one who had invited me over to their table.

I stayed up drinking with this ragtag crew well into the night on that first evening. Aaron and Corey went to their hammocks pretty early, exhausted from the day's events. I stumbled into our dorm room around four when the manager came out and told us to leave because we were being too loud.

The next night, things really started getting out of hand. As with the first night, we started off with music and cheap beer. Aaron went to bed early again, but Corey was drinking with all of us on the patio.

"Let's play flip or lick!" Damo said.

"What the hell is that?" I asked.

"It's this awesome game that Charles taught us the other noight," he said in his thick Australian accent. "You take a coin, roight? Then you pick someone else at the table. They pick heads or tails and then you flip. Whoeva wins the coin toss takes a drink. Then they tell the loser what they have to lick. If the person *refuses* to lick, they have to chug a drink. Not the rest of their drink, but a full drink. Whoever loses the coin toss gets the coin and picks someone else."

Around this time, some new people joined the table. Within moments of their arrival it became clear that they were not going to fit in with the established group.

I don't remember most of their names so we will refer to them as "BritishGirl," "BritishGuy," and the star of the night's show, another American who everyone called "Nebraska." (Since, I assume, that's the state from which he hailed.)

Nebraska was a talker. A talker and a drinker. Not a good talker or drinker, though. He was one of those kids who probably got made fun of a little too much in high school and felt like he was proving something in his later years by imbibing to excess and wearing his hat backwards. Picture fingerless gloves.

American backpackers have a deserved stereotype, I'm ashamed to admit. Many of us are loud, attention-seeking, and self-important. Nebraska fit this persona to the letter.

Damo did not like Nebraska. I think it's a fair assumption that *none* of us liked *any* of the new arrivals, but Damo really did not like Nebraska. So at the behest of our Australian friend, Nebraska was picked each time any of us got the coin.

We made him lick the floor. Door handles. Trash can lids. Slovenia's head. Damo even made him lick a stranger who was sitting on the other side of the cafe. Lisa made him lick a hostel employee who spoke no English.

I won a coin toss with him and made him lick BritishGuy's ass (the cheek, not the acorn).

BritishGirl picked me when she got the coin, but I won the toss.

"I want you to dig a beer bottle from the very bottom of the trash can and lick it," I said.

"Are you fucking kidding me dude?!" She protested.

I thought that was pretty tame compared to some of the other targets we'd seen so far, but I relented. "Fine, fine … just lick, uhhh, one of the coffee cups on the table over there."

Because I'd clearly struck a nerve she picked me again, and this time won the coin toss. "I want you to lick that ashtray," she said.

I was annoyed, but I didn't dare show it. I shrugged. "Whatever, hand it to me." I grabbed the ashtray and licked a layer of cigarette ashes off the top, realizing immediately that I should have accepted the social shame of having to chug a drink instead. I coughed and a cloud of bluish-gray ash erupted before me, triggering cacophonous laughter from the group. My mouth was blanketed in wet cigarette ash. I choked and spat. I sloshed beer around and spat some more.

Damo handed me a cigarette. "Here mate, take a shitty Egyptian cigarette. I got a whole carton of these for seven dollas in Cairo. They're the worst fucking things eva."

Hair of the dog, I suppose. They somehow helped remove the shitty taste from my mouth.

By this point in the evening, despite never once opting for a drink instead of a lick, Nebraska had consumed a prodigious amount of whiskey. He had been picked by our "team" the entire night except for only a handful of times. Once again he found himself with the coin.

"I pick the Scottish dude!" he slurred while pointing at Roddy. Nebraska lost the coin toss.

Roddy stared him down silently for a moment. The table patiently awaited his verdict. "I want you to lick the fackin toilet."

"*OHHHHH! AHHHHH! YES! YES!*" Damo shouted, already

pulling out his phone to record a video.

Nebraska could have opted to chug a drink instead and no one would have objected. However, I don't think the thought even crossed his mind. He began moving for the bathrooms without hesitation. Never underestimate the power of peer pressure.

The group followed him into the bathroom, drinks and cell phones in hand. The hostel employees watched with raised eyebrows.

We all stood in a circle and prepared to watch Nebraska perform cunnilingus on a dirty shitter. "This is going to be fucking awesome," Damo commented as he held up his cell phone.

Here's where Nebraska really blew my mind. First of all, he licked the rim—where all of the pee splatters—not the seat. On top of that, he licked a good twenty inches of porcelain. He could have just touched his tongue to the lid. *Them's the rules*. But no, he dragged that abominable slug halfway around the thing.

"*OHHHHH!*" everyone screamed. He wretched. We wretched. We poured outside in a stumbling gaggle of laughter and dry-heaves.

"That's it, game ova guys," Damo exclaimed, "there's no fucking way this could get any better than that. Fucking awesome."

At the end of the evening Roddy led the group in a Proclaimers song: "*Well I would walk five hundred miles, and I would walk five hundred more ...*" which was hilarious with his accent.

It was during this group *a cappella* that the bar staff once again came outside:

"No more *fiesta*! You go sleep. Leave now or we call *policia*!"

We had successfully closed down the "twenty-four-hour" bar two nights in a row.

3

PLATJA DE NUDISTA
BEGUR, SPAIN

July 7th

After several nights in INOUT Hostel and one in a hostel in downtown Barcelona, we plotted a course toward France. Carlos (the native Spaniard in our group at the hostel) told us about a beach in the north of Spain called Begur. "It is the most beautiful beach in all of Spain and it is not very well known. You will be able to camp there as long as you like."

After a series of confusing train connections and a bus ride of several hours, we stepped off the stop in Begur. We were confused: Carlos had described a forgotten beach, but the scene before us was a hilly, sprawling metropolis.

Aaron sighed. "Well, guess we should try to find some WiFi and pull up a map."

We walked down the hill in front of us and made it to a group of signs, each of them directing traffic to different beaches. We couldn't find any WiFi. We picked one of the signs at random and after a quick snack of bread and salami, we started walking. We stuck to the roads, walking on sidewalks when they were available. Eventually the signs took us out of town and curved into a canyon filled with houses—like suburbs clinging to a mountainside. We followed the endless switchbacks, hiking all the way down into the canyon until the road pitched back up. Walk, walk, walk … back down and then up once more.

This time Aaron was the one not handling the hike well—he was complaining most of the way. I don't blame him; it was a brutal slog. We took repeated breaks to take the load off of our backs. Eventually, we saw the road curve downward steeply. Corey rounded the bend first and saw a stone staircase leading down to a beach.

"FUCKING FINALLY."

We all made our way down the steps and collapsed onto the sand. A quick look around told us that the "remote" aspect of these beaches was utterly false. There were a lot of buildings down one direction and the other looked to be rocks. We were exhausted after the hike and decided to find a place to crash for the night and then get our bearings in the morning. Aaron went on a quick scouting mission and came back to lead us to some rocks, where we rigged up our hammocks.

• • •

Early the next morning, we stowed our hammocks and began exploring the area. A narrow trail threaded sandstone boulders around a sheer cliff. We filed into line one behind the other and hiked up it, hoping we could find a secluded area to spend a day or two and relax on the beach. As we approached the trail's apex around the cliff-edge we began hearing voices. The vista opened to a small cove. We hopped down ledges and held onto the sandstone walls for support as we followed the trail to the sandy beach inside the cove. What we saw at the bottom caused a collective gasp.

The beach was littered with gaggles of beautiful, young naked women. Lounging, reading, chatting, taking a dip. All with their breasts laid bare to dance across our retinas, each nipple releasing a jolt of dopamine. In the mere split-second snap of a bra strap I was prepared to denounce my American citizenship and swear allegiance to Spain. There was a large spray-painted message across the rocks which read, *Platja de nudista*.

Once we'd seen enough nudity to send an Amish teenager into terminal shock, we wandered to the other side of the cove, away from most of the people. We spotted a cave among the cliffs. It was too small to sleep in, but we were able to pitch our hammocks by securing them to crags in the rock wall. It was a precarious anchor, and Aaron's hammock fell multiple times during setup, at one point burying him under a miniature avalanche of stones.

As the sun's rays dulled to an orange hum, hordes of mosquitos began swarming our campsite. We started a smoky fire, but it did no good. I looked across the beach and saw the only remaining people left: a guy and two girls who looked to be in their twenties. Because we were camped in the paradise of this *platja de nudista*, they were naked as jaybirds. I walked over to them.

"*Habla Englais?*"

"Yes, we all speak English," the guy answered.

"I was just wondering if you guys have some bug spray we can use?"

"No, no spray," one of the girls said. "We made some candles, though. It is citronella plant with lemon and orange. You burn and the bugs leave."

"Ahh, that's great, thanks!"

I noticed a guitar and some percussion instruments. "You play?"

"*Sí*, we play!"

They introduced themselves. The guy's name was Krishna, from Catalonia. The dark-haired girl was Stella, from Greece, and the blonde girl was Mari, from Finland.

"We're cooking some dinner if you'd like to join us," I said.

Stella smiled. "Okay, we maybe come over."

I returned to camp and described the interaction to Corey and Aaron. Something like, "*smokkkkkin hot, dude, and titties just …*

right ... there. In my face and shit."

Later in the evening our three neighbors put some clothes on and came over to join us by the fire. We played music together late into the night. They performed a rhythmic Portuguese song in which both of the girls sang while one played guitar and the other a small drum with tambourines. We got some video footage of the song and later put it on our website. Krishna shared some chickpeas with us and made fun of our eating habits after we asked him why we couldn't find peanut butter anywhere:

"You Americans; you are obsessed with peanut butter. Peanut butter and baked beans!"

I laughed. "Well, I love both of those things and so do most of the people I know, so I think that must be a true stereotype."

After midnight they retired to their section of the beach and we settled into our hammocks. We had never established if the guy was dating one, or maybe both of the girls. I berated myself for not making any kind of move. I contemplated masturbating in the hammock. I went on to imagine the boulders above me breaking loose from the movement and shuddered at the thought of my mother getting the news: *"Your son was killed jacking off in a hammock. Bunch of boulders came off a cliff and squished him with his pecker still in his hand. The doctors aren't sure whether he died instantly or if he was able to ejaculate first."*

• • •

I woke the next morning and walked a few yards onto the beach, past the shadow of the cliffs and into the warm morning sunshine. I sat in the sand and marveled at the glistening Mediterranean Sea nestled in our rocky cove. There were magnificent rock formations jutting out of the dark blue water in the bay onto which people were clambering. They jumped to the water one at a time or in groups, laughing. Some lounged on the rocks, others on the sand of the beach. Sandy cliffs enclosed the cove like a giant stone catcher's mitt cupping the water.

Stella, Mari, and Krishna were awake and lying in the sun, nude.

To my right, Corey and Aaron packed up their sleeping gear. I looked back at the sea. I stripped off all my clothes and walked down to the water. I jumped in and swam out until I was treading the water. The uninterrupted coolness against my naked skin instilled a sense of raw, primal freedom. I swam for a short while and then walked back up the beach and sat in the sand next to my clothes. I looked over at Stella and she flashed a friendly smile.

I smiled back at her and then closed my eyes and laid back in the sand with my arms outstretched, soaking in the Mediterranean sun.

4

A SHORT AND UNPLEASANT STAY
CERBÈR, FRANCE

July 9th

We took a train from Begur to Cerbère, France, which is right across the border. From there we planned to hitchhike to Paris. My first impression of a French town was a positive one.

Cerbère is a quaint village nestled around a small inlet along the coast. It's surrounded by hills and relatively secluded. Narrow streets spiderweb between quiet residential neighborhoods, interrupted by the occasional diesel-powered car or scooter.

The catacomb-like city planning presented a problem for hitchhiking, as we couldn't tell which roads led out of town, let alone which were headed in the right direction. After a brief discussion, we decided to stay for the night and take a train the following day to Montpellier.

We looked around for somewhere to camp, but despite its small footprint, Cerbère was packed with buildings. An argument ensued during which I voted to pay for a hotel room where we could use WiFi and get a shower. Aaron didn't want to spend the money; Corey wouldn't take sides either way. Eventually Aaron relented after I pushed the issue of being able to research the next few cities.

Nestled into our cozy hotel room a few hours later, research showed an outdoors store in Montpellier where we could buy fuel for our backpacking stove. The city would be a more suitable location to start hitchhiking north toward Paris as well.

· · ·

The following day, we were waiting at the train station to head toward Montpellier. We wandered outside to smoke and noticed a baby stroller next to a group of dumpsters. It was probably covered in every bacterium known to human existence and looked like a relic from the war. The only thing convincing me that it was less than a hundred years old was the large *Hello Kitty* logo printed across its faded pink fabric.

"There ya go, dude," Aaron said, "carry your backpack in that thing."

I guess I'd been complaining about my heavy backpack more than I'd realized. I laughed. And then I seriously considered it. And then I thought to myself, *how ridiculous would that be, come on dude.* And then I pulled it out of the dumpster and sat my pack in it. It would only fit in the thing sideways, since, of course, it was designed to carry a small child.

"Hmm. Perfect."

Our fellow passengers watched with bemused curiosity as I boarded the train with the hot pink *Hello Kitty* stroller and folded it neatly into the storage compartment.

Once we arrived at Montpellier, we grabbed some WiFi at a Mc-Donald's outside the train station and pulled up a map to find the outdoors store. Aaron volunteered to get the fuel while Corey and I remained at the city center to play some music for tips.

We placed a sign in the guitar case with a message scrawled in broken French. Something like, *We are poor. Please help.* We played for only a few minutes before a ruddy-cheeked manager blew through the doors of the McDonald's and told us in no certain terms to get lost.

Not one to argue with the reasoning of corporate policies, we moved farther down the street to an area in front of the train station and set up shop again. So far no one had given us any money.

We kept smiling; we kept playing. Minutes turned into an hour. We began to get frustrated.

"You have to be fucking kidding me," I said. "Not one cent?"

We continued to pour our hearts out. Not only were people not tipping us, they were also giving us rude stares as they passed. Some would even go out of their way to bump into us.

Finally, we gave up. I started singing a song directed at the caravan of cunts streaming out of the train station:

"Fuck the French, fuck the French, they are all a bunch of dicks, they are cocks, they are cocks, they are all a bunch of frogs, etc."

Aaron returned as this was happening and chuckled. "What the hell's going on?"

Corey was taking the cajon apart. "Fuck all of these assholes."

"We didn't make one cent. Not one penny," I said.

"Not anything?"

"Nothing."

We packed our things and sat on the side of the McDonald's building—out of sight of the woman who'd kicked us out earlier. Aaron's experience hadn't been any more enjoyable than our time busking. We decided rather spontaneously as a group to say fuck Paris and fuck France.

We couldn't find any hostels nearby on Google Maps and nobody wanted to sleep in the park across the street considering how we'd been treated thus far.

I found a hotel nearby for fifty euros, but there was a catch: it was fifty euros for two people, not three. We formulated a plan:

Aaron was to wait outside, around the corner of the hotel, while Corey and I went in. We would pay for the room and come back for him after. The hardest part of this maneuver would be getting him past the front desk. Keep in mind that this is not a big chain hotel like we have in the states, but an old stone apartment building of sorts. There was only one way in and one way out, and maybe ten rooms in total.

To keep from attracting more attention, we wanted Aaron to come in without his backpack. This way, if he was spotted, we could tell them he was staying at another hotel and visiting us.

This, however, required Corey and me to bring his pack in along with us. Lest the reader forget, I was still wheeling my pack around in a bright pink, grime-covered *Hello Kitty* stroller.

I shouldered Aaron's pack while wheeling my own in the stroller. Corey and I walked through the old wooden door and approached the front desk. A mustachioed Frenchman slithered from an adjacent office and greeted us with the warmth and eagerness of a prostate exam.

"*Bonjour.*"

"*Parlez-vous Anglais?*"

"*Qui.*"

"We need a room for two." I handed him my passport.

"Two?" he asked, eyeing the third backpack seated comfortably in the Hello Kitty stroller.

"Yes, two."

"Two … no three?" His eyebrow raised.

"*Qui*, two."

"You are sure?—two?" He looked at the third backpack again and then back at me.

"Two."

He squinted his eyes and nodded his head and then produced some paperwork. He showed us a sheet with the printed price of fifty euros as had been advertised, crossed it out with a pen and wrote sixty next to it. "Your price, *monsieur.*"

Whatever. I handed him the money and we made our way to the room. Later Aaron managed to sneak in unnoticed and we tackled the politics of sleeping arrangements for three in a room for two. Aaron lost the coin toss, which meant Corey and I got the bed. After a fruitless consideration of alternatives, he strung his hammock between the front door and the bathroom door. The janky setup worked—however it required him to float overtop of Corey and me while we listened to both of the door frames squeak and groan as if the hinges which held Aaron's weight would explode at any moment.

Corey and I lay on the bed warily while he hovered over us. It was quiet for a second while we all waited for the door frames to come crashing in. Then a loud *pffffffft* sound erupted from the hammock above us. Aaron started laughing.

"Did you crop-dust us from a hammock?" Corey asked, laughing.

5
RiDiNG iN CARS WiTH SWiSS DRUG DEALERS
MONTREAX, SWiTZERLAND

July 12th

We spent more precious euros on a train to Montreux. The plan was to start hitchhiking from here. Before then, however, we still needed to gather some more supplies. We figured we would camp highway-side for a few days while we hopped rides, so we needed a stable supply of food. We also wanted to do some laundry. I had finally abandoned the ludicrous *Hello Kitty* stroller in Geneva earlier that day and it seemed like a good idea to scrub away any microscopic pets I might have adopted from it.

Google Maps showed a spot just north of the city that looked campable. The hike from the train station up and out of the city was strenuous. Montreux sits directly on a mountainside, or more appropriately, a cliff side. The hike was well worth it. When we neared the quiet mountain town's summit, moving among its traditional European stone buildings and cobblestone streets, we stopped at a wooden bridge to watch the sunset. A stream gushed beneath us toward Lake Geneva, far below. The lake hugged the far mountains, a rippling mercurial blanket with a lance of fading sunlight shimmering across its middle. It was a backdrop worthy of Theroux's deepest retrospections—or at least a few Instagram influencer photos.

We followed a hiking trail up and out of town. Just a few dozen yards past the uppermost structures, the path dodged a raised platform of rock and soil about eight feet high. We scampered onto the ledge and decided to pitch our hammocks there. We could hear a waterfall thundering nearby.

We woke up shivering in the early morning hours, realizing once again that we were woefully unprepared. It turns out the Alps get, uh, pretty cold. Who knew? We spent several days in Montreux preparing for our hitchhiking journey (or perhaps putting it off out of nervousness). Corey did our laundry in the river after being chased out of a laundromat by an angry Frenchwoman; Aaron and I did some computer work in town before being chased away from a café by an angry Frenchwoman; and we somehow managed to avoid detection in our trail-side den without upsetting any angry Frenchwomen. We later learned that the Montreux Jazz Festival was happening that weekend, which could have explained some of the hostility we encountered. Despite this we enjoyed our stay there, relaxing around camp and soaking in the views.

We also discovered a hidden Alpine treasure up there along the frontier: Nutella. Corey and I had never tried it before. After weeks of searching in vain for peanut butter, we decided for some inexplicable reason that it could be a suitable replacement. The moment this sweet chocolaty paste touched my tongue I felt a wave of euphoria wash over me. *Sweet God, what is this magical nectar of princes and kings?* Corey and I raved. Aaron was much less enthused. It was too sweet for him, although he ate it anyway because money was tight and it was cheap stuff. A Nutella sandwich: who knew such a morale boost could come from something so simple? I noted my first experience with the cocoa spread in my journal with the simple words:

"FUCKING NUTELLA."

• • •

Back in Geneva, we had talked to some folks in the tourist information center about Swiss laws regarding hitchhiking. The verdict was something like, *"Technically it's illegal, but nobody cares."* One woman who worked in the Montreux thrift shop where we bought warmer clothes implied that we would probably be kidnapped or killed: "We hear all the time of people who go to hitchhike and never come back. A bad person could pick you up and drive you into the mountains and kill you there." *Cool, thanks.*

Summoning our courage, we set out from our cozy camp next to the waterfall to give it a shot. We didn't have much of a choice really—we'd spent almost $2,000 already out of the $4,000 total we'd brought. In other words, we had managed to spend half of our ten-month budget in just two weeks. Most of our money was spent on transportation (trains and buses had cost upward of $1,000 alone) but we had spent a decent portion on hotels and hostels as well. And most of it had been dished out during our first week overseas, when we were blowing money on partying.

Two things needed to happen desperately: One, I needed to finish the website so we could start soliciting money from donations or advertising. Two, we needed to contact Couchsurfing hosts ahead of time to set up places to stay for free.

Couchsurfing.org is a website in which travelers can contact hosts within a city who will let them crash for free. Everyone has a profile, which lets potential hosts and guests leave reviews and comments for some peace of mind. It's no strings attached, free accommodation. Just what we needed.

Aaron and I disagreed on our next move. I wanted to find a place with WiFi and spend a few days working on the website and contacting potential Couchsurfing hosts in Germany. Aaron was focused on the exorbitant amount of money we had already blown and had little faith in the website's ability to make money. He couldn't justify fronting funds to give it a go. We'd bickered about this a few times in our waterfall camp. One thing we all agreed upon, however, was that we couldn't buy any more expensive train tickets. So with butterflies in our stomachs we set out to find a free ride.

We wove through the tilted streets of Montreux to a bus station, where Aaron and I once again traded jabs. The nearest suitable onramp for hitchhiking was about two kilometers uphill. Being a shriveled weakling, I wanted no part of that climb. We'd noticed that people hopped on and off the buses without swiping cards or handing fares to the driver, so I figured we could just do the same and get a free ride. Aaron countered that we'd likely get caught and have to pay. He was outvoted, however, so we gave it a shot. Fortunately our luck won out; minutes later the bus spat us out in front of a gas station next to the highway.

One of our hostelmates in the hostel in downtown Barcelona had advised us that the best way to get a ride was to stand next to (or just before) an onramp. He also instructed us to make a sign with the name of the town or direction we were heading written on it. "Also," he had said, "you must smile all the time." So that's what we did. I got out my guitar and played and sang, while Corey danced around with the sign. Aaron waved at the passing motorists; all three of us wore wide, cheesy grins. People started honking and waving as they passed, most were smiling and some laughing. We had been standing there no longer than fifteen minutes when a black Audi hatchback crossed two lanes and bounced onto the curb next to us. We looked at one another for a moment in confusion.

"He's giving us a ride!" Aaron said.

I slid my guitar into its padded case and shouldered my pack. We all ran over to the car as a short and stocky black man stepped out.

"Here, here," he gestured toward the back hatch, motioning for us to place our bags inside. We tossed in our gear as traffic wove past.

We'd decided ahead of time to rotate seating arrangements, so I volunteered to sit shotgun for the first ride. Aaron and Corey would sit in the back, both of them having their knives close at hand just in case one of our drivers turned out to be a psychopath or a Frenchman. I hopped into the passenger seat.

"Hi!" I said to the driver, who was now flashing a smile as he quickly put the car into drive and pulled back onto the road.

"*Hola*," he replied. *Hmm ... Spanish? That's weird.* "Wilson," he said, pointing at himself.

We introduced ourselves in turn.

"*Habla inglés?*" I asked.

"*No—No inglés.*"

Well ... this is going to be interesting.

"*Mi parley Spanish, French, German, Italiano ... no Englais.*"

"Wow ... I don't uhh ... *parley* ... any of those ..."

He laughed. "Where ... you?"

"Ummm where am I going?" I pointed toward the road.

"No, no ... I am ... Dominican Republic," he pointed to himself. "You?"

"Ahhh. We are from America ... U.S.A."

We managed to communicate through charades and broken phrases as he drove, discovering he'd moved to Switzerland some years ago, leaving behind his wife and daughter, to whom he regularly sent money. I conveyed to him that we were traveling the world playing music and taking pictures. His smile widened. "Ahh! I *toco* ... uhh, play ... uhh ..." he air-drummed. "*Bateria.*"

It's important for the reader to know that I will be taking some liberty with the dialogue between Wilson, Corey, Aaron, and me. In other words, he'll be speaking better English in this book than he did when we were with him. We communicated almost entirely through charades and repeated guessing of words. It seemed the only reliable arrow in his quiver was *"all good,"* which he utilized often.

Around fifteen minutes into our car ride, I looked over my shoulder and saw Aaron and Corey snoozing. I worried that if anything sketchy happened, I would have no way of warning them. Wilson seemed nice enough, but the language barrier added a layer of uneasiness—on top of the expected strange feeling of entering a stranger's car in a foreign country. There were some seriously long and awkward silences between our charade-versations.

Nonetheless, I pushed negative thoughts to the back of my mind and spent those silent moments staring out the window. Switzerland held the most breathtaking landscape I had seen on our trip thus far. Rolling green hills of short-clipped glass meandered to misty crystalized mountains. Cottages were littered across the hillsides, with country roads winding through the fields. Even the road signs seemed aesthetically appealing.

One of these gazes was interrupted by Wilson: *"You douche?"*

"Uhhh ... what?"

"You want *douche?*" he repeated as he hovered a hand over his head and then imaginarily scrubbed at his body.

"Ohhh, a shower?"

He nodded.

A shower sounded amazing. He spoke again: "I get euro ... you ... my house ... you *douche* ... uhhh, eat ... and you sleep."

Yes—yes to all of those things. We hadn't showered since our first day in France, at the hotel in Cerbère. *He wanted us to pay him though?*

"You get money—uhhh *dinero*—we go to your house?" I asked for clarification.

"You eat, sleep. All good, ehh?"

"How much? How many euros?"

He looked confused, so I repeated myself. "How much do we pay you?"

His face twisted in confusion. "No, no, you no pay. I do for you!" He laughed and held back his hand to feign a smack at me. "Pay! Haha, no!"

I was confused. I was sure he had just said something about getting money first.

"Uhhh, sure, that sounds great."

I woke up Corey and Aaron and filled them in on what was happening. Everyone was on board for free showers and a good meal. Shortly afterward, Wilson took an exit ramp into a rural area.

We'd been driving over an hour, which had brought us somewhere near Biel, about ninety-five kilometers (sixty miles) south of the German border. After several curvy roads through the Swiss countryside, we pulled onto a suburbanesque street along a row of houses. Wilson pulled into a parking spot next to another car. He waved at the car and two guys stepped out of it. He got out and motioned back at us. "Here, come, come! All good, all good."

We got out as he greeted the two men from the other car. He gestured for us to get our backpacks, which we did, and then followed him into his house. He spoke in German with the two men. They were laughing and joking, occasionally saying a word or two toward us as we stood awkwardly just inside the doorway.

I glanced around the room. There wasn't much there: a set of weights on one side of the room, a coffee table, a small couch, a TV, a computer chair …

There was a smaller room next to us in which there were piles of kids' toys and clothes, all of them brand new. There were no decorations on the walls. The house itself was clean and modern, new construction.

Wilson and the Germans gathered around the exercise equipment and were demonstrating their strength amid friendly banter. Wilson delivered his *coup-de-gras* by lifting the entire rack of weights, resulting in cheers from the other two.

He then walked over and pulled a small wooden box out from underneath the coffee table. He lifted a small bag of white powder out of the box and handed it to one of the Germans, who in turn passed Wilson a wad of folded euro bills. They shook hands, and the Germans waved at us as they walked out the door to leave.

Wilson's earlier words finally clicked: *I make euro …*

He was a drug dealer.

Corey, Aaron, and I looked at each other as he closed the door behind the Germans. He turned back around with a big smile. The dude had not stopped smiling from the moment he picked us up.

"Dinner! *Quiere* for dinner?"

Aaron spoke up. "Whatever man, we'll eat anything."

"Pasta—spaghetti … all good?"

"Sure," Aaron said. "I can cook it—you don't have to worry about it."

"Ahhh okay, okay, you cook and you can *douche* if you like." He showed us to the bathroom and laid out some towels.

The fact that Wilson was a drug dealer was at this moment irrelevant to us. I've met plenty of drug dealers in previous stages of my life. None of them matched the nefarious caricatures portrayed in movies, but certainly none of them were as clean-cut, intelligent, and friendly as Wilson appeared to be. Our more immediate concern was that we were tired, hungry, and dirty.

After hot showers and mountains of spaghetti, Wilson and I played a game of chess while the boys shared a joint with him. Then another customer arrived. This time it was a towering Italian named Alejandro, who played fingerstyle guitar for us with considerable skill. He also spoke English. Alejandro imparted some wisdom on us which I found interesting enough to write in my journal: "Life is funny, man. Sometimes have the money, but you not happy. Sometimes you happy but you no have the money. You ever have both, you a lucky motherfucker, eh!"

After Alejandro finished his business with Wilson and shared a few laughs with us, he left. Wilson closed the door behind him and turned around toward us.

"We go town, drink *cervezas!* You meet *mis amigos!*"

We looked at one another. I could tell Corey and Aaron were feeling the same way.

"Man, we're just too tired. I think maybe we'll go find a place to camp for the night."

"No, no, no! Is okay … I leave … you sleep in my bed … I come back *mañana*. Uhhh ten—I come back ten morning."

We looked at each other again. *A guy we'd met only three hours earlier was going to leave us in his house alone all night while he went out? A guy that has barely even been able to talk to us and doesn't know the first thing about us?*

"Man, we can't do that," I said. "We wouldn't feel right."

"Yes, yes you stay! All good, all good." He handed us a key. "You sleep *bien*, I see you *mañana*."

With that, he locked the door and left. It didn't take long for us to convince Aaron not to head outside and find a spot to camp, so he ended up on the couch while Corey and I settled down in Wilson's bed. It was without a doubt the best night's sleep of the trip thus far.

• • •

The next morning, as we sat around the coffee table smoking our morning cigarettes, we took the first realistic look at our situation: There was not much furniture in the house. There were grocery bags full of marijuana clippings in the kitchen. It seemed like he was mostly just selling pot, but the Germans had bought either coke, molly, or ecstasy I figured. We had no idea if anyone else lived there. The full weight of the situation hit us and Aaron and I started to become anxious.

"What if this is just a drug house? I mean, maybe he doesn't even stay here. That would explain why he had no problem staying out all night," Aaron said.

"Yeah and what if the cops just come and bust this place right now—I mean, he isn't here and there's no way they're going to believe our story. We'd be fucked," I said.

Corey waved us away. "Guys, nothing like that is gonna happen. He's a cool dude. Just relax."

"I'm just saying, we don't know shit about this dude. There's a huge pile of toys and clothes in that other room and all of it's brand new … that's just weird."

The conversation went on for some time, Aaron and I both becoming more worried and Corey remaining unbothered.

Noon rolled around and Wilson had still not returned. We sat and waited. I started to teach Corey and Aaron how to play chess. I played guitar. We wrote in our journals. Finally, around three in the afternoon, the door opened and Wilson strolled in.

"*Amigos!* You sleep well, ehh? All good?" he said, tossing his keys on the coffee table and sitting with us.

We could do nothing but smile and conceal our fears. "Yeah, man! Slept great!"

"What we do now?" he asked with his trademark smile.

"Uhh, if we could just get a ride to the highway so we can start traveling …" I made the thumbs-up motion of hitchhiking and he nodded his head.

"*Bien, bien.* First, eat! *Mi amigo* own, uhh, *ristorante, cafe.* Then to road, all good?"

"Okay, that works man!" Corey said. Aaron and I looked at one another with concern.

Wilson motioned for us to follow him to the kitchen. He started pulling things out of cabinets and handing them to us, saying *"take, take!"* Rice, chocolate, granola bars, tuna, fresh cilantro. He even gave us the portable chess set. Corey looked back at us as if to say, "See, what are you guys worried about?"

He gave us a bag to put the food in and we shouldered our packs, ready to head outside. I stopped for a moment and then looked back at Corey and Aaron in worried confusion. There was now a different car parked in front of the house. Wilson walked up and opened the back hatch.

I gestured to Wilson—"Uhhh … car?—Where's the car from yesterday?"

Wilson looked at the car, back at me, and then smiled. "Ahhh. I borrow that car from a friend. This … different friend. All good."

"But what about our food? We had bags in the back of the other car with our food in it," Aaron said as he made the universal gesture for "food."

"Food? In other car?" Wilson asked.

Not just the forty euros worth of food we'd just bought, but the expensive fuel for our backpacking stove. "Yeah, in the car from yesterday—did you get the bags out of the back?"

He waved his hand in dismissal. "Is gone."

"It can't be gone; we have fuel for our stove in there."

"Is gone. All good."

"No, not all good! You borrowed from your friend, right? Can't we just go get the bags from the car?"

"No, is gone. No worries; I buy you more."

"You won't be able to find that fuel for the stove," I said, making a motion with my hands as if to cook food.

"We find … I buy you more. Come *amigos, nos vamos.*"

We looked at each other, bewildered.

We got into the car, this time with Aaron in the front and Corey and me in the back. After careening through a series of winding country roads, we entered a small town and Wilson whipped the car into a parking spot in front of a grocery store.

"Fuel," he said as he exited the car. Several minutes later he returned empty-handed and we sped off again. This time we parked in front of a larger store, but Wilson didn't get out right away. Instead, he pulled out his phone and made a call to someone, speaking in German. He rolled the window down and yelled out of it at another car, smiling. Then he turned around to face us:

"I meet friends, all good?"

He walked over to the other car—a brand new Maserati—and spoke to two gentlemen in sunglasses and suits. They looked like the kind of folks John Wick might seek revenge upon. They stared with stern expressions and then pointed in our direction. My heart palpitated at the thought of being gunned-down in a drug deal gone wrong.

Wilson waved his hand in dismissal of us, probably telling them *"all good."* They reached into the back of the Maserati and handed Wilson two grocery bags, stuffed to the brim. After a quick handshake and a signature grin, he came back over to our car, threw open the back hatch and swung the bags in. I smelled pot.

We pulled back onto the road once again, this time for a very short amount of time, before stopping in front of a gas station. Wilson went inside and then came out a moment later, handing us each an iced coffee and a small cigar. Back onto the road we went.

My paranoia spiraled. We were driving all over the place, with two huge bags of weed in the back of the car, making all these strange and unannounced stops ... was he ever going to drop us off so we could get moving? My mind wandered toward the worst-case scenarios.

We pulled in front of an apartment complex.

"I go inside and back soon, all good?"

Without waiting for an answer, Wilson hopped out of the car, grabbed the two bags from the back and headed inside. I waited until he was out of sight before I spoke up:

"Okay seriously, what is going on? Is this guy ever going to drop us off?"

"You guys need to quit freaking out," Corey said. "He's just a cool motherfucker, nothing bad is going to happen. You're over-thinking it."

Aaron agreed with me. "Dude, I mean … what happens if we get pulled over?"

Aaron and I just wanted to be out of this strangely unnerving situation. Maybe we were overthinking it, but it just wasn't a par-ticularly comfortable position to be in. Corey didn't see any dan-ger involved—or if he did, he didn't show it.

Wilson walked back out of the apartment complex holding two *different* bags. *Our food bags!*

"I get back from *mi amigo.*"

"Thank you! But uhhh, we need to get a move on … to go … *vamos.*"

"Okay, I take you to the lake. There you can sleep and ride *mañana*. All good, all good."

"Sure, sounds good." Anything to get out of the situation we were currently in.

We left the town and zoomed through winding country roads. Wilson would stop the car every so often and motion for us to get out and take pictures of the landscape.

Before we made it to the lake, Wilson took us to a restaurant in the larger city of Biel/Bienne. This was apparently the one his friend owned, because a middle-eastern man came out to greet him the second we arrived and they shook hands with big grins.

"Tres cervesas por mis amigos!" Wilson gestured toward us.

"No *problemo*, broddah!" The man smiled again as he walked toward the bar and returned a few moments later with three large glasses of beer.

We thanked Wilson and our anxieties finally lessened as we sipped the cold drinks. Wilson disappeared with the man into the restaurant while we sat out on the patio. He was playing around on some hand drums for a while, joking around with the staff and intermittently reappearing outside to check on us.

While Wilson played the drums and conversed with the staff, the owner came out and talked with us in English for a few minutes. We told him how kind and generous Wilson had been to us, and how it was all so unexpected.

"That is just the way he is. He is always 'give, give, give' and never 'take.' He buys toys and gives them to the local children whose parents have no money. He is a good man."

I remembered the large pile of brand new toys in the spare room.

Suddenly there were sandwiches placed in front of us.

"You eat!" Wilson smiled as he sat down with a sandwich of his own. It was a delicious meal; some type of toasted wheat bread with tomato, ham, cheese dressed with a vinaigrette.

"What kind of sandwich is this?" Aaron asked.

"Hmm?" Wilson didn't understand the question.

"What is this called? The sandwich."

"Uhh … just sandwich. Dominican Republic sandwich."

Fair enough, I guess.

We finished our meals and drained our beers. Wilson offered us another round but we all declined.

"Okay, we go lake now. We walk now."

We said goodbye to the owner and then shouldered our packs and took off down the sidewalk, Wilson guiding the way. You could tell most of the buildings in this city were new in comparison to the quaint look of the typical European villages we had seen. We wandered through alleyways, past rows of shops, alongside the many other people who were out enjoying the beautiful sunny day. After a short while, we rounded a bend and a glistening lake came into view.

We walked to its shoreline and sat on a concrete bench near a group of people barbecuing food. We rested there with Wilson for a while and Corey and I played a couple of songs for him.

Finally Wilson stood up. "Okay, it is time I go now, work *mañana*. I come back, give you ride after?"

"No man, you've done more than enough, we'll be fine," Corey said.

"Okay, okay. I give you money then, *dinero*? To help with you travel?" He reached for his wallet.

"No! No we don't want any money, seriously Wilson, you've done enough."

Aaron and I stood there, flabbergasted.

"Okay, okay. Just little money?"

"No, no, no."

"How about you get a picture with us?" Aaron offered.

"Ahhh yes!"

Aaron set up the tripod and we all gathered for a photo. I held up the cardboard sign we had been holding when he had picked us up in Montreux. Afterward he gave us all a hug, told us *adios*, and he was gone. We sat in silence for a moment and watched as he rounded the bend up toward the city. No one said a word for a few moments until I finally spoke up:

"Okay, was that guy seriously just that nice? Because that's un-believable."

"I told you guys it was no big deal," Corey said with a grin.

"You did, but ... goddamn ... I just couldn't believe that there could be someone who was that genuinely nice to complete strangers. It's just insane."

At that moment I first truly realized just how good-natured the human race can be. I needed to trust people more. I needed to be more amenable to the chaotic, dynamic flow of long-term travel-ing. It would be the first of many such experiences.

6

JUANCHO VS THE NAZI OF FREIBURG
FREIBURG, GERMANY

July 15th

The friction between Aaron and me tightened. Each day we began to argue more and more about money. Even though we'd agreed to pool all of our funds together, it began to feel like he was in sole control of purse strings because he'd brought more to the table than Corey or I so far. Corey and I were confused because it had been clear from the very beginning that Aaron would contribute more money at the start: he had a full-time job and lived with his parents. I played as many gigs as possible, but lived alone and had a car payment to make on top of my housing costs. Corey worked some odd jobs, sold quite a few possessions, and any tips we made playing shows were put toward the trip as well. Since Aaron didn't expect to make any money during the trip, he worked side jobs in addition to his landscaping work so that he could contribute more at the beginning. Then as the trip went on, it was expected that Corey and I could make money playing music and that I could solicit donations and advertising through the website, making up the difference in the long run.

So it was surprising that Aaron started to act as if all the money was his to control. It felt like we needed permission to buy even a morsel of food. He complained incessantly about it; wishing to forgo any comforts imaginable to save pennies. I was all for saving money too, but at the same time I wanted to enjoy the trip. More importantly, I knew that our extreme budgeting was ironically denying me the chance to actually make money. If we never had WiFi, I'd never be able to get the website to its full potential. If we were too tired from sleeping in random places and hiking all day, we'd never have the energy to play music. And so the vicious cycle continued.

The simmering resentments boiled over after Wilson left us. We were camping on a mountainside near Lake Biel when I once again brought up my idea of staying somewhere for a few days to work on the website and contact Couchsurfing hosts.

"Yeah, but what if we spend all that money and then the website doesn't make anything?" he asked.

"Well if we don't even try then we'll be doing nothing but spending with no chance at recouping some costs. And what about Couchsurfing?"

"I just don't see us making any money from the website. And what city would we even try for Couchsurfing?"

"Well if we had WiFi, we could research that."

"I ain't spending any more money on hostels, so that's out of the question."

Corey was staring toward the ground in silence.

"Dude how is that up to you? We're all in this together—it's not a one-man show." I said.

"I'm tired of you guys trying to tell me how to spend my money. I broke my back to make this money—I earned it."

"Uhhh … first … all the money didn't come from you. And we all agreed to pool our money together anyway. So now that's not what we're doing?"

Corey finally spoke. "Yeah man. We all agreed that we'd pool our money together as a group."

"Well that was before I saw how much money we're spending. If I let you guys buy whatever you want, we'll be broke in a week."

"I'm not trying to go out and spend all our money Aaron, I just want the chance to be able to make some money and enjoy this trip as much as we can. You're making me feel like a piece of shit right now, like I'm bumming money off of you or something."

"I just wish we all would have had the same amount of money to bring from the beginning."

"Well I was busy planning this trip for us and busting my ass on the website while you did the same thing you do every day. You didn't break your back working any differently than you always did—trip or no trip."

It went on and on like that for the better part of an hour. Corey mostly stayed silent. He usually tried to be the peacekeeper between us. Eventually we both gave up and went to our hammocks. I lay there, still fuming, wondering what the rest of the trip would be like. It was becoming clear that Aaron and I were two contrasting personality types. I just hoped we could learn to live with each other.

• • •

The next day we packed up and went back to the road to hitch-hike. An older woman picked us up, who spoke not one word of English. She called her daughter and put her on speakerphone in the car to translate. She had only been planning to drive twenty minutes down the road, but offered to take us all the way across the German border to Freiburg—three hours away.

When we arrived in the city, we headed to a McDonald's for some free WiFi and I looked up nearby places to stay. There was a relatively cheap hotel right next to where we were sitting. I brought it up to Aaron, waiting for him to blow up on me. We argued about the price for a while and finally he agreed. "Wanna pay for this one with your card?"

I had mine and Corey's money in my bank account. There was around $500-600 still available at that point. When we had put our money in, Aaron didn't want to put any in the bank, opting to carry it in a money belt instead. It had seemed a bit foolish to carry all that cash around, but I didn't think much about it otherwise.

"Sure that's fine," I said. "Why don't you guys go check in and I'll see if I can make some money busking."

"Sounds good."

They sat their bags next to me as I stood near the sidewalk. I tuned up my guitar and started to play and sing. I had been playing a few moments when I saw two police officers walking over. Oh great.

"Yeah man, rock and roll!" One of them said with a grin, playing air guitar as he walked by.

A pretty young blonde walked in front of me, smiling seductively. *Nahhh. No way.* I surely had to be imagining things.

She turned around and walked back. I smiled back at her and this time she waved.

Another girl walked from across the street and this time the blonde girl turned around again and kept walking. Just as I finished the song I was playing, the second girl approached me.

"Hallo," she said with a smile and a thick German accent.

"Hi."

"Where are you from?"

"The US."

"Ahh, I love American music, is great, ya! You are very good."

"Thank you very much."

"Would you like some food?"

"Uhhh, okay."

She placed a croissant in my case along with a handful of coins as I started another song. She stood there listening as people passed by, many of them dropping coins in the case along the way.

Two more girls approached from behind where I was playing and sat Indian-style against a flowerbed to my right. I looked over and they smiled.

I finished the second song.

"You are American?"

"Yes, American."

"You know Jack Johnson?"

"Yeah, I love Jack!" I listed a few of his tunes I liked to cover and began to play one.

More tips went in the guitar case.

Just then Aaron walked out. He stopped for a moment and then smiled. I was surrounded by beautiful girls. I was probably more astonished than he was. I finished the song and he walked the rest of the way over to me.

"What the hell is going on?" he asked with a grin.

"I have no idea, dude."

"Well I'm gonna take the bags to the room. I'll send Corey down to sneak you in; we had to get a room just for two again."

"Cool, whatever man." The hotel was the last thing on my mind. I looked over at the two girls sitting to my right.

"You know I normally play for tips, but in your case I'll take a phone number."

They giggled and looked at each other.

"Oh ya?" one of them smiled, "and what you will do with my phone number?"

"I'll be in town for a few days; we could go out for a drink?" I imagined in my head Aaron telling me *"No, we can't spend money on that,"* after which I would casually round-house him in the face on my way out the door.

"I will only be in town tonight. We can meet you later if you want?" she said.

"Sounds great."

I got her phone number and went back to playing. The tips kept rolling in and I floated on a cloud. Eventually Corey came to get me and I called it a day. Once we got to the room, I opened the guitar case and counted out €15 (about $20 USD) I had made during the short thirty minutes I had been playing. It seemed like the German youth—girls and guys both included—were into acoustic music.

I ended up video chatting with my family back home most of the evening rather than calling the girl from earlier, as that would have required me to find a cell phone store and get a German SIM card—I was more excited to have a shower and a bed. I supposed when you're a poor vagabond, it's more about the chase sometimes.

• • •

The following day we booked a hostel for two nights. Again I was surprised when Aaron didn't argue against it. We took a tram there and only lost our way once—our navigation skills seemed to be slowly improving and I even found a cell phone store right next to the tram stop, where I was able to reactivate my cell phone with a German SIM card so we could use Google maps.

We entered the guesthouse via an elevator. An old man with a bent posture and a warm smile greeted us at the front desk. After checking in, he took us to a four-bed dorm which would be our room for the next two nights.

"You have one more person in here," he told us as he handed us a key. We settled into the room and cooked a dinner of rice and tuna on the balcony. (I consumed more rice and tuna during the next few months than the average person probably eats in a lifetime.) We were smoking cigarettes after our meal when the door to our room opened and a stranger walked in—a younger, Spanish-looking man with short, neat hair and a dark blue t-shirt that was too large for him.

"Ayyyye, guys!" he grinned as he extended a hand. "I am Juancho."

We introduced ourselves and asked where Juancho was from.

"I am from Canary Islands, is near Spain. And you guys are American?"

"Yes." I noticed a guitar in the corner. "You play?" I pointed toward it.

"Yes man, I love to play! You as well?"

"Yeah, we should jam sometime!"

I spent the first day working on the website while Corey talked to his girlfriend on Facebook and Aaron edited photos he'd taken.

In the afternoon I took a tram into town by myself to busk and once again made a decent bit of money. We went out for a couple beers with Juancho that evening, where he and I played guitar on the street.

The next night we took the tram downtown with our new friend to do some real drinking. We all loved Juancho. We scuttled into a hole-in-the-wall bar to get some to-go beers. I approached the counter and asked the woman to "give me the cheapest, shittiest beer you have."

She handed me a bottle. I took a drink. It was delicious. "You have to be kidding me—Germany is fucking awesome." We got a few beers apiece and stuffed them in our pockets.

Afterward, we gathered around a bench along one side of the cobblestone street. Juancho and I played some tunes while Corey kept time with the shakers. We were dancing around, following each other's songs. A large group of people gathered around us to listen. Only bicycles used the street we were on, so most of the crowd grouped right there in the middle. We jumped up on the bench and continued to jam as the growing crowd clapped along. We finished the song with a dramatic display of jumping up and down and were met with a large round of applause afterward. We laughed and hugged and then jumped down from the bench. A group of younger kids walked up to us.

"You guys must come with us to the big party!" They said.

"Where at?" Corey asked.

"Right down the street; here, walk with us."

We followed them down the cobblestones and into an alley, surrounded on both sides by the characteristic old-stone buildings of Freiburg. It was a picturesque city, undoubtedly rich with history.

The end of the alley opened to a forum filled with hundreds of young kids, all sitting on the street. They were speaking quietly, but the sheer number of their whispers created a blanketing static of sibilance. The group of kids who brought us there quickly melted into the crowd and we sat down at the edge of the gathering.

I took out my guitar when a teenager sitting next to us turned to me. "You cannot play that here, they will arrest you."

"Arrest me?"

"We are permitted to gather here, but after nine there is no noise allowed."

I shrugged. I started to play anyway. I hadn't even gotten through the first song when a boot clocked me in the shoulder. Corey, Aaron, and Juancho looked behind me with widened eyes. I turned to see three police officers in tactical vests standing behind me.

"Passport, now."

"Okay, okay, hold on." I reached into my pocket, fumbling for the little book.

"You cannot do this here—it is not allowed. I can arrest you and take your guitar, you know."

"I'm sorry," I said with an innocent face as I handed him my passport. "I didn't know," I lied.

Another of the officers, a young woman with blonde hair in a tight bun, snatched my guitar out of my hands. "Whoa!" I yelled in protest as I began to stand up.

"Sit!" The first cop pushed me back onto the ground. "You understand we can arrest you right now if we choose?!"

"Listen, I'm really sorry. It won't happen again, I promise. I don't want to go to jail."

He looked at the officer holding my guitar and then back toward me. "I will let you go with a warning this time since I do not think you knew about the rule. But if I catch you again, you will go to jail."

"Thank you sir, I really appreciate it."

They returned my guitar and then walked away. *I can be arrested for playing music? What is this, the town from Footloose?*

"You guys want to go somewhere else?" Juancho asked.

"Yeah, fuck this," Corey said.

We all stood up to leave. We walked back down the alley from which we had arrived until we noticed a door to a small bar at the bottom of a basement staircase. We heard loud music coming from inside. I walked in behind the others and we all grabbed a seat at the bar. The source of the loud music was karaoke, happening on a small stage at the end of the long, narrow tavern. I got a beer and walked up to the sign-in sheet where I was accosted by a young British guy—"Ah you singing, mahn?" he slurred.

"I think so."

"Let's do one togethuhhh, yeah?" His shaggy blond hair fell to one side.

"Okay. What song?"

"Fuck, man! Uhhh, The Beatles?"

"Are you really gonna be a stereotypical British guy right now?"

"Hey, fuck you mate!"

"No, no, I like the Beatles!"

I sang with the drunken British man and then finished my beer. I ordered another and then headed outside for a smoke. I'd been carrying my guitar on my back this whole time, and as I walked up the stairs a college-aged guy noticed it. "Hey guitar-man, play a song for us!"

I took the guitar out of its case and played a song to the guy and his friends—another guy and three girls, one of whom was catching my eye. I was chatting with the group when Juancho, Corey, and Aaron emerged from the bar.

"Hey guys, these are my new friends," I said. The boys lit up a smoke and sipped from their beers while I played another song. After I finished, one of the girls spoke up:

"We are going to a dance club, you want to come with us?"

I looked at Corey, Aaron and Juancho.

"The tram quits running in like fifteen minutes …" Corey said.

"Yeah, that's a pretty long way to walk if we miss it," I said. "But, I mean … it's not like we have our packs or anything."

"I will do whatever you guys want to do," Juancho said with a smile.

Aaron shrugged. "Yeah, sure."

I looked at Corey. We both nodded our heads: "Fuck it."

We followed the young Germans down the alley and back onto the same cobblestone street from earlier, and then down yet another alleyway on the other side. This one led to a small door where a man stood checking IDs. We handed him our passports and then entered a long hallway which led to the club.

One of the girls called back as we walked—"Tonight they are playing only 90's and 2000's music."

We entered the club, which reminded me of the small-town roller-skating rinks from my childhood (except with alcohol). It was a circular shape, with a DJ on one end and a bar on the other.

Smash Mouth's "Walking On The Sun" blared as young Germans danced and drank.

Aaron grabbed beers and brought them to us. "Where's Quencho?"

"You mean Juancho?" Corey busted out laughing … "Queso."

I looked around, but didn't see him anywhere. "He was behind me when I gave the door guy my passport."

Aaron shrugged. "I'm sure he'll be in."

"… Taco." Corey was still laughing.

We walked up to our new friends, who were already dancing. Corey and I stopped for a moment and then looked at each other with raised eyebrows … These kids couldn't dance worth a good goddamn. It was terrible. It was like watching Rock 'Em Sock 'Em Robots try to gang-bang a ballerina. They were lifting their arms up and swaying back and forth like balloons tied to a mailbox.

50 Cent's "In Da Club" came on. I sat down the guitar and started fist pumping. Corey followed behind me and laid down some serious moves. This was our shit. (Or at least it was when we were in high school.)

I started doing the lawnmower—where you pretend to be starting a push-mower with a pull-chain. Corey busted out the shopping cart move. Even aside from the stupid dance moves, we were really getting down.

Let me pause to say that I'm not a good dancer (as you may have surmised from my lawnmower move). I have rhythm, but all my moves are painfully "white-boyish." That said, the people in that club made me look like Justin fucking Timberlake. Corey, who is a legitimately good dancer, was like a god to these people. At one point, while we were dancing to "How Bizarre" by OMC, one of the German guys came up to him and said, and I quote, *"YOU*

ARE THE COOLEST MOTHERFUCKER IN THIS CLUB RIGHT NOW, BRO!"

After over an hour of dancing our asses off, we decided to call it a night. I wasn't sure how, but Corey and I somehow convinced Aaron to let us get a taxi back to the guesthouse rather than walk.

We entered our room to find that Juancho was still nowhere to be found.

"Where the hell is Quesadilla?!" Corey said.

I couldn't stop laughing. We were genuinely concerned about Juancho, but there wasn't much we could do. We stood on the balcony and smoked a cigarette before heading to bed.

We had no sooner shut off the lights when Juancho flung open the door.

We all yelled simultaneously.

"Dude what happened?" Aaron asked.

He was covered in a film of sweat. "Ohhh, guys. When we get to club, I think *'hey man, this place is not for me.'* I decide I want to walk back to here. Man, it took forever. I thought I would never make it back. At one point I saw a child's bicycle and I think to myself *'Hey Juancho, you could take this bike and ride it back, no one will ever know.'* But I cannot do this, ahhh, I would be … how is it you say … a 'dickhead' … so I keep walking instead and here I am."

•   •   •

The next morning Juancho offered to buy us each a beer and breakfast before we parted ways. We would be headed toward a highway onramp nearby, hoping to catch a ride to Heidelberg. Dennis from the hostel in Barcelona had a friend there who'd agreed to let us crash for a couple nights. Aaron and Juancho went into a small market while Corey and I waited outside and shared a cigarette.

"Do you think it's weird Aaron has suddenly been cool with us getting hostels and stuff?" I asked Corey.

"Uhh, yeah. About that," Corey said.

"What?"

"He said made a comment when we were checking into that hotel the other day. Something like, "Hey if Tom wants to spend all his money I don't care.""

My face flushed. Not only was I offering the money in my account for the whole group just as we had agreed upon, *but he was also thinking he was taking advantage of me?* He clearly saw all of our money as separate at this point. I knew I would make more money eventually, but I still had plenty of work to do on the website and the past few days had admittedly drained a lot of the money in my bank account, diminishing any upper hand Corey or I may have had in decisions. Aaron had snuck his way into taking full control of our finances.

7

JOHANNES, ISABEL, AND THE KING IS DEAD!
HEIDELBERG, GERMANY

July 19th

We arrived on the outskirts of Heidelberg after a long day of hitchhiking from Freiburg. Our last ride of the day, a laid-back and smelly Swedish guy driving a seventies Volkswagen van dropped us off on the side of the highway. We set up our hammocks in some bushes for the night.

The next morning we emerged from our highway-side cocoons with tousled hair and baggy eyes. All through the night vehicles had screamed down the highway, waking us up every few minutes. After stowing our hammocks, we walked toward downtown, better known as the "historical sector" of Heidelberg where we were to meet our host. We didn't know much about him other than his name (Johannes) and that he ran a local theater group.

Heidelberg looked old, almost medieval even: most of the buildings were constructed in traditional German fashion, with large stones accented by dark wooden framework. The streets were cobblestone and intersected by plazas, usually featuring a fountain or statue of some sort in the middle. The people we spoke to were all friendly—we had to ask directions a few times on our quest to find the park where we were to meet our host.

We arrived at said park during the afternoon and collapsed on some benches. We were all feeling the effects of our sleepless night. I powered up my phone and was met with a low-batter warning. I sent Johannes a message:

"We are sitting on the benches under the trees in Uniplatz by all the bicycles. My phone is dying, but you'll know us by the backpacks and the beards."

Just as I hit the send button, my phone died. I didn't even know whether or not the message went through. "Well, let's just hope for the best," I said.

We ended up falling asleep on the benches for a few peaceful moments before a voice awakened us: "Hello, guys?" I pulled the bandanna from over my eyes to see a young guy with dreadlocks tied in a small ponytail. He was dressed in a threadbare t-shirt, sitting atop a bicycle.

"Joe ... hans?" Corey said.

"*Yo-han-ness,*" he said with a smile and outstretched hand. We introduced ourselves in turn and then he motioned toward our packs. "If you want to grab your things, you can follow me to my apartment. Afterward we are having practice for the play if you would like to join."

We followed Johannes down the cobblestone streets as he pushed his bike and gave us our own personal tour: "Heidelberg was first built over 1,000 years ago ... there is a castle still standing that was built around 1500 AD! There are many buildings in the city that are quite old. It was one of the only major German cities to escape bombardment during the war."

We arrived in front of a door that opened up to a small foyer containing a staircase and a narrow hallway. Johannes stashed his bike along the hallway and we followed him up four steep flights of stairs. We were panting and gasping by the time we reached his apartment door. When he opened it, we were met with a sweltering, humid pillow of air. At one point later in our stay, Aaron checked a mini thermometer he carried with him and it read ninety-three degrees in the apartment.

This was worsened every night when we were about to go to sleep: Johannes would walk over to the only source of redemption from drowning in your own ball sweat—a small oscillating fan—and quietly say, "Hey guys … I am going to turn the fan off now, okay?"

Of course we'd say okay, no problem. But inside I was thinking, *Please for the love of Hades, don't turn off that magnificent oscillating angel.* Corey mentioned it as we were leaving the city a few days later: "Every time Johannes asked if he could turn off that fan I wanted to punch him right in the face." Of course if we'd asked Johannes, there is no doubt he would have left the fan on. But we were new to Couchsurfing and weren't confident enough to ask for anything we didn't consider normal routine for the household.

Other than its Mercurial temperature, the apartment was awesome. Each window was a picture frame of tiled rooftops and nostalgic European architecture. It was a studio apartment, but his bed was separated from the living area by a long bookcase and a tapestry strategically hung as a pseudo-doorway. We slept on mattresses on the floor, which more than contented us.

Johannes shared the apartment with his girlfriend Isabel, a short, attractive woman who was a hair stylist.

• • •

We made an important decision upon arriving in Heidelberg: we had to quit smoking cigarettes. We'd been spending a lot of money on tobacco and had actually planned to quit before we'd even left the States. I had a few nicotine patches with me that I'd bought at home. I offered to split what I had with the group to lessen the cravings and side effects of quitting. Corey accepted, but Aaron opted to do it without aid.

"Are you sure, man?" I asked. "They really help."

"Nah, I'll be all right. I'd rather just kinda taper off of em."

"Dude, I know how that works—you're gonna have to quit cold turkey or it's not gonna happen."

"Nah, I'll be all right," he urged. "You guys do the patches and I'll just cut down and smoke the rest of what I've got in my bag," he said, referring to the small pouch of tobacco we carried and rolled from.

"Okay, man; whatever you say ..."

• • •

A local theater festival was in just a few days' time. Johannes was helping to direct a play for it, called *The King Is Dead!* We spent our first few days in the city watching the rehearsals and getting to know Johannes's friend group.

There were two British guys, Leo and Alex. Leo had short red hair and was the more humorous and laid-back of the two, while Alex, with his long hair and brown corduroy pants worn with a white dress shirt and brown vest, was more serious. He was attending the university for his PhD. He spoke fluent German and Leo spoke a bit as well.

There was Alixe, an American girl who wasn't in the play but was hanging out with the group as well, and Katharina, with brown, curly hair, who was German.

Other German friends were Tomas, a skinny and surfer-haired guy who cracked jokes, Thibaud, a quiet, reserved artist, and finally Simon, who looked like a frat guy but displayed a personality opposite.

We sat and drank beers while they rehearsed. The play was in German of course, so we weren't entirely sure what was going on. That said, it seemed like they were talented actors.

• • •

The next day, everyone went to look at the castle. I was stuck inside working on the website while they were out. I was rebuilding the entire thing with WordPress, which would A.) look better, and B.) be easier to manage.

It was a tedious job which would take more than a full day of work. Did I mention that it's hot in Johannes's apartment? I sat in a pool of my own sweat for hours on end, typing away at that damn site. At one point I thought maybe my penis had actually melted like a candle in the oven otherwise known as my shorts. It was just a mess down there. I eventually took a cold shower and changed clothes, and then decided maybe it wasn't the best idea to keep the computer on my lap. I hope they burned that chair after I left.

• • •

Johannes's English was exceptional. He was active in politics, even writing speeches for local politicians on occasion. You would never think it looking at the guy, with his dreads and generally dirty, disheveled appearance. He took good care of us and tried to involve us in everything he was doing, especially stuff with the play. He also gave us heaps of travel advice for everything from hitchhiking and busking, to planning for our next big trips. He had traveled extensively himself—Nepal, most of Europe, the United States ... Isabel held an even more impressive collection of passport stamps, having traveled by herself through Russia, China, Israel, Mongolia, and Jordan with only a small handbag. They planned to go traveling together permanently after saving money for a year or two.

He and I held discussions, sometimes on political issues about which we disagreed, but regardless of each of our views, the debates were always handled matter-of-factly. I really liked that he was not afraid to disagree and tell us what he really thought. If I asked his opinion on something I was doing—whether it be the website, or something travel related—he would tell me if it sucked, and then tell me why it sucked. I respected and appreciated that.

8
BIG BEERS AND MOUNTAIN SCOOTER RIDES WITH PRETTY GERMAN GIRLS

HEIDELBERG, GERMANY

July 20th

I spent most of Saturday finishing up the website in Johanne's sauna—I mean apartment. There was still a lot to be done if we were to make any money from advertising, but the core design was finished, so all I had to do was write some articles and create video content. The big play wasn't until the next afternoon, so we had the whole evening to do whatever we pleased.

One of Isabel's friends was having a going-away party in the local park, so we agreed to tag along. I brought my guitar and Johannes brought some small drums.

We stopped on the way to grab some beers from a local micro-brewery near Johannes's apartment called Vedder. They sold huge one-and-a-half liter beers in a cork-top bottle. It was an insane deal given beer prices in Europe—something like three euros per bottle, and if you returned the bottle you even got one euro back. After grabbing a Vedder for each of us, we headed toward the park.

Quitting cigarettes had gone as expected. Aaron smoked through the rest of the bag of tobacco and started picking up butts off the ground and rolling them. We were pretty sure he'd bought another bag and was hiding it from us. It made it hard for Corey and me not to smoke when he was lighting up right next to us. I relapsed multiple times, including during the walk to the park.

We had just crossed the historic stone bridge over the river when we were joined unexpectedly by a short blonde girl. I thought she must have known Johannes. She asked him—motioning toward our instruments—"Have you already played, or are you going to play now?"

He replied that we were heading to the park for a party. She struck up a conversation with him and upon mentioning that she had spent almost three years traveling through Southeast Asia and Australia, he introduced her to me: "You should talk to this girl, Tom, she has traveled quite a lot where you will be going!"

Rahel [pronounced Rackk-ell] told me about her travels while we walked along a narrow dirt path toward the park. Her journey infatuated me: having spent all that time away from home, living without money, sometimes in remote corners of the world. As our conversation continued, we finally arrived at the party.

Aaron, Corey, and I didn't know anyone there since it was mostly Isabel's friends, but it didn't take us long to become part of the group. We started playing music and trading the instruments so others could play. While someone was borrowing my guitar, I talked to Rahel a bit more. The noise from the instruments was loud, so I suggested we go for a walk. I told Johannes and the others I would be back in a while, and off we went.

We walked along the shoreline and eventually found a spot to sit. The Neckar river passed quietly in front of us, the streetlights on the other side casting a splash of watercolors.

Time passed as we got to know each other. Whether minutes or hours, I'm not sure. Eventually we decided we should head back and join the others. When we returned to the circle, Aaron, Corey, Johannes, and the others were nowhere to be seen. We asked the group if they knew where they had gone.

"They left about twenty minutes ago," one of the girls said. "They didn't know when you would be back."

"Interesting," I said. I knew how to get back to Johannes's apartment from where we were, but I was still enjoying Rahel's company and wasn't quite ready to part ways.

She sensed my hesitation. "If you would like, you can stay with me at my house."

I thought for a moment … Johannes and everyone wouldn't know where I was. They did however, leave me here most likely under the assumption that I can take care of myself, so they probably wouldn't be too worried. Also I was pretty sure "stay with me at my house" meant I was going to get laid.

"Sure, why not."

"Good! We can make a campfire and talk more. The only thing is, I drive a motor scooter—and I live in the mountains."

"A scooter?" I asked.

"Yes, and I don't have an extra helmet which is a problem in Germany. If you see police, you must duck behind me."

Duck behind you? You're like five feet tall. And forget the police, how about my head bashing off of a guardrail in the middle of the goddamn mountains?

"Uhh, okay."

I accepted my fate with little worry—which probably had a lot to do with the amount of Vedders I had consumed by that point. As we walked toward her scooter, conversation on travel continued until she brought my alcohol-induced confidence in her scooter-captaining abilities to a screeching halt:

"I am quite worried; this is the first time I have driven the scooter with another person … especially in the mountains … and in the dark."

"But you're European … I thought you guys learned how to drive these things when you're like five years old?"

"No, I have just learned to drive when I was in Thailand."

I weighed my options. On one hand, I could possibly die in a fiery scooter crash. On the other hand, maybe I was about to make love to this gorgeous German woman.

"Just don't kill me, please."

"I will try my best!"

What more can you ask for?

We made it to the scooter, which was parked on a sidewalk. I popped the cork back into my bottle of beer and stuffed it in the under-seat compartment, then hopped into place behind her.

"Okay, here we go!" she called back to me.

We bounced off the sidewalk and onto the road, zipping toward the mountains. I was holding onto her waist as the lights of the city dissolved into a blur of dark-green forest. The light of the moon filtered through the branches, casting webs of shadow across the road. Chilled air whipped against my face and the scooter's motor growled as we climbed. After what seemed like only a few minutes, she stopped the scooter in the middle of the road and it idled, puttering. She pointed to the left. "Heidelberg!" she yelled through her helmet. We had gained altitude fast. You could see a circle of city lights nestled in the hills below, the soft sparkle of their reflection on the Neckar River running through its middle.

A short while later we stopped again, this time at a gravel pull-off. Clear spring water flowed from a pipe jutting out of the side of the mountain into an ancient-looking iron grate. She filled a water bottle.

"Try!" she said, handing me the bottle. It was some of the best water I've ever tasted.

We hopped back on the scooter. Farther down the road we entered a small mountain town, which seemed to have sprung up out of nowhere. This is where my backseat ride got sketchy; I was gripping on for dear life as she sped us through intersections and buzzed around corners, heading for the outskirts of the village— obviously trying to make it through the city without being confronted by police. We finally pulled in front of a picturesque cottage and I attempted to pry my deadlocked fingers from her sides.

"HOLY SHIT, I'M ALIVE!"

She laughed as she shut off the scooter and opened up the seat compartment. I grabbed my beer and she led me around the side of the house to the backyard. She asked if I knew how to start a fire, to which I scoffed and grumbled something about my competency as a man's man.

Rahel went inside while I started a small fire. By the time I had it burning, she came back with a small, tattered book.

"My journal, from traveling."

Over the next few hours we flipped through its worn pages while she told me her story. She had originally gone to Thailand for just a short trip. She became friends with a woman while she was there and went shopping with her one day. After they picked out clothes, her friend realized she had forgotten her money. She asked Rahel if she could just borrow some cash and then pay her back later. The price of the shopping venture was rather high, but she agreed to help her out if she promised she would pay back the money. The girl promised, and Rahel paid the bill.

Shortly afterward, her friend disappeared. She never heard from her again. The money she had loaned her was going to help pay for her ticket home, among other things. She was heartbroken. She felt she had no choice but to stay in Thailand for the time being, at least until she could figure something out. She decided to forgive her former friend, at least in her own conscience, and move on.

There were days without food, and there were lonely times, but things always seemed to work out. People offered to let her stay in their homes without her even having to ask, right when she was down to her last penny. She was given food and even money, eventually finding a job on one of the southern islands where she stayed for another eight months. She enjoyed her life there, making many close friends.

When Rahel decided it was time to move on and leave Thailand, she headed for Australia. There she worked as a laborer on a few different farms and met more and more people who helped her along the way.

Her journal documented the many highs and lows of her adventure with emotional entries from moments when she on her own and loneliness took over. Entombed between artwork and poems, you would find scribbled in black crayon: *"Scared … alone … please help"*—written as if she were merely pleading to herself to gain the will to persevere.

In Australia she became friends with a girl who was traveling as well. They were together for a few months, and eventually the other girl decided she was going to leave the country to return home. Upon her departure, she gave Rahel a gift: her car. *The girl gave her a damn car.* She lived in that car for the next year and a half while continuing to work on farms and meet new people, who filled pages of her journals when they parted ways.

"Rahel, you are the most amazing person I have ever met. You have changed my life, and I will always love you."

After a while, she again decided to move on. She went back to Thailand, to the island of Koh Tao where she had resided and made many friends on the first leg of her journey. She lived there for the next few months, and then finally decided it was time to come home.

After we had flipped through her journal, we sat in silence for a moment, watching the flames, listening to the crackling and popping.

"I think it is time for sleep," she said.

I put out the fire and followed her into the house. She left the sliding back door cracked open, explaining that I *"might see a cat come in during the night."*

"Do you … have a cat?"

"No."

"… Okay? …"

"I take care of him. Sometimes he likes to come in and lay with me."

"Why doesn't that surprise me."

During the short amount of time spent with her by the fire, my whole demeanor had changed. When I'd got there, I was—and this will shock you—thinking I was about to have sex with a beautiful blonde foreigner. But for the first time in many months, loveless lovemaking wasn't the high I was chasing. The night with Rahel sewed the first restorative stich in my broken heart. As my faith in humanity had been restored by hitchhiking, now too was my faith in love beginning to return.

· · ·

The next morning we sat together at a white plastic table on her back porch. It was one of those perfect summer mid-mornings. The early sun warmed our skin, teased by whispers of a cool breeze. Our hair smelled of last night's campfire smoke. We each had a cigarette and tea, along with some blueberries and strawberries from her garden. I thought to myself, *I could spend the rest of my life in this moment.*

Then, I remembered: *THE PLAY.* It was in an hour.

"Fuck!"

"What?! What's wrong?"

"I say this knowing full well it could result in my untimely death: I need you to get me back down this mountain as quickly as possible."

I gathered my things and we jumped onto the scooter. We sped down the mountain, stopping only at the spring for a quick drink. Before I knew it we were back on the streets of Heidelberg. We hopped onto the same curb we'd left during the night prior and she turned off the scooter. We paused to take a picture together next to the river and then walked toward the bridge. She decided to head into work early, which led her directly past Johannes's apartment. So we walked together until we reached the door in front of his stairway.

"If you'd like, you can stay at my house for a while. As long as you'd like really."

My heartstrings tightened. "That would be awesome, but ..."

"I don't have the room for your friends—so I apologize that I would not be able to keep them as well—but you can stay if you would like."

I looked into her eyes. "I just ... I really can't leave them. We've pooled all of our money together and we're kind of like ... a team. I really want to stay with you, though."

Even as the words were leaving my lips, I wanted to draw them back. My gaze lowered and I let out an exasperated sigh.

"You must travel for you, Tom. Not for anyone else."

My heart told me to stay. Not because I had fallen in love with her or anything so dramatic, but because I didn't feel like it was time to move on just yet. The city had a hold on me. Johannes and all of our other new friends were there. Hell, the place even had cheap beer! I wanted to stay there for months longer. I wanted to, but I didn't. It wouldn't have been right to split up from Aaron and Corey.

We said our goodbyes, not knowing whether we would see each other again. I watched as she rounded the corner, then turned and walked upstairs in somewhat of a smitten daze, playing over the events of the previous night. The daydream ended the moment I opened the door to Johannes's apartment.

"TOM!" he threw up his arms in relief. "We were worried you would not show up!"

They prodded me for details about my night, but I couldn't put it into words just yet. The questions didn't last long anyway, because we didn't have time. They were literally walking toward the door to leave for the play when I'd walked in. Corey handed me my gear, which he'd already loaded into my daypack, and we walked toward Heidelberg University Square. We arrived just in time to set up our equipment.

The play was a success, as was our recording. I was proud of my new group of friends. The crowd loved them and I was honored to have been a part of the experience.

We spent another day with Johannes before leaving Heidelberg, during which time we mostly just relaxed. Johannes gave us more advice for hitchhiking and saving money while vagabonding around Europe, and we all sat around joking and talking about future plans and the usual traveler banter.

When I left Heidelberg, I thought to myself, someday you'll come back here and see these people again—and to this day, I hope I will.

9

JOURNEY SOUTH
HEIDELBERG, GERMANY TO BASEL, SWITZERLAND

July 23rd

We left Heidelberg late in the afternoon. Johannes had recommended we head to a gas station by the highway and ask people for rides rather than stand by the onramp with our sign. We figured we'd give it a shot.

  After taking a train out of the city, we found a bike path that crawled toward our destination through miles of farmland. Without shade, the midday sun broiled the pavement under our feet and beat down on us in unrelenting waves. At this point though, I had begun to find a rhythm in my hiking abilities. I was tired, but I wasn't about to collapse onto the pavement in a melting pile of disappointment like earlier in the trip. I was listening to the familiar sound of cicadas in the fields, thinking of home. One foot in front of the other, then repeat: *step, step, step.* Aaron, on the other hand, had backpedaled. His backpack straps were less padded than Corey's and my own. Despite this, he refused to use his waist strap, which transfers weight from the shoulders to the hips. He would stop every ten or fifteen minutes to lean forward and take the weight off his shoulders. "Hold up guys, lemme give my shoulders a little rest here." Corey and I would stand there, ready to keep moving, getting more exhausted all the while. I had this mentality that the quicker I walked, the sooner I would be able to rest. Corey felt the same way. So eventually we gave up on waiting for Aaron to take his breaks and just kept walking. When Corey and I finally reached a tunnel under a roadway, we turned to see Aaron—a tiny dot far in the distance—leaning forward with his pack rested.

It was then, standing next to the highway with no gas station in sight, that we started to think we had somehow ended up in the wrong place. When Aaron caught up with us, resting in the shade of the tunnel, he told us that he had come to the same conclusion.

We decided to continue on the bike path, which went across a narrow bridge over the highway and ended at what looked like an American military base on the other side.

We shouldered our packs and walked across the bridge. Cars zipped along the autobahn beneath us. On the other side we turned toward the base, where we hoped one of our fellow Americans could point us in the right direction.

We got within about fifty yards of the entrance when an uncharacteristically chubby soldier standing at the gate snapped to attention, fumbled with his M-16 and then pointed it at us— "STOP! Stop where you are, NOW!"

I quickly raised my hands in surrender and almost coughed up my testicles as they jumped into my chest cavity. "We're Americans! Please don't fuckin shoot us, man!"

"BACK AWAY FROM THE PERIMETER!"

"Listen man, we just need directions fo—"

"BACK AWAY FROM THE PERIMETER!"

"Okay we're leaving, we're leaving."

This guy was like Farve from the movie Super Troopers. You could tell he was just so excited for something to happen to him, *finally*. Oh well … thanks for nothing, US Army.

We turned around and walked back over the bridge to the tunnel. It was starting to get dark, which, as you can imagine, is *no bueno* when it comes to hitchhiking. It's hard enough getting rides when you're three bearded, dirty-looking guys on the side of the road in the daytime.

"Looks like this is where we're sleeping tonight," Aaron said.

"Yup."

That night was ridiculous.

Before leaving Ohio, I had repeatedly uttered a phrase when all my friends would ask if we would have enough money to make it: "I'll sleep under a bridge, I don't give a shit!"

Here I was, months later, sleeping bag laid out on the hard asphalt of a bike path tunnel, thinking, *You stupid motherfucker.* Turns out I do give a shit, and let me tell you, sleeping in a tunnel sucks. We were lying on one side, against the wall, and people were riding their bikes along the other— all night long. I would wake up to a blinding bicycle light and a *ding ding!* as they pedaled past. Then there was the massive thunderstorm that hit us in the middle of the night, misting our sleeping bags.

We woke up with the sun and unanimously decided that the fabled gas station Johannes had shown us might as well have been in Ethiopia. So we headed to the closest onramp to try our usual technique for catching rides.

We were tired. We were grumpy. But still we smiled. I played guitar and Corey held up the sign, dancing around. Aaron started making some sandwiches behind us. I noticed some weird expressions from the drivers as they sped by us. *What the hell is going on?* I wondered.

I looked over my shoulder and saw Aaron sharpening his knife to make the sandwiches. "Uhhh Aaron. I'm gonna go out on a limb here and say that there is no way in hell anyone's going to pick us up if you're standing back there sharpening a killing instrument."

Corey looked back and bent over with laughter. "Aaron, you've got to be kidding me."

He hadn't even thought about it. All three of us laughed for a good while, just imagining driving down the autobahn and seeing three strange guys standing there, two grinning and waving and one slowly sharpening a knife.

Aaron put away the knife, but still no one was stopping. No one was even waving or really acknowledging our existence at all for that matter. We finally realized that since it was eight o-clock in the morning, all of these people were probably on their way to work. You know which kind of people had usually picked us up so far? Hippies. You know who probably doesn't wake up early? Hippies. We came to the conclusion that it wasn't going to happen.

We walked along the highway until we found a shaded spot by some trees and spread out Corey's rain fly to lie down on. I put in my earbuds and slipped a bandanna over my eyes. I have an app on my phone for traveling which plays a fan noise that's usually pretty good at drowning out background noise. But here, next to the screaming cars on the autobahn, it didn't do a damn thing. Fortunately, I was so tired that I still fell asleep within minutes.

I was awoken not long afterward by a gentle kick in the ribs. I didn't hear anything but the static noise of traffic and the fan app. I pulled the bandanna up from my eyes. There were two German police officers standing over me. They were yelling at me, but I couldn't hear a word they were saying. I took out my headphones.

"Hello, officers," I said, smiling for some dumb reason.

They looked at me as if I were a complete moron. "You know you cannot sleep here, yah? Zat is zee autobahn over there. You cannot sleep on zee autobahn."

"Oh, we can't?" Aaron asked innocently. This was something we did every time we were in situations like this … play dumb.

"No, you cannot. Do you have any drugs?"

"No sir." *Can't stress that enough, sir.*

"Okay. You must leave now or ve can arrest you, okay? You walk down farther, maybe four kilometers, and you vill find a gas station. You can find a ride from zhere."

The damn gas station …

We packed up and started walking—pretty much back in the same general direction from whence we had come. After an hour, Corey and I reached the gas station and looked back. Aaron was bent over, resting, far behind us. "He's gonna have to figure something out with that pack," Corey commented. One huge oversight during the packing phase of our preparation was the negligence to leave space for carrying food. Because of this, we were forced to carry all of our food in grocery bags. Since Aaron had the lightest pack, he was delegated to carry these bags. Of course, that didn't stop him from pawning off as many items as possible to Corey and me. "We all use the stuff," he would say.

I was carrying all of the computer equipment and Corey carrying the extra camping equipment which benefited all of us as well. But when I told this to Aaron, the concept of splitting up our labor was lost on him. Sticks in the stream, much like pooling our money together had been. So alas, I was forced to carry heavy bags of rice or extra water on top of my already heavier pack while Aaron's grocery bags would be lighted to less than ten pounds. Oh well. *Step, step step.*

We stood in front of that gas station for six hours, asking just about everyone who walked by. No one wanted to give us a ride. We met a couple of girls in their early twenties who were also hitchhiking. They were walking around and asking everyone in German for rides. *If they aren't getting rides, then we stand no chance*, I thought. We sat along a wall next to the restrooms with a cardboard sign sitting in front of us. Since the girls would surely get a ride before we did, we gave up for the time being. I wrote in my journal, played guitar, and smoked probably a hundred cigarettes. It was during the lattermost of those activities that a comically small police car sped up and skidded to a stop in front of us. Out jumped two officers who swaggered over and took the cigarette right out of my mouth, throwing it on the ground and stomping it out.

"Passports!" one of them demanded. They didn't look like they were here to fuck around: physically fit, with tactical clothing, tactical vests, and tactical mustaches.

"Okay, give us a second," I said, opening up my backpack.

"You have drugs, no?"

"No," Aaron said. "No drugs."

"You have drugs—marijuana?"

"No drugs."

They looked directly at Corey this time. His long hair, bandanna, and huge beard were not working his favor. It was posed as a statement rather than a question when he moved on to him: "You do drugs."

"No sir." He quickly shook his head back and forth.

"You have marijuana?" he asked.

"Nope."

"Have you ever smoked marijuana or tried any drugs?"

"Nope. Never once in my life."

"Hmmm …"

Aaron spoke up again—"You can search our bags, man. We don't have anything."

He finally relented, and nodded at the quiet one who then held out our passports and said, "You don't smoke here. Go away from gas station for that." He nodded at the pumps, and then raised both of his arms above his head—"Boom."

"Oh … yeah, that's a good point."

They got back in their car, but slowly drove in circles around the gas station. After a while, a Lexus SUV pulled in next to us. They screeched to a halt behind it as a skinny, short guy with a buzz-cut stepped out.

They spoke in German, so I wasn't sure exactly what was being said, but it looked like they were putting him through the same rounds as us. The next thing I knew they were searching through his vehicle and assumedly asking him whether or not he possessed drugs currently or had ever done drugs. He was eventually cleared and they got in their car to leave.

As the man was walking into the gas station he dropped his ID and Aaron ran over and grabbed it. "Hey bro, you dropped your card."

"Ahh, thanks," the guy said.

"Hey, where are you headed?"

"South, to Switzerland."

"You think we could catch a ride? We're trying to make it as far south as we can and we haven't had any luck so far."

He looked at us and pondered for a second, then he shrugged—
"Ahh sure, why not." He turned around and opened up the hatch
to his SUV so we could load our bags in while he went into the
store. He returned as we were getting in the car. "I'm Alex," he
said as he sat in the driver's seat. We introduced ourselves in turn.

"Is that normal? For police to do that?" I asked.

"Yeah man," he replied as he slipped on a pair of Oakley sunglasses and put the car in reverse. "That is how they try to solve
the drug problem here in Germany: they just ask if you have ever
done drugs, and if you're stupid enough to tell them, yes, then
they can arrest you."

"So if I tell them I smoked a joint five years ago, they can arrest me?"

"Yes. To them, that is the admission of a crime."

"That's insane."

"Ahh yes, but it's pretty much useless for actually finding drugs
or marijuana, so for me it is no problem." He reached into his
pocket. "I had this on me the whole time," he held up a blunt.
"You guys smoke?"

Corey spoke up from the back: "We do."

Alex lit the blunt as we sped down the highway.

He was a booking agent for a living. He explained to us that he
had just left the police station because of an altercation he had
gotten into earlier that day. He'd booked an act at a local club
and the manager had canceled at the last minute. He wanted his
deposit back and had attempted to actually kidnap Alex and ran-
som the money.

The manager asked him to meet up so they could "talk" and the
next thing he knew, his vehicle was blocked-in and a bunch of big
Armenians were standing with the club owner. They were trying
to throw him into a trunk to take him back to some other country
I can't remember the name of, but luckily were stopped by a rather large guy that Alex happened to have with him at the time. He
jumped back into his car and called the police, which fortunately
was enough to make the would-be kidnappers flee. I was a little

wary believing the story at that point: all that for what, probably a five hundred euro deposit?

His cell phone rang—"Yeah … No man, fuck you, okay? You gonna pull some shit like that on me, I can pull some shit too. I already talked to my lawyers, bro … I was gonna give you the 50,000 back and just be done with your stupid ass … but that's not happening now. You signed a contract …"

Did he just say 50,000? 50,000 euros?!

He hung up the phone. "See—this fucking asshole, man. He read some shit on a tabloid that Akon is canceling his European tour or something. I told that stupid fuck it was bullshit. He believes that shit over me."

"Wait—so who do you do booking for?" Corey asked from the back seat.

"A bunch of people, man—hip-hop artists mainly: Akon, 50 Cent, Lil' Kim, Wu Tang Clan … I did Snoop Dogg and Dre back in the nineties."

"Holy shit, dude!"

"Yeah, this asshole paid his deposit and now he canceled the show and wants his money back. That's why he tried to take me and shit, to make me pay."

"50,000 euros is the deposit?" I asked.

"Yeah, with Akon they pay fifty percent up front and the other fifty percent at the performance, plus all the incidentals and shit."

"What does that mean?"

"Here, you can look through his rider if you want … the shit they ask for can get crazy, man …" he handed me a stack of papers.

I flipped through them. The first couple pages were the details of the show—when and where it was, how much (100,000 euros) and all of that. There was a huge list of food and drink requests on the third or fourth page: one case of Fiji water, chilled; one case of Fiji water, room temperature; four Pizza Hut pizzas, one pepperoni and cheese, etc.; three buckets of KFC chicken, etc.; four Snickers bars; one bottle of Cristal for Akon's dressing room; one bottle of Cristal for band dressing room. It went on and on like that and then it moved on to furniture: Akon's dressing room:

one black couch, one black love seat; one black coffee table with glass top. It continued with first-class airfare, limos, just about anything you could imagine.

"They will usually pay about 100,000 euros for the show, then another 50 or 100,000 or so for shit like that—and man, the acts don't even touch half of it," he told us. "Such a fucking waste sometimes."

"Wait, is it like … someone's job to go buy all of this shit?"

"Oh yeah, man. I used to work with Mariah Carey. That bitch was crazy. She had to have an all-white dressing room, with all white furniture, and four white puppies in it."

"Four white puppies?!" Aaron said with a laugh.

"Four fuckin white puppies, bro," he confirmed.

Around this time he mentioned the name of his business—which I won't repeat in order to protect him from any liabilities—and I inconspicuously looked it up on my phone.

Sure as shit, there he was. His picture and everything, along with a lot of the aforementioned clients.

"Hey, do you guys have somewhere to stay tonight?" he asked.

"No man, wherever we can find really." Corey said.

"Well if my wife is cool with it, I'll let you stay at my house tonight and then drive you farther tomorrow."

"Oh man, that would be fantastic."

He took out his phone and spoke in German for a few moments, and well, let's just say you don't need to know German to understand the universal language of a man trying in vain to reason with his wife.

"Yeah, that's not happening." Apparently his wife thought there was something sketchy about bringing three foreign hitchhikers back to their house.

"Well, I'll tell you what, guys. I know of a little park a few miles away from my house. I can drop you off there to sleep tonight and then I'll pick you up tomorrow and run you back to the highway. How's that?"

Upon arrival at said park, I got Alex's number and saved it in my phone. He told us he'd return sometime in the afternoon the next day to pick us up, and then he got back in his SUV and headed down the road.

We left the parking area and walked down rough-cut stone steps to a copse of trees nestled between stone retaining walls. The park bordered a slow-moving river, upon which a family of orange and brown ducks floated. We hung our hammocks between the trees after our nightly dinner of rice and tuna—this time with a desert of watermelon we'd purchased from a market up the street.

Despite the ride from Alex, we considered Johannes's "sit-and-talk" method of hitchhiking a failure. The next day, we planned to go back to dancing alongside onramps. The only question was whether Alex would actually come back to get us. He had driven us relatively far into this town and we didn't really have much of a clue how to make it back to the highway. We knew the general direction it was in, but that was about it. I fell asleep hoping he would keep his promise.

10

KiNGS OF THE ROAD: HiTCHHiKERS EXTRAORDiNAiRE

BASEL, SWiTZERLAND TO MiLAN, ITALY

July 25th

The next day, my phone calls to Alex went unanswered. We waited until the afternoon before leaving. The problem, as mentioned previously, was that we weren't sure exactly where we were. So we set off in the general direction whence we'd come and hoped we'd spot an onramp.

About ten minutes into the hike, the skies darkened and rain dotted the pavement. Within five minutes it increased to a torrent. I suggested we stop and hitch under a bridge that the road passed through, but Aaron wanted to keep walking farther out of town.

Corey yelled over the static of the downpour: "But it's raining, man."

"Yeah but I think we'll just have better luck out there," he pointed, squinting against the rain.

"There," was about a hundred feet farther down the road.

"Ugh. Whatever."

Because Aaron and I both had a natural inclination toward leadership, a hairline fracture in the group was beginning to compound. Ego aside, my grievance was that I felt he lacked the ability to navigate us in the right direction. Some of the shit he would say was baffling to me: for example, choosing to stand out in the pouring rain rather than taking shelter a mere one hundred feet away. Recently his suggestions started to feel more like barked orders and the delicate balance of power teetered toward implosion. Corey and I secretly nicknamed him "The Lieutenant."

Having stood on the shoulder of the road for close to an hour with no luck getting a ride, the rain finally let up. We decided to keep moving. If only it were that simple ...

"Let's just walk farther down and jump onto the highway there. I bet there'll be a gas station or something eventually," Aaron suggested, pointing to a busy highway that ran perpendicular to the road we were on.

"We can't even see where that goes, though," I said. "Plus there's not really anywhere to walk alongside it. It'd be super dangerous." There was a large barrier next to the highway, which left about five feet between it and the traffic that would be speeding by—not much walking room. "What if we just walked back to the first road in town and walked along that to an onramp?"

It was an argument of which I'll spare you the details, because it went on for a while before Aaron finally just turned and started walking down the road. Corey and I continued to protest as we followed behind. Careening vehicles brushed our shoulders as we pounded pavement toward destination unknown. People were honking as they passed, probably telling us to get the hell off of the side of the highway. We walked for almost a mile like this before finally reaching an exit with a rest stop.

"See, told you guys ..." Aaron stated as we approached the rest stop.

"Aaron you just completely fucking guessed and led us down a highway where we almost got flattened by trucks every five seconds. You didn't tell us shit. This is why we vote on these things—you're not the dictator."

"Well it's always you guys versus me when we vote on shit."

"Nahhh man," Corey spoke up. "I tend to agree with Tom more—I'll give you that—but I side with you on some stuff too."

"He agrees with me most of the time because your ideas are fucking stupid, Aaron."

We walked over to the gas station at the rest stop and sat along a wall. I went into the restroom and filled up all of our water bottles in the sink while Corey and Aaron waited outside. When I came back out and sat down, Corey motioned toward a tiny Fiat Panda (a small car about the size of a Mini-Cooper). "Wait till you see the girl that gets into that car."

"Hot?"

"Smoking hot."

A few minutes later he elbowed me and gestured. He wasn't lying. She was short and thin, with long brown hair and black-rimmed glasses. Instead of walking back to her car, she walked directly over to us. "Hallo … Do you guys need ride?"

The three of us stared blankly.

"You … you need ride?" she repeated.

"Uhhhh … yeah?"

"I can give you ride …" she said, with a slight laugh at our awkwardness.

"You can? … Ohhh … really?" Corey finally figured out what was happening.

"Yes, no problem—if you can all fit."

We collected our things and followed her to the tiny car. We all squeezed into the Fiat with our packs on our laps and my guitar and Corey's foldable drum in the back hatch.

This girl, who turned out to be only nineteen years old, drove us for a couple hours and ended up buying us dinner at the next rest stop restaurant.

It was getting dark when we said goodbye and thanked her for her generosity. We were at yet another gas station. We sat a cardboard sign in front of us with the name of the next city. Corey and I played chess. Aaron wrote in his journal. Then he and Corey played chess while I read a book. Then I played guitar. Before we knew it, the sun was setting. No one had paid the least bit of attention to us.

"We're gonna have to sleep here." Corey said.

There was a brief and fruitless discussion about the logistics of doing so. There wasn't really anywhere to disappear. The entire area was fenced off on the highway side. Behind the rest stop was a steep drop-off into a swamplike area. All we could find was a group of bushes directly next to the gas station. It would have to work.

We laid our sleeping bags down and tied our packs to them, just in case someone tried to grab them in the middle of the night. We were not hidden by any means. Anyone who looked toward the bushes would surely see us. The back door to the gas station was only about three feet away from Aaron and there was no cover between us and that door. To one side of us was a road which led to the highway. To the other was a road that ran parallel to the parking lot. Ahead of us was a connector between the two. We were essentially sleeping on a tiny grass peninsula between three heavily trafficked areas. *Would we be robbed? Arrested? Fined?*

I was tired, though, and a group of trucks idling nearby made for perfect ambient noise. I slept like a baby.

Unfortunately, that sleep didn't last long. Aaron woke me three or four hours later, right before dawn. "Hey man, I think we should get up. There's people moving around and shit." I woke up Corey and we gathered our gear. Aaron had been too worried to sleep at all.

Corey was the king of sleeping anywhere. You could put that dude inside of a monster truck tire, drive it over a field of land-mines, and he would be snoring inside. I was improving, but would never reach his level of professional hobo sleepery.

We caught a ride that afternoon with an older woman who took us to yet another gas station. We decided to take a lunch break. Aaron spotted a river nearby, so we decided to try our hand at a fresh meal: After lifting up some big rocks and sourcing a few earthworms, Aaron took a spool of fishing line and hooks to the bank to try his luck. Corey and I cooked rice while he was doing that. After he'd declared the fishing unsuccessful and we'd eaten our rice, we headed back out to the highway and caught another ride from a woman and her adolescent kid. They took us to the next big city where we purchased more food from a supermarket.

When we headed back to the highway, we found ourselves playing a game of Frogger: due to construction going on, the onramp we needed to reach was on the other side of the highway. This required us to shuffle with our packs and bags/guitar/cajon through a narrow channel between two fences. Then, we had to duck under a section of fence, come out on the other side directly in the middle of a single lane of traffic, and quickly run to the other side. We took turns waiting for a space between cars, scurrying under the fence and onto the road, and then running across.

Once we all crossed safely, we set up shop along the onramp. We were in a particularly goofy mood; this time we had headphones in and were dancing around like a bunch of idiots while we held up our signs. People were laughing and honking and waving as they passed.

Two young women in a big SUV pulled up to the intersection and offered us a ride, which we gladly accepted. The girl driving had a flat-brim hat and gauged ears, dressing with a kind of "scene" fashion, and the other was a skinny black girl who dressed more conservatively. They both had awesome tattoos.

We rode with them into the Alps, where the woman driving swerved in and out of traffic along the narrow mountain passes without giving two shits or a fart whether we lived or died. She didn't speak very much English (her native language was Italian), but the girl in the passenger seat did. We talked to them about music and the history of the area we were passing through: the driver pointed out some of the oldest Roman ruins known to modern archaeology—an old bridge nestled into the mountainside.

I wasn't aware until I visited the country, but three main languages are spoken in Switzerland—German in the north, French in the middle and Italian in the south. To the best of my knowledge, there is no "Swiss" language, although the accents of Swiss people differ from their respective counterparts. Most people we met could speak at least two of those languages as well as English.

Apparently the driver noticed our fingers wrapped around the armrests like boa constrictors securing a meal.

"She say … don't worry about her driving … she knows these roads very well," the girl in the passenger seat translated.

"Sure, yeah." I pulled my seatbelt tighter.

They dropped us off in a town called Bellinzona, Switzerland. We were getting close to the Italian border—around twenty-five more miles. They told us if we hiked down and out of the city we'd reach a river, which should be perfect for camping. We said goodbye to them and started walking. It was quite the trek from where they dropped us off—several miles. It was a steep decline and I couldn't help but think how shitty the hike back up would be in the morning.

Eventually we reached the river and walked along its bank until we found a secluded sandy spot along the bank. The rippling water was mountain runoff—icy turquoise in the middle and crystal clear along the calmer shallows. Spray from the passing water teased the air with the smell of fresh rain. Coupled with the surrounding pine trees, the calming scent would make a Bath and Bodyworks candle that could drive white women to delirious murder.

We took advantage of the cool river water to bathe after four days of strenuous, dirty travel. Then we washed our clothes using sand against large stones and laid them out on the shore to dry before going to sleep.

I slept-in the next day. Even though my quality of sleep had been pretty good the past few days, I'd gotten nowhere near enough of it. I felt rejuvenated when I woke up. We hit the trail in the early afternoon and hiked back up the mountain toward the highway. The hike was a slog, and as usual Aaron brushed off the idea of grabbing one of the numerous buses lumbering uphill. That was frustrating enough, but coupled with his complaining about his shoulder straps or aching feet or disintegrating back, it drove me to madness. *If we're going to hike up this mountain because you're too cheap to drop three euros on a bus fare, fine. But that means you deal with it. Put one foot in front of the other and suck it up.* I don't remember Corey complaining more than once or twice during these hikes—he would eventually earn the nickname "The Mule." We loaded that cajon bag (carrying the foldable cajon drum) with so much bullshit it was surprising he could even walk without leaning toward whichever side it hung on.

After two hours of heaving and sweating, we finally reached the summit of our alpine jag. We posted up at a gas station, where we once again made a visit to the super classy shitter to top-off our water bottles with impeccably clean and tasty public restroom sink water.

It didn't take us long to thumb a ride from this location. The gas station was sitting at an intersection with a set of traffic lights leading directly to a highway onramp. A young woman pulled over to the side and flipped on her hazard lights. Another Fiat Panda.

"Hello!" she said with a big smile. "If you can fi—"

Corey interrupted her, throwing up his hand with a grin—"We got this—we rode in one yesterday."

"Oh, good!" she said with a laugh. She opened up the back hatch and a German Shepherd hopped out. *Oh, shit ... that's a curveball.*

"Well, there wasn't a dog in the one that picked us up last time," I said.

"We got this ..." Corey's optimism never failed.

It was more cramped than last time—I had to have my pack and guitar between my legs and on my lap, which required Aaron to shut my door for me since I couldn't reach the handle. The poor dog was holed up in the back hatch along with the cajon drum.

This woman spoke English well, but was a native Italian speaker. I took the opportunity to learn my first bit of Italian, which was, ironically, "How do you ask someone if they speak English?"

"Ahh, it is: *'Parli inglese?'*"

I repeated the phrase in my best Italian accent.

She laughed at me. "I am sorry—you spoke very well, but you sound like Italian man from far in the south of Italy. Is just funny."

We told her of our plans to continue hitchhiking all the way to

Rome. She was skeptical. "I don't think you will have much luck from Lugano, where I am taking you. You would be much better taking a train from there. People will not want to drive you."

We had heard this kind of stuff before—about not being able to catch rides—but we entertained the idea by agreeing to at least price-check some train tickets.

I learned more Italian as she drove us out of the mountains and into the town of Lugano, seated along the southern Swiss border. There she helped us unload our gear, much to her pup's satisfaction. She and the dog posed with us for a picture and then she and Aaron headed into the train station to ask about tickets. Corey and I dogsat. "Sit. Sit, boy," Corey commanded. The dog stood there, panting and staring blankly.

"Uhhh, I don't think he speaks English," I said.

"Shit." He laughed. "I didn't even think of that. Uhhh, *seetooo*, boy. Whatever the Italian word for 'sit' is, do it." The dog continued to stare at him. "Thought shepherds were supposed to be smart and shit …"

"Don't you dare speak about him that way. He's doing his best."

Aaron and our driver walked out of the train station with tickets, which surprised me. I figured there was no way in hell Aaron would buy them, regardless of the cost. I don't remember the price exactly, but it turned out they were pretty cheap. The tickets would take us to Milan, and from there we could either hitch again or buy another train ticket.

We thanked the young woman for all of her help, and she loaded the dog into the car and drove off. Once in the train station, we were having trouble finding our platform. When time began to run out, Corey finally asked a police officer near the tracks to ask if he could direct us. This was their conversation:

Corey: "Excuse me, sir. Can you show me which train—"

"You have drugs?!"

"What? No, I just need to fi—"

"Do you have drugs?!"

"No I don't have drugs. I need to find my train. If you could ju—"

"Do you have your passport?!"

"Yeah, I have my passport. Listen we're really late, sir ... I just n—"

"Come with me," the officer said as he grabbed Corey by the arm and led him to a back room. Aaron and I watched from a few yards away with our mouths open.

"Well, Corey's arrested," I said.

"What the fuck ..."

Corey emerged after a few moments and ran over to us. "Jesus Christ, that was ridiculous. Dude was asking me if I've ever done drugs and shit, just like in Germany. I guess our platform is over there."

As I followed him to our train, I felt relieved that we were finally going to have a solid ride without having to worry. Maybe hitch-hiking was over? The generous and selfless things that people did for us during that time never once ceased to amaze me: people driving out of their way to take us further, buying or giving us food, putting us up in their houses, giving us beer, all of it. It was humbling. I'd gained a whole new outlook on life and humanity for the umpteenth time on our journey so far.

11

TRAIN HOPPING HOBOS
BASEL, SWITZERLAND TO MILAN, ITALY

July 27th

The train we boarded out of Lugano broke down in the middle of the tracks. One minute we were moving, the next minute we were learning local swear words as people groaned at no one in particular. We sat there for something like thirty minutes and despite asking a few people around us, we never did find out exactly what was going on. Although I didn't know it at the time, I'd learned two valuable lessons about Italy right from the start:

Nothing runs on time—or is even guaranteed to run at all for that matter.

The Italian heat is a sweltering, humid blanket akin to being boiled alive.

Due to the first train's holdup, we missed our connecting train to Genova. We had to wait for the next one in Milan, which was conveniently four hours later. The plus side was that the train station had WiFi. I hadn't been able to contact anyone at home since we'd left Heidelberg some five days prior, so I used this time to let all my friends and family know that I wasn't dead or anything.

Our second train ride was uneventful. We arrived in Genova hoping for good luck, but were disappointed. Despite our blissful riverside respite, it seemed like we couldn't catch a damn break. I was starting to think we were cursed somehow. We left the train station and walked around for a while, hoping to find a cheap hostel or hotel. We didn't have any luck. It was getting late and we were all hungry, so we had a seat on the grass in the middle of a tiny park next to the train station and cooked some rice. There were homeless people everywhere, sleeping wherever they wanted—a good sign for us.

We managed to pick up a WiFi signal in the park and used it to try to locate somewhere to sleep. It didn't look promising. There was no way we were going to be able to make it out of the city. It was late—around one in the morning—and all the trains had stopped for the night. We had two options: either sleep somewhere on the street or shell out the money for a hotel. All three of us agreed that the hotels around the area were way too expensive, so we opted for the street. Or, more specifically, the train station. We walked all the way to the farthest terminal and found some benches. The dozen-or-so vagrants occupying the terminal did not look like a friendly bunch. In fact, we were just setting our bags down on some benches when two English-speaking police officers approached us:

"Hey guys," one of them said, "you should be careful, okay? These are dangerous people—they will steal from you if you are not careful. Watch your bags very close, okay?"

"Thank you, sir," Corey answered. The cop nodded his head and walked the other way. At least the police in Italy seemed friendlier than Germany's Gestapo forces.

"I'll watch the stuff if you guys wanna sleep," Aaron offered.

"We can take turns," I said.

"I'm not gonna be able to sleep anyway."

I didn't think *any* of us were going to be able to sleep. We walked over to the train schedule and inspected it: the next train was set to depart at five in the morning. By that time it was two, so that gave us three hours to doze before we could disembark. From Genova we planned to head farther south where we could hopefully find somewhere to set up our hammocks and get at least one good night's sleep, since it was apparent that we were going to be up all night. There was one small addition to this plan that changed the course of our travel in Italy from then on out:

"You know," I said, "I noticed no one checked our tickets on either one of those trains. We should just hop on this thing tomorrow; I bet they don't even check."

"I noticed that too," Corey said.

"But what if we get caught?" Aaron said.

"I don't think we will—I mean if we do, fuck it. We could talk our way out of it, I think."

"I don't know. I think we should just buy the tickets," Aaron said. "I don't think it's a good idea."

"Listen man, you're always bitching about money. Here's your chance to save some. I guarantee they aren't gonna check shit."

In the end democracy won out; Aaron agreed to give it a try. All that was left to do was try and get some sleep. I laid out my sleeping bag on one side of a concrete bench. Each bench had two sides, separated by the backrest in the middle. Corey was situated one bench farther down and Aaron was on the other side of mine. Ours were the only benches left available.

"We should put all our bags together by me," Aaron said. "I can watch them while you guys sleep."

"That's a good idea," Corey agreed. He grabbed his bag and brought it over to our bench, where he started to dig through it for his sleeping bag. About this time, a sketchy looking guy in a tattered black t-shirt and baggy jeans walked past us, glaring with crazy eyes. He walked over to the bench Corey had planned on sleeping on, looked back toward us, and then plopped right down on it. Corey looked up at me. "You have to be kidding me."

We couldn't help but laugh.

"You can have my side here Corey," Aaron offered. "I'm not gonna be sleeping anyway."

Corey accepted. The guy that had taken his bench was lying

there, staring at us. We spoke to each other loudly: "HEY AARON, DO YOU HAVE YOUR KNIFE BY YOU? THE BIG ONE?"

"YEP, I'M GONNA KEEP IT RIGHT HERE NEXT TO ME ... DO YOU HAVE YOUR KNIFE?"

"SURE DO—I'M GONNA PUT IT HERE RIGHT BY MY HAND SO IT'S READY. COREY, YOU HAVE YOUR KNIFE?"

"YEP, I'M GONNA GO AHEAD AND GET IT OUT OF THE SHEATH SO IT'S READY TO STAB A MOTHERFUCKER, JUST IN CASE."

By the end of this conversation, the shady dude surely understood that he was going to get stabbed right in the face if he came anywhere near us or our shit. I figured it didn't matter whether he spoke English, considering we were waving our knives around like goddamned pirates.

I didn't sleep more than an hour between the time I finally laid down and when I awoke to leave. When Aaron roused us at four-thirty I was hungry; I was tired; I was angry ... I wanted to be in a bed. One with a pillowtop mattress, not concrete and chewed-up bubble gum.

We walked to our designated terminal and leaned our bags against a bench. I smoked my third cigarette in a half hour while I drew pictures of food in my journal. Pizza, hot-dogs, hamburgers, everything. All we had left was some rice (which we didn't have time to cook), a dollop of Nutella, and a few slices of bread, which we needed to save if we wanted to have anything to eat for lunch. The hunger pangs were made all the more unbearable by the fact that we had money with which we could have bought food. Aaron would have thrown a fit if I'd wanted to go buy breakfast somewhere, though. I didn't even ask.

Five rolled around and our train still hadn't shown up. Aaron looked at his wristwatch. "Where the hell is this thing?"

"Who fucking cares," I grumbled. "I want to die."

Corey walked over and looked at a big board containing the train schedules. "Uhhh ... what the hell were we looking at last night? This train doesn't even run today."

"Huhh?" Aaron walked over.

"Kill me …" I whispered as I sank down against the dirty wall next to the tracks. My head throbbed.

"Today is Sunday—the next train doesn't come for another hour."

"Ah, fuck me."

I sighed.

When the train finally did show up an hour later, we boarded it with no problems. No one asked for a ticket, just as Corey and I had hoped. The plan was to get off at a little town called Deiva Marina, which sits along the northwestern coast of Italy. On Google Maps, we had seen an area adjacent to the village with plenty of trees and grass, suitable for a hobo campsite.

We weren't sure which stop we were supposed to take, as there wasn't any kind of monitor or sign with the stop schedule. Instead, we looked out the window and read the signs at each stop. As exhausted as I was, the views out the window of the train lifted my spirits. Here was the true Italian coastline right at arm's length: rocky cliffsides jutting from choppy-blue Mediterranean water, sparkling in the early morning sun. We passed sporadic towns and villages—tiny cottages on a ridge here or a hillside there; honeycomb communities of stucco or brick buildings, which seemed almost as if they were carved into the seaside coves during earth's creation.

The problem was, I didn't see a single tree anywhere. There was plenty of shrubbery, but nothing suitable for setting up a campsite. I hoped Deiva Marina would be different.

Aaron said he would let us know when to get off the train, so I pulled out a book. I was dull from lack of sleep, losing myself in its pages and periodically nodding off.

Aaron must have zoned out as well because at one point he kind of just looked up, stared outside for a minute and then said, "I think we missed our stop."

"Sounds about right," Corey said.

"We'll have to get off at the next stop and then head back in the other direction. I think it was just one or two stops back," Aaron told us.

We hopped off the train at the next stop and decided to look around for a place to sleep there. There was no particular reason we had been heading to Deiva Marina, it had simply looked the most suitable for camping when we'd looked at the map.

We climbed up and down (mostly down) the hot gray paths of the village for about twenty minutes before deciding to give up. The whole town was situated on a steep cliffside, with buildings and roads packed densely among it. The muscles in my legs screamed as we climbed back up to the train station. We decided we should eat something before we hopped back on the train.

We finished off the rest of the Nutella along with some stale bread. Getting some food in my belly drastically improved my mood. Aaron, on the other hand, was groggy eyed and grumpier than ever. I'm sure it didn't help that he hadn't slept at all while Corey and I had at least gotten an hour or two of shuteye.

He rolled his eyes when Corey and I dipped our fingers in the Nutella jar to get as much of its delicious goodness out as possible before throwing the jar away. Now granted, I had been a total smartass and sarcastically asked him permission, since he had thrown such a huge fit about us eating directly out of the jar in Germany. The final straw was when Corey came up with the idea of filling the almost-empty Nutella jar with water and shaking it up to try and make a chocolate drink of some kind.

"Fucking brilliant," I said.

"I know right ... I'm a goddamn genius."

"Are you done playing around so we can get moving?" Aaron snapped from behind us.

"Just chill man, we're almost done," I said.

"Well I'm going back to the train station, I'll see you guys there."

Corey was focused on the jar of Nutella which he was slowly filling with water. "Whatever," he said as Aaron shouldered his pack and then walked away.

"What a dick ..."

"He's just tired. Here we go, dude," he closed the lid on the jar and shook it furiously. "Best ... idea ... ever."

He unscrewed the cap and handed it to me. "First dibs?"

I took a sip. "Fuck me … that is amazing. A lot better than I expected it to be."

"When are you going to learn that there is no way to make Nutella not taste good?"

We walked back to the train station and sat on a bench next to Aaron, who had his headphones in and was staring straight ahead.

This is stupid, I thought. We're never going to be able to carry on like this. The arguments about money was driving us apart and I worried if we spent another month in Europe we might end up killing each other. After ten or fifteen minutes, an idea suddenly struck me. I tapped Aaron on the shoulder.

"Why don't we just leave Europe early?" I asked.

"What, like … change our flights to Thailand?"

"Yeah. I mean, we aren't really seeing much anyway. At least in Southeast Asia we might actually be able to afford shit."

In Thailand, a night in a hostel could cost as little as $1.00 USD per night, compared to Western Europe's bare minimum of $12 on a good day.

Aaron eyed the ground in contemplation. "That's actually not a bad idea." He raised his head. "What do you think Corey?"

"If that means I can eat a real fuckin meal and sleep in a real fuckin bed, then I don't give a shit what we do."

"And you don't care if you don't get to see much of Italy?" Aaron asked me.

"Look at what we're doing, man. I haven't been able to see even a tiny percentage of the stuff I had wanted to see in Europe … money is ruining this trip as far as I'm concerned. All I ask is that I get to have at least one Italian meal in a decent restaurant."

"Well … I say we try to find WiFi tomorrow and email them. Maybe book the flight for next week."

"Deal."

I instantly felt relieved. Once we made it to Thailand, we would be able to afford to enjoy our trip without guilt. Donations had been rolling in from the website—around $300 had been given to us by our friends and family members back home who wanted to help out. I was confident they would keep trickling in and that I could make some decent money if I could have WiFi for a reliable amount of time. But I had given up trying to convince Aaron of this. By then he'd made it clear that he didn't believe we'd ever see money from my computer work. But in Thailand, we could afford to stay in a hostel every night. We could get a meal in a decent restaurant for one or two bucks. My spirits were lifted—soon we would escape our homeless lifestyle. I wrote in my journal as we waited for the train to arrive and take us someplace we could try and sleep. It was around one in the afternoon at that point, and I was a zombie: *I am so done with sleeping in strange, dangerous places, and surviving on little sustenance. Thailand can't come soon enough.*

12

DEE, THE FRIENDLY NEIGHBORHOOD EMU
DEIVA MARINA, ITALY

July 28th

Much like the other villages I'd seen from the train, Deiva Marina was devoid of suitable vegetation for campsites. We walked through the city to the outskirts on the other side and spotted a bridge with a dried-up creek bed underneath it. We all agreed that it was more than suitable to get some rest under.

We exited the footpath after crossing the bridge and descented a steep berm, forging a path through weeds as tall as our shoulders and finding footholds on large rocks embedded in the earth. At the bottom we entered a dry creek bed. There were two massive concrete walls which supported the bridge and a relatively flat area alongside one of them with finer, pea-sized gravel. It looked as good a campsite as any.

We took a long nap that afternoon and woke up in the early I figured maybe getting my frustrations out on paper was a better way of venting than continuing to jab Aaron with sarcastic comments. Something needed to change. His attitudes on money and life constantly grated my nerves. Corey was getting sick of it as well, but being a much more laid-back individual, he absorbed it without much fuss. I decided that Corey's approach was better for all involved. Getting to Thailand earlier would help, but I needed to make a real effort to get along with Aaron if I wanted this trip to improve. I nudged him awake.

"Hey man, it's like six in the afternoon. We should probably get up."

He rubbed his eyes and sat up. I continued—"I think we should talk, man. Listen... I know I've been kind of a d—HOLY SHIT, DUDE."

"What?!"

"There's a gigantic bird behind you."

"Huh?!" Aaron turned around and saw the massive ostrich-like bird standing a few feet away from him.

"What the hell is that?!" I asked.

The bird stood there and looked at us. *"Hmmpff..."* It made a weird noise and casually walked a few feet further.

"Corey ... wake up and look at this shit." I shook him.

"Uhhhh," he yawned and sat up rather quickly. "See wh—HOLY SHIT. That's a big-ass bird."

"What the hell is that thing? An ostrich?" I asked again.

"No, I think it's an emu," Aaron said calmly as he turned on his camera to take some pictures. "Pretty sure they're native to Australia."

"Well, what the fuck is it doing under this bridge then?"

Corey chuckled. "That's a great question ... that I don't think any of us have the answer to."

Just then we heard voices above us on the bridge, followed by a loud *THUMP* a few yards away. A potato ... someone had just thrown a potato off of the bridge above us. *THUMP!* ...another one. *THUMPTHUMPTHUMP...* they apparently emptied the whole sack into the creek bed.

"This thing must be like the town mascot or something," Corey said. "Wonder what kind of dipshit thinks a bird is going to eat a potato though."

Aaron walked over to the potatoes, which had landed amidst a smattering of other food items people had "donated" to the emu. "This is a perfectly good orange!" He held up a navel orange from somewhere in the pile and peeled the skin off. He took a bite and then held it out towards us. "You want some?"

"Aaron," Corey started to say as he lifted his hand to his brow in bemusement, "you're telling me you won't eat Nutella or peanut butter out of a jar after Tom and I have dipped our spoons in it because you're afraid of germs ... but you'll eat a skank-nasty orange that someone threw off of a goddamn BRIDGE?!"

"Yea, but that's different."

"I'm not even gonna address how outlandish that is, Aaron."

"The potatoes look good too." he picked a few up.

"Get the fuck outta here, dude," I laughed. "But yea, grab a couple of those potatoes because we're cookin' those bitches up tonight."

• • •

Amidst the very real argument that started just after the afore-mentioned conversation, I told Aaron that I was going to try my best not to get into with him anymore. This, as I explained it, would basically consist of me just keeping my opinions to myself when he dragged us into some insane situation. He decided that was as good a time as any to air another grievance with Corey and me, telling us that he'd prefer it if we didn't say the word "god-damn" around him.

We hadn't known before the trip that he was religious, but began to wonder along the way when he brought up his Cath-olic upbringing. He'd gone to Catholic school almost his whole life and his parents were devout. Now I don't have any problems with anyone believing whatever they want to believe, but I'm not a huge fan of having it intrude on my life or the lives of other uninvolved parties. For example, telling people who they can love or who god wants them to kill. Or, less hyperbolically and more relevant, tellinga couple of grown-ass men the swear words they can and can't use. Despite this, and putting aside my annoyance that Aaron had quite immediately taken the inch I'd given him and asked for a mile, I figured I'd humor him simply for the sake of keeping the peace. "Sure," I said. "Whatever. I'll try."

"I fuckin' won't," Corey said. "Sorry Aaron, but I'm not religious. If you don't want to say certain spooky words, go for it, but it's not my problem."

Aaron shrugged it off with a muttering under his breath and that was that.

We still hadn't gotten any proper food, so I volunteered to sit at the camp with our stuff while Corey and Aaron checked out the town and grabbed some groceries. I also gave them my phone so they could try to find WiFi and shoot an email to our travel agent about changing the date of our flight to Southeast Asia.

That night we cooked up the first good meal we'd had since the hot girl had bought us food at a rest stop restaurant in Switzerland. Aaron and Corey had picked up some pork from the store and we cooked it up along with the "bridge potatoes" and a can of corn. While we cooked, we came up with a name for our new roommate living just on the other side of the concrete barrier. Aaron told us that the emu was a female, so we named it "Dee," after a character from the popular television show *It's Always Sunny in Philadelphia*. The character on the show is constantly referred to as having "birdlike" features and is even portrayed in one episode as a literal ostrich, so it seemed to fit.

We stuffed ourselves with pork and potatoes and then settled back down to sleep. The plan was to wake up early, check our email to see if our travel agent had messaged us back, and then hop on the rails again and head for Rome. Aside from the fact that I was lying on a pile of rocks under a bridge, I slept pretty well that night.

The next morning, however, was a different story. I woke up around five-thirty. A soft morning light filtered into the valley ahead of our cozy Air BnBridge. The dew gently evaporated from creek-side foliage. My stomach was filled with angry bees. I sat up quickly and groaned. I drank some water and then lay back down, but could only focus on the bubbling brew in my midsection. I finally worked up the energy to reach for my pack and dig out some antacid tablets. I crunched down on three or four of them and then rested my head on my pillow again. I was still tired and wanted nothing more than to go back to sleep. I tried sitting up, leaning my pack against the concrete wall and then lying back against it with my small travel pillow against my neck. I finally fell back asleep this way.

About ten minutes later I awoke with a start. I wretched. my body kicked forward with a *yackkkk* sound erupting involuntarily from my mouth. I unzipped my sleeping bag in a panic and ran over to the other side of the bridge, where I started blowing chunks everywhere. I stood on a concrete platform and held onto the graffiti-covered bridge support as I continued to puke my guts out.

The only other time in my life I can remember puking like this was the first time I ever tried hallucinogenic mushrooms. I had a bad trip and my body attempted to relieve my delirium by ejecting liquid fire from my mouth like a dragon. I was on all fours and arched my back downwards as vomit projected from me to an unbelievably far distance, in what my cousin Blake later claimed looked, "just like that scene from The Exorcist."

This was pretty close to that. I thought I was losing internal organs in this mess. I leaned hard against the wall in one final heave and then collapsed onto the ledge in exhaustion. I lay there for a moment, breathing heavily.

Eventually I pulled myself back up and stumbled back to my sleeping bag. Somehow neither Corey nor Aaron had been disturbed by my body turning inside out on the other side of the bridge. I slid back into my bag and closed my eyes...

I woke up an hour or so later and repeated the whole process, complete with falling onto the ledge. My whole body shook and ached as I made my way back to my sleeping area. This time both my companions woke up.

"You okay, man?" Aaron asked.

"No dude. I'm pretty sure I have a fever."

Corey grabbed the thermometer from our medical kit and I

took my temperature... 101.5.

I laid the thermometer back down. "That was the second time I've ralphed this morning."

I fell asleep for a couple more hours. This time I woke up to the sound of thunder. It was going to storm. *At least we're under cover from the bridge*, I thought. A few seconds later it started to rain, the wind blowing it right under the bridge and onto me. *You've got to be kidding me.* It was like something out of a movie.

I was so exhausted that I couldn't even move myself farther under the bridge. I pulled the sleeping bag over my whole head and rolled onto my side. I fell back asleep.

I woke up an hour or so later to see the sun shining again. I leaned forward to grab one of the water bottles...

"You feel any better, man?" Corey asked as I was taking a sip from the old, worn-out plastic bottle we'd reused a hundred times.

"No."

"You want to try and eat some food?" Aaron asked.

"No."

I lay back down just long enough to feel my stomach twist again. The good news was that I didn't feel like I was going to puke again. The bad news is that it was going to come out the other end. The *really* bad news is that I'd need to walk clear down the creek bed about 50 yards to an enclosure of bushes to be able to relieve myself. Puking on the other end of the bridge was one thing, but I figured this operation would leave certain smells a little too close for comfort if you get what I'm saying. I slipped out of my sleeping bag quickly. This wasn't going to be a sit with the newspaper type of shit. This was going to be a napalm drop.

"TOILET PAPER." I yelled.

"There's only like two wipes-worth," Corey said as he handed me a small wad of T.P.

There was no time. "SORRY!" I said as I grabbed a pair of his socks sitting on the ledge. I started sprinting through the creek bed, or more accurately, waddling like a caffeinated penguin. I didn't even check to see if there was anyone watching me from the walkway that followed most of the creek as I ran along with my hand on my ass. Halfway there, my waddle turned into a desperate Forrest Gump-before-the-leg-braces-came-off-style run. I reached a small creek and jumped over it. As the muscles in my legs sprang to life, the muscles in my sphincter relaxed for one unfortunate moment. I did an air-drop onto the water about halfway over as a turd slipped out of my shorts leg. I stumbled the rest of the way to the bushes. I ripped off my shorts and underwear and threw them a few feet away for safety. And then it started. I've never experienced anything so terrifyingly awful in my life. I thought I was actually going to poop out my skeleton. It was everywhere on the grass. It looked like someone had tossed dynamite into a septic tank under me.

I finally took a deep breath and walked over to the small creek where I proceeded to wash my feet and legs. I walked back over to grab my shorts but I apparently wasn't done yet. I ran back over and repeated the whole process again, this time at least avoiding hitting myself with the shrapnel. I looked down at the toilet paper Corey had handed me. I winced. It was gone in no time, as well as the socks I'd stolen from Corey moments earlier. By the time I was done, my underwear lay on top of the pile as well.

After I'd finally finished the whole disgusting process, I walked back over to my shorts. If you haven't fully grasped the image, I had been completely naked during this entire process. Still no word on whether anyone was watching from the walkway above. Just imagine walking through your local park and seeing some naked hippie screaming and spraying shit out of his asshole all over your nice community creek bed. Oh god am I deeply sorry to any unfortunate soul who discovered the residual carnage from that scene.

I slowly walked back to the bridge and then crawled back into my sleeping bag and rested my head on my pillow. Despite the midday heat, my body shivered inside the bag.

"Are we still gonna try to keep moving south today?" Aaron asked. I turned my head and glared at him. My eyes cut into his soul like a barbed spear into flesh.

He held up his hands in defeat. "I was just wondering."

I rolled back over and closed my eyes.

An hour or so later, I finally spoke with a low, raspy voice. "Aaron. I can't do this, man. I'm sick as fuck … under a bridge. Can we please just get a hotel for one night?"

He looked down at the ground. I knew what was coming. "I mean … what do you think that will accomplish?"

"I just want a bed. A toilet. I'm fucking miserable."

"I don't think you're gonna get over it any quicker because of those things, man. I saw a sign up there for a hotel and it was like 40 bucks..."

"40 fucking dollars Aaron. I would kill you right now for five."

"I get what he's saying man," Corey spoke to Aaron. "I mean look at the motherfucker. One night isn't gonna make us go broke."

"We're not spendin' 40 bucks on a damn hotel," Aaron said. "You'll be okay, man. Just drink some more water and try to sleep."

I wanted to kill him. I didn't have the energy to fight with him though, so I just tried to sleep. I decided at that moment that if things didn't improve by the time we got to Thailand, I was going to go my own way. Corey could come with me if he wanted, but I wasn't going to travel with Aaron like this if he was going to keep being such a crazy person about money. I'd rather go broke and have a great time than spend the next year or so like this.

Early in the afternoon, Corey started to experience the same symptoms of illness that I was going through. Luckily for him, he didn't have it nearly as bad—he never threw up, just felt terrible and had the runs. Aaron decided to walk farther down the creek bed to the beach and check it out while Corey and I lay there in our sleeping bags. You know, instead of offering to help out by getting some tea or fruit, or anything really. He said he was bored. He expressed not even the slightest amount of empathy for our plight, and offered little-to-no assistance to us. On the contrary, it felt almost as if it was a pain in his ass that we had gotten sick.

He returned a couple of hours later with an armful of stuff. "What the hell is all that?" I asked. Corey turned over in his sleeping bag and had a look.

Aaron sat everything down in front of him. "I found this place where some homeless guy stashed all his shit. Check it out, I got an umbrella, an extra sleeping bag and also this little laptop bag we can put our food in."

"You stole from a homeless guy?" Corey asked.

"It isn't really stealing. I mean *he* obviously got it from somewhere. I'm sure he didn't buy it," he said.

"He probably dug that stuff out of the trash, man," I said. "You absolutely stole it."

"You don't want me to say a special word that offends you, but it's okay for you to steal from a fucking homeless person?" Corey said.

Aaron stuck by his defense and justified his actions to himself, but it never sat right with Corey or me. Considering all the bad luck we'd had so far, we didn't need the kind of bad karma that comes from stealing three things from a person who probably has like, I don't know, eight things total to their name. Plus I didn't even want to be within fifteen feet of that disgusting sleeping bag. The thing looked like an archeological relic that had been eaten and subsequently shat-out by a dinosaur. "Well, enjoy the lice and scabies," was all I could say to him.

• • •

I finally started feeling a little better late in the evening, sometime after dark. I ate some rice and played a game of chess with Corey, whose condition was also improving. I was just lighting up a cigarette when I heard voices farther down the creek bed. "Shhh," I held up my hand to Corey as he was moving a piece. "I think there's someone down here."

We sat quietly while the voices came closer. Three young guys, each with a beer in his hand, stepped out from the bushes talking amongst each other. They were there for a few seconds before one of them happened to notice us and stop talking mid-sentence.

I spoke first—"Hello... welcome to Vagabond Bridge."

"Uhhh, hey," one of the guys answered in a British accent. Then he kind of laughed uncomfortably. "What are you guys doing down here?"

"We're ... well I guess we're living here at the moment. We're traveling to Rome."

"Uhh, that's cool. You guys smoke weed?"

"Yes, we most certainly do," Corey answered.

"Well we came down here to smoke a bowl if you wanna join."

We sat and talked with them for the better part of an hour. They were from London, staying in a relative's house for the summer. They seemed like spoiled rich kids, but they were cool for the most part. At one point one of the guys walked over to the other side of the bridge to take a leak. "Holy shit!" he jumped backwards. "There's a big-ass bird over here!"

We had forgotten to tell him. "Oh yea, that's Dee."

"What the fuck..."

"She keeps to herself over there, you're fine."

"Uhhh, okay..."

After a while the guys headed on their way, back up the creek bed from whence they had come, and we settled down to try and get some sleep. We were planning on leaving the next day to continue south. Aaron and Corey had made the daily trip to fetch water earlier in the day and received a promising response from our travel agency that they'd be sending the price of the fee to change our flight, so we'd be checking email and heading on our way.

As we were lying down to sleep, we heard a loud noise just up the creek bed from us. It sounded like some kind of animal coming towards us.

"What the hell is that?" Corey whispered. It ran closer.

"That's a fuckin' wild boar!" Aaron yelled. He threw a rock at the pig and it ran back up the creek. A few minutes later there were two of them coming toward us. We guessed they were trying to get the food people had thrown off of the bridge. "Dammit!" Aaron yelled. "Get the hell outta here!" he threw another rock. A few minutes later they were creeping closer again. This time we heard a rustling noise on the other side of the wall:

"AAAAACKKKKK!" Dee came running out towards the boars,

her useless little wings spread as wide as they woul go. The boars took off running in the other direction, squealing the whole way. We heard them splashing through the creek farther down this time as they fled the scene entirely.

"Damnnnn, Dee's a badass!" Corey laughed. "That's my girl. Tell those motherfuckers who runs this bitch."

We didn't see them the rest of the night.

· · ·

The next morning Aaron and I walked up to the town to get water and check my email. I jumped on a WiFi connection as I stood outside of a little restaurant and pulled up my email. I read the first lines of the email and my face fell.

"They're saying we can't switch the flight..." I told Aaron.

"What?"

"Yea, I mean we can, but they want like $600 a person."

"How is that?"

"I guess we have to pay the difference between flights on top of the fees and everything."

"So basically the girl that sold us the tickets lied to us?"

"Yea, that's what it's sounding like to me," I said. "I need to get my computer up here so I can chat with them." It looked like we weren't leaving the bridge for at least another night.

Aaron and I brought our computers up to the restaurant and asked them if it would be okay to use their WiFi for a while if I bought something. After their consent, we grabbed a couple gelatos and had a seat. I pulled up a chat window with a representative from the travel company.

After a lengthy, furious debate, a final verdict was reached: It was not going to happen. They wanted to charge an exorbitant amount of money per person to change the tickets. We were stuck. Worse, we were stuck with nowhere to stay for the next month.

We sat in the restaurant for a few hours, researching different options. I applied online to writing jobs while Aaron researched farms we could possibly work at. Neither of us was making any real headway. All of the farms we were looking at had already hired help for the year. Those were jobs you needed to apply for well ahead of time.

The best idea we could come up with was to at least try and break even financially for the next month. If we could find a place to camp somewhere, Corey and I could play music for money and Aaron could get a temporary job at a restaurant or something. We'd camp for five or six days and then spend one or two in a hostel where we could get WiFi and showers. We looked up a hostel in Rome where we could research a place to camp somewhere nearby. Morale was at rock bottom that evening. Our dreams of finally being able to enjoy the luxuries of Southeast Asia were crushed... back to the bridge we went.

That night the boars returned just as we were drifting off to sleep. Dee engaged them in a full-on fight this time. That crazy bird was chasing the pigs all over the creek bed for a good twenty minutes or so before they finally gave up and retreated. To this day, I swear that damn emu thought it was protecting us. It came over to our side of the bridge all the time during the day and just stood there next to us, as if it was guarding us.

• • •

The next morning we woke up to find Aaron hunched over in his sleeping bag. He looked pale as a ghost.

"You alright, man?" Corey asked.

"I think I have that same thing you guys had," he grumbled.

I wanted to jump up and down laughing at him. I wanted to poke him in the ribs and dance in a circle around him while I cackled with joy. After the way he had treated both Corey and me when we were sick, I wanted him to shit until he met his god. But, I kept these evil thoughts to myself. Instead, I said, "Do you want us to go get you some fruit or something?"

"That would be great."

"No problem." I knew exactly how he was feeling. Even though he'd been a dick to Corey and me, we both knew what he was going through. Wouldn't you know it though—this meant we were stuck under this goddamn bridge for yet another night. That would be four nights and five days calling that place home. Corey and I were walking into town when I mentioned—"Oh pleeee-ase, let that motherfucker ask if we can get a hotel. I'll rip him to shreds."

"I was thinking the same thing. You can lay there on the rocks and suffer just like we did. He knows better than to ask that, I'd say."

We got him fruit juice as well as an apple and some fresh water and tea. By early afternoon he was starting to feel better. He didn't have it as bad as Corey and certainly nowhere near as bad as me, I could tell that pretty easily. Eventually he said he was ready to travel. I'll give him one thing; the guy was resilient.

We left the bridge behind and hopped more trains south, passing Cinque Terra and Pisa along the coast, getting ever-closer to Rome. Along the way, we decided to try and quit smoking again. We all agreed, in the interest of our finances—our favorite topic of conversation and debate—that it was truly imperative that we stick to it this time. None of us were happy about it, though. We divvied up what little tobacco remained, amounting to three or four small cigarettes apiece. It was up to each individual to save or smoke it how he pleased. But then that was it. We weren't buying any more tobacco. That was the rule.

We were within an hour or two of arrival in Rome when we decided we should find somewhere to camp for the night. We knew from experience that we weren't going to be able to find a place to sleep anywhere in the city (not for free, anyway). We'd have better luck hopping off the train in a rural area, camping somewhere, and then coming back into the city in the morning. So we got off at a random stop, which as far as we knew, was in the middle of nowhere. At least that's what it looked like from the train window.

However, when we stepped out and investigated, we realized we'd made a serious error. This place was heavily populated. We couldn't find a single place to bed down away from active streets or residences. We sat on a little concrete barrier next to the train tracks and pondered our options. It was around one in the morning, so we knew that no more trains would be stopping there until morning. Aaron suggested we sleep in the only area of refuge in sight—a big culvert next to the train tracks that everyone had thrown their trash into. It was well hidden by brush and located down a steep incline that ran parallel to the parking lot we were sitting in. There really wasn't any other choice. We formed a chain down the steep incline and handed packs to the bottom. Once I made it down with the other two, I surveyed our situation...

The spot was no doubt our worst yet. There was trash littered everywhere: bottles, old fast food wrappers and bags, buckets, cans, and even a jug of kerosene that had spilled all over the ground. The fumes tickled our nostrils as we dumped our packs. There were itchy nettles growing everywhere. I laid my sleeping bag on the ground and attempted to situate my pillow so my head would be as far as possible from the spilled kerosene. I was angled downhill, but I couldn't switch the other way because the majority of the fuel spill was located at that end. Instead I angled my bag part way up the incline and lay in an awkward "L" shape. I ached for a cigarette, although in retrospect it's probably a good thing that I didn't smoke one, given the whole kerosene thing.

I wanted to break down and weep at our situation. The train tracks were less than twenty feet away and every ten or twenty minutes a cargo train would come careening down the tracks and shake the earth around us. The deafening cacophony of screeches and grumbles would end up waking me over and over. It seemed I was always hungry. It had been eight days since our last shower—and since our last bed for that matter. I reeked of body odor and kerosene. *What is the point of being here if I have to live like this?* I thought. I didn't meet anyone or see anything new living under bridges and culverts. There had been nothing enjoyable about the past few days... That night I wrote in my journal:

My spirit is broken. Just when I think things can't get worse, the powers-that-be find some clever new torture. We are sleeping in a culvert. Nettles & weeds & trash everywhere. When will this bad luck end? I'm depressed, and having great difficulty finding opti-

mism, which is very unlike me. I am exhausted & despondent. I don't want to do this anymore. I hate this. At least these kerosene fumes are probably killing a bunch of my brain cells. Maybe I won't even remember this next week.

13

¡ROMA, FINALMENTE!
ROME, ITALY

August 3rd

Our first couple days in Rome were a welcome reprieve. We booked beds in the Hostel Happy Days Roma near Vatican City. We had showers, made awesome new friends, enjoyed a free pasta dinner cooked by the friendly staff each night, and Corey and I even made a good bit of money busking in the evenings. In the mornings, the hostel gave each guest free coffee and a pastry. It was paradise compared to our previous living conditions and didn't cost that much by European standards—about $9 USD per person each night. We became friends with the hostel manager, Alex, who was a short, rail-thin fellow from somewhere in the Middle East. We had already booked another hostel farther out of town, but when we left Hostel Happy Days, we told him we'd be back at some point when we took our next break from "vag-abonding."

The idea was that if we stayed a campground—specifically the Tiber Campground Hostel—we could disappear into the woods nearby to camp for free. It turned out to be a bust after we realized that we wouldn't be able to busk without first paying for a private bus line to take us back to the city, but we did stay there for a couple nights and worked on Internet-related tasks.

I should note that we arrived in Rome during a record heat wave. Temperatures were reaching well above a hundred degrees Fahrenheit each day and there was no air conditioning anywhere that we could find so far. Especially not in the summer-camp-style dorms of this hostel. The upside was that we had almost the whole dorm to ourselves, save one other person—a German guy named Hannes who occupied one room. The dorms were separated by sexes, so there were several male dorms and several female ones. Each dorm was huge, and separated into smaller "rooms" which were more like cubicles, as the walls only came up to about five or six feet, leaving the area above open—assumedly to help air flow. Each section had two bunk beds, one on each side.

To cool down I went to the showers about three or four times a day, as cold as the water would get, and walked back to the dorms without even toweling myself off. I would be relieved for about ten minutes before my body was sweaty again, my skin sticking to anything it touched. I'd sit on one of the bunk beds, leaning against the wall and typing out articles for the website, and when I'd get up, there would be a sweat-spot running all the way down from where my shoulders had been to the floor.

• • •

The first night there we met this girl named Kassel, a short, blonde girl from Canada who was living in northern Italy and working as an au pair for a wealthy family. She had it made—all she had to do was teach them English, and the kids were both older, in their teens, so she basically just talked to them in English while she lived there. Oh, and "there" was actually a fucking castle. So she lived in this castle, riding horses and hanging out all day, chatting with spoiled rich kids, and they paid her to do it. She was on a vacation from the au pair job, which had brought her to Rome, and to our campground-hostel near the Tiber.

We hit it off with her, as well as Hannes. He and Aaron played some intense games of chess—Corey and Aaron were improving after learning how to play under the bridge, but this guy was really good. I spent most of the evening chatting with Kassel about music and such, and eventually Corey and I got out our instruments and started to play. Another group of people came over and joined our table—some British guy I vaguely remember who kept buying us beers and a couple of others who stayed mostly quiet.

This was the first time we'd really been able to enjoy ourselves since Heidelberg, so we reveled in it. Everyone else went to bed around one or two in the morning, while Corey, Kassel and I remained at our table outside. The British guy had bought a bunch of beer and abandoned it on the table … there wasn't any sense in letting it go to waste, of course.

We had been talking about religion earlier, and Kassel had made a few jokes about Catholicism. I had seen Aaron stare ahead quietly in the background so I thought I'd bring it up for his sake now that he'd gone to bed. "Hey I didn't want to like, call him out earlier or anything, but you should know that Aaron is pretty religious," I told her. "I mean … just letting you know, I guess."

She shrugged. "I would say there is a one hundred percent chance I offended him then."

"Yeah, probably. I just thought I'd let you know for future reference."

Around three we started cleaning up the area before bed. "Ugh … I hate those sorority bitches in the female dorm," Kassel said as she dumped an armful of beer cans into the garbage. "Do you guys care if I stay in your dorm instead? I have to wake up at like eight in the morning to go to the city with Hannes anyway."

"I don't care," I said. "It's not like there's anyone in there watching over the place." There was a noticeable lack of employee involvement or interest in anything at the campground.

"All right, I'll go grab my stuff and then meet you back here."

"Cool," I replied as she walked toward the female dorms. When she rounded the corner, I turned to Corey. "You gotta go to bed, bro. I think I'm gonna make a move here."

"I read ya loud and clear, man," Corey said. He finished his beer. "Good luck!" ... Such a good friend.

Kassel came back with her things and we went into the dorm. At some point between the table outside and the door to the dorm, the idea was settled to build a really badass blanket fort in one of the bunk rooms. We went into one of the empty bunk sections and hung sheets across the beds, creating a tent into which we then drunkenly crawled. We were being obnoxiously loud during the entire exchange. As we settled into the tent, Aaron sighed loudly from a couple sections over and then got up and stormed outside.

"Whoops, we pissed off Bible Boy," Kassel said. I tried not to laugh, but was unsuccessful.

"Okay seriously, we should try to be quiet," I said.

We stayed up for a while longer, blundering our attempts to talk softly. Aaron had returned shortly after.

Eventually, sometime around six, we fell asleep. I didn't make a move with her because, well, I can't really tell you why. Normally I'm fairly confident, but there's just something about being a mangy hitchhiker for a couple weeks that really knocks you down a peg or two.

The next morning my slumber was broken by a loud voice and sudden, blinding daylight. Aaron tore down the cotton ramparts of my sheet fort as he yelled—"Get the fuck up! We can't just sleep all day!" He walked back to his section to pack up his stuff. Kassel's bed was empty; she had left with Hannes sometime earlier in the morning.

My whole body ached. It was approximately the temperature of a demon's taint in the dorm and my head felt like it was filled with a bag of hammers.

"Aaron," I gasped as I clawed for a nearby bottle of water. "What time is it?"

"TIME TO GET UP. It's ten a.m., GET YOUR ASS UP." He sounded like a drill sergeant.

I sat up on the bed and rested my forehead in my hand. My vision was swimming. I pulled myself up and drunk-shuffled to the section where Aaron was packing his stuff. Leaning against the wall, I grumbled, "Dude … what the hell is your problem?"

"MY PROBLEM?! MY PROBLEM? YOU AND THAT GIRL KEPT ME UP ALL FUCKIN NIGHT—THAT'S MY PROBLEM."

"Aaron … I'm sorry about that. I really am. But you're being an asshole right now."

"I'M AN ASSHOLE? YOU DON'T CARE ABOUT ANYONE BUT YOURSELF. YOU SAT IN THERE AND—"

"You know what. Fuck all this noise." I cut him off. "I'm going back to bed. Do whatever you want." I was too hung over to argue with him.

"OHHH NO," he followed me back to my bed as I plopped down on top of the sheets. "WE NEED TO LEAVE. YOU AREN'T GOING BACK TO SLEEP. YOU SHOULDN'T HAVE STAYED UP SO LATE DRINKING."

"You can do whatever the fuck you want, man. I know for a fact that no one is gonna come here and check this place. I guarantee we can stay here again tonight without paying and nobody will say a goddamn word. I'm staying." I just wanted the argument to be over with so I could go back to sleep.

"WELL WE NEED TO TALK."

"Okay honey, what do you want to talk about?" I said, in a patronizing voice.

"YOU'RE SO SELFISH … YOU—YOU KEPT ME UP ALL FUCKIN NIGHT," he repeated. "AND WHAT'S WITH THAT GIRL CALLING ME BIBLE BOY?"

Corey's laughter echoed from three sections over. It was the first noise he'd made during the entire altercation.

"OH, YOU THINK THAT'S FUNNY COREY?"

There was a silent pause. "… Yes."

"Aaron," I said with my eyes closed and hand rested on my forehead again, "how in the fuck is it my fault she said that?"

"YOU LAUGHED."

"It was funny. I'm sorry. Kind of."

"HOW DID SHE EVEN KNOW I'M RELIGIOUS THOUGH?"

"I told her, because I thought she wouldn't make so many religious jokes around you that would make you feel uncomfortable—which, clearly didn't work, but—the point is, believe it or not, I was actually trying to help. Listen, man … can you stop fucking yelling at me? I feel like shit. I'll talk to you about all this, but give it a rest already."

He let out a deep sigh, and then spoke at a normal volume. "Something's going to have to change. This isn't some big party. I'd like to get some rest at some point."

"Are you kidding me Aaron? Some big party?! We've been living under bridges and shit. This is the first time we've drank in weeks. We are in no way partying all of the time."

"You guys were staying up late with the Australian girls at the last hostel too."

"Listen man, if you want to spend ninety percent of this trip in some ditch or field in the middle of nowhere, then you're gonna have to get used to me having a good time when we're actually around people. There is no way I'll apologize to you for having a good time."

Corey appeared in the doorway to my bunk room. "Aaron, I'm gonna party with people when I can, dude. It's not like we get to do this often."

"Well I didn't get any sleep because you guys were making all kinds of noise last night."

"Aaron I told you I'm sorry and I really mean that. I knew we woke you up the first time and then we tried to be quiet. We really did."

He scoffed. "Yeah, I'm sure you did. I'm just saying, if something doesn't change I don't know what's going to happen."

"What—like you're gonna go off by yourself?"

"Maybe I will."

"Go for it. See if I care. Just leave my backpacking stove next to the bed here and I'll go back to sleep."

He nodded his head with a sarcastic half-grin. "Yeah, you wouldn't make it anywhere without my money. That's the only reason you even traveled with me."

"I don't give a shit about your money," I said. "I've never once been worried about it. I've told you, shit like this always works out. I'll make money once I have Wi-Fi for a reliable amount of time … or I'll busk for it. The difference is, you don't have any more ways of making money and you're such a goddamned Amish person that you don't even own a debit card to have anyone send you money."

"Yeah well we'll see if you actually make any money."

"Whatever man. Are you leaving or not? Because I'm going back to sleep."

"I just wish we all would have brought the same amount of money, that's all I'm saying."

"Well, there's nothing we can do about it now. Yes, you brought more money at the beginning but I guarantee I'll end up bringing more to the table in the long run. You know what the difference is though? I don't really care. At all. You'll never hear me say a word about it if I do."

"Yeah, well, I bet it'd be different if it was switched around and you had brought more money."

"No, it wouldn't. I've gone on two different trips now where I've paid for other people to go, and I never bitched once. That's just the difference between you and me, I guess. You're so obsessed with money that you'd rather have pieces of paper sitting at home in a box than enjoy yourself on a once in a lifetime trip. We're fundamentally different people.

"Look, I'm sorry about last night. But I'm not doing this anymore. Either you're with us or not. I'm done arguing with you."

He was silent for a moment, and then sighed. "I mean, I guess I'll stay—but that doesn't mean this is over."

"I think you need to go take a nap. You're obviously pretty upset," I said.

"So we're staying here again tonight?"

"That's what I'm doing. There's no way I'm carrying that pack in this godawful heat. You can do whatever you want."

He stayed—and took a nap, thank god.

. . .

Later that day we did some research and found what looked like a suitable place for camping near the Mediterranean, about thirty miles west of Rome: a nature preserve that was close enough to the nearby towns of Ostia and Litoranea that we could find places to busk. We also figured Aaron could find a temporary job in either of the towns washing dishes or something.

The mood remained tense throughout the rest of the day, not helped in the slightest by our nicotine withdrawals. We had smoked a couple cigarettes given to us by people who were staying at the hostel, but we still hadn't bought any more tobacco. I craved them constantly. I didn't want to quit anymore at that point, but I was going along with the plan.

We started finding butts on the ground, emptying tobacco into a new paper, and rolling them up—as Aaron had done in Germany. Yes, it was gross. We didn't care. You're talking to the guys who ate "bridge potatoes."

We woke up early the next morning and took a private bus line back to the city. From there we hopped on a train west which took us to Litoranea, a town situated right on the coast. We exited the train station and picked up a few half-smoked cigarettes from the pavement outside the terminal. Multiple bus lines stopped at the train station. Figuring out which one we needed to take was a chore, given that the place we'd spotted on the map wouldn't be listed on the scheduled stops. It was just a nature preserve on the opposite side of the road from the sea, which looked full of trees in the satellite images. We knew that it was toward Litoranea itself, so we hopped on a bus headed that way and hoped for the best.

We'd noticed a pattern within the Italian bus system—or all the bus systems in Europe for that matter: if there were two or more sets of doors (one by the driver and one in the middle), you could hop on without paying. You were supposed to scan some card thing or give cash to the driver when you got on the bus, but we just never did. We'd hop on whenever we pleased and hop off whenever we pleased. No one ever said a word to us.

Unfortunately, the Roman metro system was more organized, consisting of a ticket and gate system: you buy a ticket from a kiosk, and then you put it into a slot among a row of motion activated gates. Basically the gates won't open until you put the ticket in the slot. It didn't take us long to learn from the locals and adopt a way to circumvent this as well, though: we saw a group of Italian boys insert one ticket into the slot, and then follow closely behind one another so the motion sensor would remain tripped and the doors couldn't shut. The computer in the gate machine probably thought, *Wow, that was the fattest guy ever*. It was kind of sketchy sometimes (there was usually a police shack among the gates). But we were never caught and only had a couple close calls. One time I went to the exiting side, to a row of those spinny-bar things— you know, the ones they have at amusement parks and the like with the three little bars that spin and make the clink sound as you walk through? I just hopped right over and kept moving. Once on the other side, I saw an officer approach Aaron and Corey, telling them that "This is the exit gate, the entrance gate is over there, *blah blah blah*," but I just kept on walking toward the platform and somehow got away with it.

From the train station we took a bus, which drove along the coastal beaches with reckless abandon for the lives of the passengers. The driver sped around turns and screeched to a halt at stops; and you would see a stinky Italian man go flying into another stinky Italian man. The three stinky American men held on for dear life.

After about ten minutes we saw a campground, so we thought, *Hey this is as good a spot as any*, and hopped off when the bus slid to a stop. We entered the aforementioned campground, where a tall, balding man quoted us a price of thirty euros per night. We laughed directly in his face and turn around. Directly across the street was the entrance to the nature preserve. It was a wide paved road with a vehicle gate blocking the entrance for any cars, bordered by trees on both sides.

We ran across the small highway to the other side, dodging the madmen bus drivers who were careening down it, and walked past the vehicle gate.

I went into the trees next to the entrance to take a leak, but stumbled back, stunned. "Oh my god. You guys have to see this."

There were condoms everywhere. I'm not exaggerating when I say there were probably over a thousand of them. Used, nasty condoms. It was like someone drove a slut-truck back there and exploded it. Corey took pictures—"No one's gonna believe this otherwise ... the sheer number of them ... just astonishing."

We heaved our packs down the paved road, until we were out of sight of anyone driving along the highway or otherwise, and then ducked through pine boughs and walked along a dirt path. It took a couple hours of investigation to find a spot that looked hidden from view from any of the trails. It was an open circle of pine trees with a crawling, ancient oak tree in the middle.

"Home?"

"Home."

14
THE NATURE PRESERVE
OSTIA & LITORANEA, ITALY

August 6th

Our makeshift home turned out to be quite an interesting spot. First of all, there were the sex workers. Early on in our stay we discovered them, while walking across the road to the campground to fetch [steal] some water. They sat along the highway in plastic lawn chairs, usually tapping away at their phones. A car would pull up, they'd hop in, give the guy a peck on the cheek and off they'd go. Or, the guy would get out and they'd disappear into the bushes together. This aptly explained the nest of condoms we had discovered, or "Cum Canyon," as we had coined it.

Unbeknownst to them, these women solved one of our biggest problems: We had absolutely nothing to sit on in our hobo campsite. So one day, when Corey and I went to get water and saw one of them hopping into a car, we thought, *Hey, just look at that chair sitting there, ready for the taking*. We repeated this sequence four times over the course of the next several days. Every day we would steal a chair and the next day there'd be a new one. *Where were they coming from?* They certainly weren't new—some were already broken when we snatched them. It may forever remain a mystery.

They knew we were taking them, too. They had to. Corey and I talked to one of them almost every day on our way to "work," busking in Ostia.

We'd be on our way back to the campsite from the bus stop, and the conversation would usually go something like this:

"Ciao," Corey or I would say. "How are you today?"

"I'm good, how are you guys?"

"Great, it's hot as hell."

"Ugh yes, and is very slow day today. How did you guys do?"

"Not too bad, enough to buy some food. You?"

"Ahh, not many customers today, hopefully better luck tomorrow."

It took a while to get the hang of busking in Ostia. We had been playing music on the street here or there throughout the trip, but this was different. We were playing almost every single day here, five or six hours per day. On top of that, bus travel made the experience unnecessarily stressful. As previously mentioned, the Italian bus system is unreliable at best. In my journal, I called it "absolute chaos and disorder." Every day we'd walk out to the bus stop outside of the nature preserve, have a friendly chat with the sex worker, and wait. Sometimes we'd wait five minutes, sometimes an hour. Usually around thirty minutes. We'd pass the time by sitting there and flipping rocks toward the opposite curb in a game we'd invented—a testament to our boredom. This bus would take us back to the train station. From there, we had to walk about a half mile to another bus stop, then finally catch a bus to Ostia. Neither of these stops had anywhere to sit and both of them were directly in the sun.

That wasn't the worst part of the daily commute though: the tricky business was getting back to the nature preserve. The buses stopped running around ten. The prime-time for busking, we discovered, was from eight to ten. So if we wanted to make the maximum amount of money each day, we'd have to play until nine-thirty then pack up swiftly, run to the nearby bus stop, and hope we didn't miss it. Problem number two: *did I mention how unreliable the bus system was?* Sometimes the bus would come at nine-thirty, right as we were running up, and other times it would come a half an hour later. This wouldn't have been that much of an issue, but there was still the other bus we had to catch. So if the first bus showed up late, you could find us running as fast as we could with our instruments to the next bus stop. There were quite a few close calls, and one time we actually missed it, which sucked. We had to walk two miles back to the nature preserve after busking out in the hot sun all day. All of this was timed almost perfectly to coincide with the closing of the little campground store just across the road. There we would buy dinner for the night (we kept a large store of pantry goods in the preserve with us, but we usually wanted some type of meat to go with our daily pasta dinner).

All this while trying to dodge the campground manager who would often stop and harass us: "If you are going to camp here, you need to register at the office."

"We aren't camping here."

"But then ..." he would ponder for a moment; there was literally nowhere else for miles that we could be staying, to the best of his knowledge. "Why you here?"

"We're buying food."

We eventually learned to avoid him, running past the office when he wasn't looking or ducking behind shelves when he entered the general store. My favorite part was sneaking behind the office and ducking below the window where we filled up our water bottles from their hose. The water tasted disgusting, but it was the only fresh water source available to us within a reasonable distance of our pirate camp.

We learned all of this over time, of course. In the end we would spend a total of three weeks living in the nature preserve. The original plan was for Corey and me to busk while Aaron worked a temp job, but it faltered from the very beginning. Aaron didn't want to get a job—which he made apparent. My argument was that, seeing as he was the one so obsessed with money, here was his chance to do something about it. He was negative about the whole situation from the very beginning.

"Nobody is gonna hire me around here."

"Well, you have to try man. Everyone has to pull their weight," Corey told him.

"I already earned my money."

"If you're so worried about money, that wouldn't matter to you," I said.

I felt like his father. He didn't want to take the buses alone at first. So I had to go with him. I figured it was best that way anyway, because I knew if I wasn't there to supervise him he would probably just go lie on the beach and then come back and tell us he couldn't find anywhere to apply. I took him to Litoranea, where I went in and asked for him. I had been learning quite a bit of Italian using smartphone apps when I had the opportunity. So I taught him how to ask if they spoke English and how to say "work?" in Italian.

The next day he went by himself to Ostia to look and came back empty-handed.

"There aren't even any restaurants up there really."

Corey and I followed his tracks the next day to go busking and counted over twenty of them! But it didn't matter. He gave up after that second day. Two days. He refused to look anymore. Instead, he just sat in the camp all day while Corey and I went to play music. He whittled things out of wood and wrote in his journal. Hell, I don't really know what he did to pass all of that time. Then he would bitch about it to us, that he was bored sitting there all day. *Well then go get a job.* I think it was more an issue of pride. He felt like he had already paid his dues, so he didn't think he should have to do anything else.

Corey and I, however, wasted no time in our efforts to reach our goal of breaking even for the month. During the first week we spent every day trying out new places to play: street corners, storefronts, places like that. We had trouble at first, often getting kicked out and asked to move on. After a while we found a perfect spot, on a corner in a four-way intersection. People had to stop there to wait for traffic, and in the evening all the beach-goers walked right by us on their way to a train station nearby.

I had found it when I walked into a store to ask to fill up our water bottles. The manager asked what we were doing, and I told him we were playing music for money to eat and travel.

"*Ahhh, mi amico!*" he'd exclaimed. "You can play out front of my store any time! I love de *musica.*"

We played there for a week and a half or so and he'd come out every single day and throw money in our tip case. He'd even urge anyone walking by to throw in money as well. Every day we'd get off the bus, head to our spot and he would greet us—"Heyyy, my friends! *Come stai?*"

"*Molto bene, gratzie!*"

We were averaging about twenty euros a day for four or five hours of work and two hours of travel there and back.

One notable tip we received at that location was from someone on a third-story balcony. We heard someone yell "Heyyyy, music guys!" from somewhere above after we finished a song. I walked out onto the street and saw a man leaning from his balcony on the other side. "For you!" he held out a ball of aluminum foil and tossed it down to me. I caught it, and inside was a pile of coins and a five euro bill. I thanked him and returned to our spot on the corner.

We had good days and bad days out there, but at least we made something every single day. I hopped another bus to Litoranea at one point—a ten-minute bus ride south of our campground—where I had seen a bar/restaurant with a sign for music. My Italian wasn't advanced enough for salesmanship, so I did a bit of research on my phone before walking in and asking for the manager. They introduced me to the owner, whom they said was named Salvadore.

"*Ciao,*" he said with a smile as he walked from the kitchen and shook my hand.

"*Ciao,*" I replied, "*parli inglese?*"

"Mmm, no, *picollo inglese,*" he answered, holding his finger and thumb up to signify very little.

Well, shit ... here we go. I spewed forth the Italian I had rehearsed: *I play music. I am from America. I will play here for euro, etc.*

He was nodding his head as I talked. *Holy shit, this is working ... he's actually understanding what the hell I'm saying.*

"*Sí,*" he smiled, "*gioca,*" meaning you play. "*Sí, sí.*"

"*Molto bene!*" I exclaimed.

"*Quanto?*" he asked. *How much?*

I hadn't even thought of the price, I'd been so worried about just being able to communicate with the guy. "*Uhh, cento euro.*" *One hundred euros.*

He shook his head in disagreement. "No, no ... *sessanta?*" *Sixty euros.*

"*Sessanta euros e cibo e birra?*" I countered. *Sixty euros and food and beer?*

He outstretched his hand with a smile. "Deal!"

"Yes, deal!"

We scheduled the show for the following Friday. In total, Corey and I ended up making over $500 from music during our three weeks in the nature preserve. We were literally playing music to keep food in our bellies. I had been getting along better with Aaron for the most part; it helped that we weren't spending so much time together and that we had a routine and some scrap of normality during our stay in the nature reserve. Every day Corey and I would head off to work, while Aaron stayed behind to watch the camp. When we returned in the evenings, he would have pasta ready for the sauce and meat we'd picked up from the store.

I had lashed together a table out of branches, upon which we organized our food and played chess and card games. In the mornings, we each enjoyed a piece of fruit and a pastry of some sort, and for lunch we'd usually have a Nutella and peanut butter or tuna sandwich. Although later in our stay, when Corey and I realized that we were making decent money and doing all the work, we secretly treated ourselves to ice cream or fast food while we were out busking.

The dynamic of the group began to shift. Aaron could see that we were finally bringing in money. Any time we needed to pay for something—whether it be a short one- or two-day hostel break, food, or anything else, he wanted us to spend the busking money. I started to become suspicious that he was preserving the cash in his money belt—which he considered his and his alone—for Thailand, so he could control everything again. I went along with it, because I honestly didn't care about the money unless we were starving somewhere or dying under a bridge and he wouldn't spend any. It came to a head though, when he brought up Australia one evening:

"I think when we get to Australia, I'm gonna get a job in one of the mines there. I guess you make like thirty dollars an hour. I'm thinkin I could work for a few months and save up some money to bring home."

"Uhhh okay," Corey said, "have fun with that."

"Yeah," I said. "You can do whatever you want, but I'm not spending my time in Australia working in a damn mine. I'm gonna enjoy it. It's fine if that's what you want to do, but we'll probably have to split up, because I'm gonna want to stay in Perth where I can do some busking and stuff."

"Well, you'll still share the money from the website with me though, right?" he asked.

I was flabbergasted. "Uhhh … no. I'm sorry, but no way. I have no problem sharing with you while we're in this together, but I'm not going to sacrifice money that Corey and I will need just so you can have more money to take home with you—especially when you'd be making more than enough to get by on your own."

"Well that's not really fair is it? That's all of our money."

"Excuse me?" I'd waited to hear those words since Corey and I had started bringing more money to the table. "I seem to remember you talking about how you had *your* money and we had *ours* … well this is money I've earned. I built the website, I maintain it, I write the content, I edit it. I do all the work."

"I didn't mean like, *myyy* money when I said that, I just meant that I had earned it myself."

"No, no, don't try to backpedal now dude—that's exactly what you said and how you meant it. You made Corey and I feel like pieces of shit, like we were bumming money from you or something, and now you see us making money and suddenly want to go back to it being everyone's money. You can't just switch it around whenever it benefits you."

Corey stood up and walked over to his hammock, avoiding the altercation.

Aaron rebutted again—"When did I ever tell you 'no,' you couldn't spend money on something?"

"How about when I was dying under a fuckin bridge a couple weeks ago?"

"I meant—I mean—I was talking about how I broke my back for this money. I worked my ass off for it."

I stood up, knocking my chair into the leaves. "Aaron, you did literally the same thing you always do. The same job, everything! I not only worked my ass off day in day out building the website, planning everything and playing music, but Corey and I also sold off virtually everything we owned for this trip."

"Yeah, bu—"

"No, dude. I know you have money at home still, even though you won't admit it … you're gonna go back and live at your parents' house, with no bills and a stack of cash—regardless of whether you work in Australia or not—and I'm going to go home with nothing, but with a house and vehicle to pay for. I don't bitch, though. This trip is worth it to me. I don't give a shit that I'm going home broke. But I'm not going to give you money I'm working hard to earn, money that I *need*, so you can have more stashed away in a box at home."

His face was beat red. He shook his head in anger, searching for words. "Well, my photography work is on the website."

"If we split up, I'll remove your photography, split everything I have in my account from the website up to that point fifty-fifty, and then that would be it."

It went on and on like this for a long time. It was the worst argument we'd gotten in thus far. It came to a head with us screaming at each other across the camp, both of us red in the face. I stood my ground, though. There was no way I was going to give him money that I needed to survive if he was making more than enough, and not even traveling with me for that matter. I just didn't understand him. When it comes to traveling, I want to enjoy the experience. I don't really care if I go home broke, as long as I have a good time on the trip. I didn't even know why he took the trip up to that point; he was genuinely more concerned with having money when he got home than he was with having a good time.

He told me and Corey he'd never been to a concert. That he had only went out to a restaurant a handful of times in his life because it was way cheaper to just go to the grocery store and get food. He just never wanted to spend money on anything. Arguments aside, we tried to talk some sense into him every single day of our journey. Just to try to get him to loosen up a bit and enjoy life. But we weren't having much luck.

That argument left me infuriated for days. I finally said something to Corey one day when we were waiting for the bus to come:

"I think I'm splitting up when we get to Thailand," I told him.

"Like, going home?"

"No. Just leaving Aaron. You're more than welcome to join me. I just can't take it anymore, man. I don't think we'll ever be able to get along. I'm gonna wait and see what happens, but it's not looking good."

"Honestly I'd probably just go home if you do that."

"Why?"

"I don't know, I think we just started it as a team and if it's not that any more then I'm out."

"That doesn't make sense at all. You just want to go back to Katie don't you?" I was referring to his girlfriend back home. He'd been homesick recently.

"No, that's not it. I just don't think it would be the same if it wasn't the three of us."

"Whatever man." I knew he was lying. "You can do what you want, just know that I'd be more than happy to have you with me."

"We'll see what happens if it comes to that."

• • •

Once again, the attempt to quit smoking failed in a blaze of glory—pun intended. What had started as picking up a half-burned cigarette here or there turned into walking alongside the highway outside of the nature preserve and hunting butts. Then, when there were no more to be found along the road, we took buses to the train station and searched there. One particularly effective tactic was to wait until a group of buses was about to leave, and watching as people threw half-smoked cigarettes onto the ground before jumping on. This would often yield much more tobacco than your usual butt, which is smoked almost down to the filter. I had eagle eyes when it came to the sport of butt-hunting. I could spot a half-cigarette from twenty yards away. We'd return to our camp with a worn-out tobacco bag full of stinky old cigarette butts and empty all the tobacco onto a notebook. Then we would roll up our hobo-stogies and light up for a moment of revolting bliss.

After a couple weeks of this, I finally put an end to it, telling Aaron and Corey that I was buying a bag of tobacco. Surprisingly, it was Corey who put up resistance. I told him the sad truth: cigarettes were all I had left. Food was decided by the group. Sleeping was inhibited. Water was from a dirty hose. We took shits in a shallow hole in the ground. I jizzed into dirty socks. But I could smoke cigarettes whenever I wanted. He relented and I took a bus to the store right away to get some sweet, sweet store-bought nicotine. And that was it. We were smokers again.

We had a great show at the restaurant in Litoranea, called Albatross, and hit it off with the staff there. They were a fun bunch, teaching me all kinds of Italian swear words the language apps left out. We all had such a great time that the owner offered to book us again for the following Friday. We gladly accepted. After our show was over and the restaurant closed for the night, Salvadore cooked a huge feast for the staff and invited us to eat with them. Then we got a lift back to the nature preserve from Adriano and his girlfriend Tonia, who also worked at the restaurant.

Even aside from our shows at Albatross, music was going great. We had moved to another busking spot, on a pier in Ostia a few blocks from our old corner. We were averaging more money there and it was conveniently located near a gelato shop and a McDonald's. The phrase "cheat meal" gained a whole different meaning as Corey and I enjoyed secret meals at McDonald's on some days, or cups of ice cream and a cold can of Coke to share on others. I'd also discovered that I could recharge my phone with my laptop at the nature preserve, so every few days we would bring all the electronics to the McDonald's and charge them while we ate.

After eating and charging the phones, we would head to the pier and play until exactly nine-thirty. Then we'd toss the guitar and cajon into their cases and run to the bus stop. This was our life now.

Since our devices could now be charged somewhat regularly, I transferred copies of *The Sopranos* to my phone and we spent our evenings huddled together around the tiny screen, watching an episode or three before bed. We set up half of the box-like cajon drum and sat the phone in the corner of the wooden pieces to create a sound amplifier.

The days slipped by as we settled into our routine. At the same time, Aaron's laziness became more frustrating. When we finally relented on the whole job thing, our only ask had been that he make the morning trip to get water from the campground, do the cooking, and get groceries while we were gone. It didn't take him long to talk us into taking the water bottles with us so we could stop at a fountain and fill them up before returning to camp in the evening. This just created more shit we had to carry each day to go to work, but it wasn't worth the argument.

15
RETURN TO HAPPY DAYS
ROME, ITALY

August 31st

Our return to Hostel Happy Days in Rome was a jovial one. Showers, toilets, coffee, and the company of other people were welcome luxuries.

There was much to do during the five-days before we left Europe. The website had been neglected (not surprising, considering we had been living in a damn nature preserve for three whole weeks). We still needed to make money busking each day. We also still needed to do book a hostel for our arrival in Thailand and form a game plan for the following weeks. On the agenda was a Thai massage, gorging ourselves on food each day, and at least one night of drunken shenanigans.

Aaron researched Bangkok while I worked on the website during the day and busked with Corey in the evenings. Aaron was good at that kind of stuff. It made me wish I had asked him to help more during the initial planning of the whole trip, because it really helped during our time in Rome and afterward. It took a lot of pressure off me since I was so busy working on the website and everything else.

Alex, the manager I mentioned a while back, really took a liking to us. According to hostel policy, all guests had to leave from noon until some time in the evening so the staff could clean. Most travelers didn't care since they spent most of their days out seeing the city. We didn't have that luxury considering our dismal funds, so it would've been a real bummer if we couldn't stick around and get work done. This was a seriously weird rule that I never saw anywhere else, but it was strictly enforced. You had to leave at noon.

But the staff made an exception for us. When I told Alex about our predicament, he told me, *"No prollem, no prollem man. You just come out and work in the lobby when they come to change your bed."*

He came into the room early one morning with a huge—and I mean comically gigantic—bottle of liquor in his hand and cups in the other, and yelled with a huge smile, "Coffee and vodka?!"

Everyone got up and followed him to the kitchen where coffee and vodka evolved into breakfast shots of vodka chased with coffee and more vodka. The cleaning staff joined in on this as well. Those guys were great too. They barely spoke English (they were Middle Eastern too), but they always managed to make me laugh. I watched one of them convince a girl one evening that she had to eat her dinner inside of the tiny elevator near the stairwell.

"What do you mean? I cannot eat here?" the poor French girl wondered.

"No, no, no. You go outside. Everyone in line here—they pay extra for food, they eat inside. You eat in elevator, yeah."

"But I don't understand—I thought the dinner was free for everyone?"

This exchange went on for a few minutes. She was walking toward the door with her plate of pasta when they finally told her it was a joke.

We were able on one occasion to make it out into the city to see the Colosseum, which we all had mandated as necessary before leaving. I had also wanted to see the Forum, Vatican, and countless other locations for which my inner history nerd desperately yearned. But it was not to be. I stood outside the Vatican and got some pictures from about five hundred yards away. We didn't get to go inside of the Colosseum either, which was a disappointment. I wasn't expecting much at this point anyway. A month prior I had decided I would definitely return to Europe to see all that I had originally wanted. Our plan to travel on our extremely limited budget and do all the touristy things along the way was naïve to say the least.

We *were* able to experience real Italian cuisine on one evening. A couple of my relatives sent us $100 and told us we had to spend it on a nice meal of genuine Italian food or at least several nights in a hostel. Since our busking tips had already earned us the hostel stay, we opted for a delicious dinner. Not surprisingly, Aaron attempted an alternative at first:

"I think I'll just save my portion of it and use it in Thailand."

"What do you mean?" I asked. "They gave us this money to go have a nice meal in Rome."

"Well I just can't see the sense in spending the money here when it could go a lot further in Southeast Asia."

"I understand what you're saying, but I wouldn't feel right about that. They gave us this money for a reason. Why can't you just enjoy yourself for once, you're in Rome for fuck's sake!"

"I mean you guys can go out to eat; I'll just hold on to my portion."

I finally put my foot down and said, "Look man, either you come with us and eat tonight or I'm dropping this whole hundred bucks between Corey and me. It's not right for you to take the money and use it for something else. That's not why they gave it to us."

He agreed to join us for the meal. We found a picturesque restaurant in a side alley near the Trevi Fountain and got whatever our vagabond hearts desired. I had the chicken with peppers and potatoes, Corey had pasta alfredo and Aaron ordered a shrimp and clam pasta. It was a fine meal that we washed down with a glass of local Roman wine each.

. . .

On our last day, we hopped on the bus and headed for Roma Termini, the central train station which would direct us toward the airport. *This is it,* I thought. *No more bullshit. No more insane amounts of money spent every day. We're about to live like kings.* I was in a state of euphoria when we reached Roma Termini and made our way to the platforms. We looked at the train schedule and found a private line headed for the airport. There was the usual discussion that happened before every single train we hopped: Aaron would present his fears of being caught and reprimanded. Corey and I would both vote that we take the risk and save the money. After several minutes of back-and-forth, we would eventually cajole Aaron into to hopping on the train without tickets. I found it fascinating given the great lengths he would usually go to save money. This time around was no different. We eventually persuaded Aaron to hop onto the train and then sat down in some open seats. We made it no further than a hundred yards out of the station before I saw a guy walking through the aisles with a ticket puncher. Oh, fuck.

He approached us. *"Biglietti?"*

I quickly feigned surprise. "Tickets? I thought this was a free shuttle?"

"No, you must have tickets."

Aaron played along. "A guy at the station told us this was a free train to the airport?"

"No. You will be fined if you do not have tickets."

We argued with the man for a while, clinging to our made-up story of a man at the train station who'd told us the train was free.

"You pay fine … Two hundred American dollars."

Aaron exploded—"TWO HUNDRED FUCKING DOLLARS?!"

"You pay, or I call the police and they arrest you at the airport."

It was no use to argue. We handed the worker two one hundred dollar bills and sank into our seats. I put in my headphones and listened to music while Corey and Aaron did the same. None of us said a word for the rest of the ride. Once the train stopped, I went to grab my luggage and noticed a white Cabana-style hat sitting next to my bag. Everyone else had already left the train and since it was with our luggage, I assumed it had been sitting there for quite a while. I grabbed it and walked off of the train.

"Check it out." I held up the hat as we walked away from the train. "A two-hundred-dollar hat."

Corey laughed. "There ya go, bud. Hey excuse me, train station worker guy … do you have some lipstick? I like to look pretty before I get FUCKED."

We both kept cracking jokes. Aaron was not amused. "Are you guys really joking about this?" he asked as we continued to walk toward the outside platform where we could grab a smoke.

"Dude, this is just how we handle bad shit," I answered.

"Well, I don't think it's funny. I told you guys this would happen."

Corey interjected. "Aaron, you've said that every single time we've hopped a train. That would be like telling someone every day of their life that they're going to get in a car wreck if they drive, and then one day they just happen to get in one and you say 'See! Told you!' It just doesn't work."

"Yeah, well now we just spent two hundred dollars on nothing basically."

"Actually," I said, "if you think about it, we still saved money in the long run—compared to what we would have spent on tickets if we'd paid each time we got on a train."

Corey made another joke, and we both laughed.

"Just stop with the fuckin jokes, okay?" Aaron snapped. "I don't wanna listen to it."

"You're just jealous you don't have this expensive hat to show off to your buddies back home," I said as I slipped the Cuban cap on my head with a flip.

"Whatever …"

Again I brooded over our endless friction as the trip continued onto its next leg. I had made up my mind that if we couldn't find a way to get along soon, I'd go my own way. Corey still had another two months before he was scheduled to go home and I hoped that if I decided to split, he would come with me. I imagined continuing on with Aaron and not having Corey there to mediate between us. He was usually the middle ground and although he did side with me on a lot of stuff, he was fair and generally unbiased about it. Sometimes he would disagree with me, but it never escalated. What would happen without a third party there to keep me and Aaron from being at each other's throats constantly?

As we waited for our flight, I thought back on how things had changed during the past few weeks. We hadn't had the chance to get to know many other guests during our second stay at Hostel Happy Days. We were too busy preparing for the upcoming flight and trying to make money. For the first time in the trip, I noticed another significant change in me. I felt alienated from other backpackers. I watched as they went out on tours, spent their evenings drinking or going to dinners at restaurants, and relaxing and having a good time. I watched all of this from my bed, hidden behind my computer screen, as I labored on the website and worried whether I could make enough tips from busking that evening to keep us in the black. They were busy choosing which bar to drink Peroni beer at that evening, while I was hoping I could slip an extra pastry from the grocery store for me, Corey, and Aaron to split; I was hungry all the time. They counted down the days when they would have to return home from their vacation, while I looked with dread at my bank account and counted the days in my head until we would be reduced to true homelessness. I was angry at them for being so careless with their money and for being so touristy. I once overheard one tell another that he'd had it rough on his previous trip, "staying in hostels instead of hotels every night and only going out to dinner, like, five or six times during the whole two weeks." I laughed in my head; in my eyes he looked like a tourist as he sat there in his flip flops, eating gelato and setting down a bag full of souvenirs next to his brand-new-looking backpack. I didn't feel like a tourist. I didn't feel like a local either, though. I felt like a traveler.

16
BANGKOK BONANZA
BANGKOK, THAILAND

September 4th

We spent our first week in Southeast Asia binge eating. I applied for freelance computer jobs. Aaron downloaded movies on his computer. Corey either FaceTimed with this girlfriend or messed around on Facebook. I pirated episodes of *Seinfeld* when I wasn't working.

Three times a day we would either walk to Silom Road where endless dishes of Thai food were readily available from vendors, visit a fried rice vendor across the street, or head to the 7-Eleven that was just two blocks away. *Food, food, food.* I couldn't get enough after practically starving myself in Europe. I returned from 7-Eleven with bags of junk food: candy bars, chips, banana muffins, mystery snacks with Thai writing on them.

We took a special interest in the local produce selection and became obsessed with an extra-sweet fruit called mangosteen. It was about double the size of a golf ball and purpley-brown. The outer layer was thick and spongy and inedible so far as we knew, but when it was peeled away, it revealed a gelatinous, sugary white pulp that tasted delicious. It was a bright, sweet medley of flavors, comparable to strawberries, peaches, and vanilla ice cream combined. There was also dragon fruit, which looked awesome—a bright pink oval with neon green spikes all over it—but tasted bland, to our disappointment.

We tried new foods regularly, but my favorite was the fried rice vendor across the street. A heavyset Thai kid stood behind the table. Probably in his early thirties, he was a musician like Corey and myself. It didn't take long for us to strike a friendship with him. Every time we approached his stand, he'd shout over the heads of other customers, "Hey! American friends!" with a big smile as he motioned for us to come forward.

Every morning one or two of us would walk to the 7-Eleven and return with iced coffee, snacks, fruit, and cigarettes. It was all so cheap. Cigarettes were a dollar a pack (which meant we weren't picking up butts and rolling them up anymore), most food cost about a dollar a meal, and our hostel was only two or three US dollars per night. After our first week there, we decided we really needed the rest and recuperation after Europe, so we opted to pay for another two weeks. It was cheaper that way, and we had the option of our own room—which ended up being a whole dorm to ourselves because they ran out of private ones.

During our first week we became friends with a group of young guys from India who were staying in the adjacent room. They showed us the ropes around Bangkok and became a frequent presence.

Aaron and Corey went out on the town to see the sights during the day on several occasions. I would have loved to join, but I was on a desperate mission to bring in money online. The cheaper cost of living in Southeast Asia came with a price: No more busking money. We felt it wouldn't be right to try to busk there, where the average citizen was barely squeezing by to begin with. This also meant the bars weren't going to be paying more than about twenty dollars for hours and hours of playing. So the answer was the Internet. With my computer, I hoped to earn a first world income while paying for third world living expenses for three people. Aaron still had some money and Corey's mom had sent him some cash. Neither sum was anywhere near sufficient to make it another six or seven months until our return home. Our fate depended entirely on donations from the website at that point. We had made around $500 in donations so far from friends and family members back home. I had a feeling more would keep coming in, but they weren't reliable enough to depend on entirely, and it would be nice to become self-sufficient. I came to realize eventually that the website itself wasn't going to generate much money for quite some time. Besides the donations, Aaron had been right all along on that score. I had barely been able to put any time into it while we were in Europe—and even if I had, it would be a long time before we reached enough readership to attract advertisers or sponsors. In retrospect, I had—yet again—been naïve and ignorant.

Thus, there was freelancing.

The majority of my time in Bangkok was spent applying to jobs on Odesk or Elance (they've now merged into Upwork). These are websites on which clients search for freelancers to complete jobs, ranging from graphic design to writing to voiceover work. Basically anything you can do with a computer and an Internet connection. There were two downsides to these websites: The first and most important was the insignificant amount of income it generated: most freelancers were based in countries with a low cost of living, such as India or even Thailand, where I was. That meant most of the jobs that pay about $30-100 per hour in the US were paying only $3-20 on the freelancing websites (the latter number being rare). Luckily, since I happened to be *living* in one of those low-income countries, that part wasn't too big of a deal. I was already used to working my ass off for peanuts back on the pier in Italy. But the second downside was that it was difficult to get started. I needed to take a ton of skills tests, ranging from spelling and grammar to Photoshop competency. I also needed a decent portfolio, which I didn't really have at the time.

I wasn't sure which of my meager skills would draw the most

clients. I applied to several writing and graphic design jobs, but the latter became the winning option. I had taught myself design here and there over the years and then really dove headfirst into it when I was building the website.

So for days on end, I sat in front of my computer. Again. I was on the top level of one of the bunk beds where one of the few ceiling fans in our room could gently caress me with pitiful waves of stale, musty hostel air. My body was fueled solely by coffee, cigarettes, and fried rice. The work was tedious and I didn't see any results for quite a while.

Fortunately, I hit a stroke of luck elsewhere. I had joined several groups of travel bloggers on Facebook before we'd left. I posted one or two things in there and browsed a few times, but hadn't participated other than that. It suddenly occurred to me one night that most of those people probably didn't do their own graphic design work. I could charge them about half of what they were used to paying and still make considerably more than what Odesk or Elance clients were offering. Additionally, I'd be working for other bloggers who may be able to offer insight into the industry. So I posted something in all the groups I could find, offering my design services at affordable rates with a small portfolio available upon request. I got a few messages within the first day or two and by the time we left Bangkok a week later I had a decent bit of work coming in. Those people told their friends, and so on and so forth. It wasn't enough to put us in a luxury hotel, but for the moment at least, a weight was lifted.

17

THE PUSSY SHOW
BANGKOK. THAILAND

September 16th

Commonly referred to by Westerners as a "Ping Pong Show," the Pussy Show is a surreal experience in which a live audience witnesses scantily clad young women strut around a stage and perform carnival-like acts with their vaginas. You've probably seen some kind of spoof of this in a comedy movie before, where a girl is shooting Ping Pong balls out of her ham cannon at a surprised crowd and laughter ensues. Turns out this is actually a real thing, and it also turns out that popping Ping Pong balls across the room isn't the only carnie-magic a vagina can perform. Such events are advertised by short Thai men who run up to you at Patpong—the night market in Bangkok—and pass out flyers.

"Ahhh, you Merican guy, you my special frien, come see pussy show! Ping Pong, pickle, darts … You my special frien, you come for free!"

No matter how many times you say tell them *no thanks,* they will continue to follow you through the market, flapping their flyer in your face. I half-expected to see swag items next. Maybe a shirt that reads, "My friends went to a pussy show in Bangkok, and all I got was this lousy syphilis!"

Eventually we decided to see what the fuss was about. So we walked to Patpong and made it about twenty feet into the market before one of the flyer guys ran up to us, yelling, "Pussy show! Pussy show, Merican friend! You come free!"

"Okay then," Corey said. "Lead the way."

His eyebrows lifted and he dropped his arms, as if thinking, *Holy shit, it worked ...*

We followed him onto a side street and stopped in front of a narrow door. He unlocked it with a key and we followed him inside, up a narrow set of stairs. When we reached the top level, we came into a dark room with a strip-club/opium den vibe. There was a stage in the middle that looked like a boxing ring without the side ropes, with a small staircase leading up to it. A bar sat against the far wall on the other side of the stage, tended by a Thai woman who was reminiscent of Frankenstein's monster. The room was surrounded with benches and small stadium-style seats. A topless woman danced on the stage. Several others in rarified dress either hung out in front of the bar or sat on the small steps to the stage.

Flyer Guy led us to a bench. "You sit heeya." With that, he scampered down the stairs to search for more customers. I was already feeling weird about the situation. We were the only customers in the whole place. One of the girls approached us:

"Drink for my friends?" her bare breasts jiggled as she rested her elbows on the counter, and I tried not to stare.

"Yeah, drinks!" Aaron said. Soon the girl returned with three *Chang* beers. We thanked her, but she didn't leave. Instead, she sat down with Aaron and rubbed his leg.

"You cute! You buy me Coke?"

"Uhh ... no?"

Soon Corey and I had girls sitting next to us as well all asking for a "Coke." We politely turned them down..

Deep Blue Something's *Breakfast at Tiffany's* began crackling over the speakers. An announcer began shouting in Thai—similar to what you would hear at a boxing or wrestling match. A nude girl walked on stage.

The first girl sat down on the stage, leaned back on her elbows, and spread her legs wide. Then she inserted a full dill pickle into herself and with a "*hwah!*" shot it out of her crotch at us. It bounced across the floor toward me like a skipped rock across a pond. My fight or flight response induced a jerk sideways in my seat.

The girl sitting next to me laughed and said, "Aww, you scared, you scared!"

Goddamn right I'm scared. I'm not trying to get an STD from a pickle.

She placed another pickle in her vagina just as another group of people were walking in the door. "*Hwah!*" It shot across the room at them and they all jumped back to escape it. They were ushered to a bench diagonally from us. "*Hwah!*" Another pickle skipped across the floor. She was spinning in circles on her butt and shooting them in all directions as fast as she could manage.

Another girl was walking around with a bucket and tongs and placing the pickles in it. She held one up at Corey's face as she walked by: "Ahhhh!" she exclaimed with a laugh as he jumped backward. The girls we were sitting with all continued to laugh at us.

The pickle girl left, and another woman took her place. This one began pulling a long string of razor blades out of her vagina. We were aghast. "WHAAAT!" I heard Aaron scream as she pulled the blades out, one by one, on a string. This was followed by another string, with small plastic flowers that bloomed as she birthed them. "Ahh …" we all sighed in relief. She then pulled out a big permanent marker. We gawked, waiting to see what would happen next.

The marker was inserted exactly where you guessed, with the tip protruding downward. She sat a piece of paper on the floor and squatted over it while moving her hips around in a controlled circular motion. Then she humped forward a couple of times and did a *swoop* motion with her ass. We were on the edge of our seats. She held up the paper, which bore a perfect smiley-face. I couldn't have drawn the thing better with my *hand,* let alone if someone shoved a Sharpie up my ass. We all clapped. She bowed, pen still in place.

The girl sitting next to me started rubbing my leg. I swatted her hand away and took another swig of my beer. She reached again, and this time slid her hand up my shorts leg. I swatted harder—"NO."

"Ahh, come on, I bet you have big dick, yeah?"

"It's tiny."

"I feel it and find out!" she clawed at my crotch. I grabbed her arm again.

"I'm not interested. Thanks, but no."

"Come on—I sucky for 1,000 baht!" she said with a seductive smile.

I thought for a moment. First, I wondered if there had been any recent advances in curing herpes, AIDs or any of the other "you're stuck with it" types of diseases. Then I thought, *Damn, that's actually a pretty good deal. I mean seriously, that's like twenty-six American dollars. I could get a blowjob from this girl for less money than a parking spot in New York.* Then I thought of my family doctor back home, and his words as I would drop my undies in his office for inspection:

"Ahh, I see what's going on here. Looks like a hooker sucked you off, huh? What you're seeing there is actually your penis detaching from your body. You see, the hooker spit has lodged itself up under your shaft there and it's causing your cock to eat itself from the bottom up. I gotta show this to my secretary. Hey Carol, come in and look at this guy's dick!"

"Oh my god, is there anything you can do?"

"Well there're a couple ways you can take care of it. Your best bet is gonna be flying back to Thailand and killing the hooker who gave it to you. That would stop its power-source. Or we can inject some Catholic-girl spit in there along with the hooker saliva and let the two just duke it out. That procedure is a little riskier. Odds are, the Catholic girl's blowjob is gonna be nowhere near as good as someone more experienced like a hooker."

"I gi-you blowjob for 1,000 baht!" she repeated, snapping me out of my trance.

"Thanks, but I'm gonna have to pass."

Corey directed his girl over to us by telling her that he had a girlfriend, but that Aaron and I were both interested.

Aaron's girl gave up on him early on, probably in fear of the whole Catholic-spit thing destroying her.

A new girl walked onto the stage as we continued to battle the sex workers. Pickle Girl and Sharpie Girl approached us—much to the catty dismay of the current lingerers. Every female in the place was a working girl, it seemed, aside from the Terminator behind the bar.

The new performer held a long, thin tube between her fingers on one hand and inserted it into her vagina. She lifted one leg high in the air, raised her hips and yelled out a short but high-pitched *"Yah!"*—A balloon popped. She was shooting a blowgun out of her vagina. We applauded heavily. *Pop!* Another balloon exploded amidst cheers from the small audience. She kept going and hit nine out of ten balloons before missing. I was thoroughly impressed.

She turned and walked away as another girl got up on stage with a glass bottle of soda. She shook it up and sat it in front of her. She spit on her hand and rubbed herself, and then slowly sat over the bottle, holding the bottom in place with her feet. She paused for a moment. The small crowd went silent … and then—*POP!*—she snapped her hips backward and the bottle top popped off, releasing a geyser of soda into the air. A dozen mouths collectively gaped.

"Are you fucking kidding me …" Corey commented.

"Oh my GODDDD," Aaron exclaimed. I was speechless. We clapped and cheered. Then the mountain of a woman who'd been behind the bar approached us.

"Show over, time you go," she barked.

"Oh … okay…" Aaron looked over at us, both equally puzzled.

We stood up.

"Five hunnit baht each."

"Huh?" We'd each only had one beer, about sixty baht each.

"Five hunnit baht. You pay now."

"Uhhh, the guy that brought us here said it was free?" Corey said.

"No, no free. You pay—five hunnit baht each."

"Three hunnit baht. Three hunnit baht each then."

"No. No three hundred baht."

"You buy Coke for girls?"

"No …?"

"You?" she looked at Corey and Aaron. They both shook their heads.

"Then five hunnit baht."

All the women had gathered around us in a circle with the Mama-San towering over them. They yelled in frustration behind her: "You no buy Coke!"

"Is the Coca-Cola company fuckin sponsoring this thing?" I asked.

"A hundred baht each," Aaron said.

"No—no hunnit baht. Hmm. Three hunnit baht each." She stepped forward and a few of the girls behind her began hurling insults toward us, to up their arms. It looked like a riot was about to ensue.

"Fine—fine, we'll give you three hundred baht." I motioned to Aaron who counted out the money and handed it to her.

"Now you leave, show over."

We slithered to the stairwell in shame and took two steps at a time to the bottom. After re-emerging into Patpong, with its neon lights, raw smells, and chattering sounds, our embarrassment was replaced with the jangling, chaotic excitement of budding adventure.

Aaron suggested we pick up some whiskey to take back to the hostel. I'm not a big liquor-drinker, so I opted for a four-pack of Chang while he and Corey grabbed two bottles of rot-gut liquor and some mixers. Aaron popped open the whiskey on the steps outside of a 7-Eleven and mixed Corey and himself a drink for the long walk home. As we threaded the busy sidewalks, he sipped from his Coke bottle and gradually added more whiskey to it. About a block from the hostel, he was getting a bit wobbly.

"Aaron, you might wanna slow down on that stuff, bud," Corey suggested. "It'll sneak up on ya."

"Ahh I'm good man! I sip on this stuff all the time at home!" He was giggly and careless.

"Allll right man," Corey said. "Just saying, our tolerance is probably fucked considering how little we've drank over the past couple months."

"I'll be all right."

We made it back to the hostel without getting smashed by one of the rickety buses careening around the city and were greeted by our only hostelmates—three Indian guys with whom we'd been regularly partying. So much so that we'd dubbed them the IndiAnimals.

They were the first Indian people I'd met and they were some of the friendliest people I've ever met. Although, at times, they may have been a little *too* friendly. For example, in America, if you're walking around holding hands with another man, people will think you are homosexual. In India, it would be akin to seeing Joe and Ted hold their hand on the way to the car after slamming back a few Buds and throwing some darts: a simple show of friendship. The first time we saw them doing it, we were confused. *Are they gay? I thought one had a girlfriend back home?* Finally Corey asked, and they filled us in.

There was Sajeer, a tall guy in his mid-twenties with a small goatee, who always wore a pair of aviator sunglasses. He was *The Fonz* of the group. Laid-back and chill. Then there was Jamshad, or "Jam" as we all called him. I had the hardest time understanding him out of any of them. He spoke English almost as if he was underwater. I had to have him repeat almost everything he said at least once. This was made especially humorous one day when I asked him what he did for a living in Bangkok: "I teach ... Eennngleeesh." *Dear god.* Jam was a short guy with short curly hair and a baby-face. He was a little more "friendly" than the other guys: he kissed me on the cheek as I was playing guitar one night (he was shit-hammered) and laid his head on my shoulder, saying over and over, "You are my *bosom friend*."

Then there was Praeful, who they just called Matthew. He was the most reserved of the group, rarely speaking unless directly addressed.

"Party time!" Sajeer smiled as we made our way up the steps to our rooms.

"Yeah, party!" Aaron cheered. I cracked open one of the Changs and had a seat on one of the beds. The IndiAnimals went to their own room and returned with more alcohol and some fried chicken and other foods. Aaron sat on the floor and mixed up another drink. I noticed that the first bottle of whiskey was almost completely gone.

"Aaron, you might wanna have some of that food," I said.

"Yeah bro, that's probably not a bad idea if you're planning on making it through the night ... seriously." Corey said.

"Whaaat? I'm not even drunk yet! You guys ain't even *seen* me get drunk before," he said. I swear his eyes crossed as he was telling me that. He was shit-hammered.

I laughed. "Whatever you say dude."

At the behest of Jam, we got out the instruments and started playing some tunes. Aaron began cheering belligerently as he rocked back and forth and lolling his head from side to side. "Sajeer! Sajeer, I love you duuude! Take a shot with me!"

Corey and I played several more songs before Aaron was on the floor, shirtless, rolling from side to side and shouting, "Woo! Yeah! Uhhhh, fuck ... yeah!"

Then he sat up quickly. His head tipped forward and his eyes drooped. He stood up and then fell into a bed frame. He stumbled the other way and smacked an oscillating fan into a precarious totter. Then the vomiting began. He spewed whiskey and Coke across the room with the velocity of a firehose. He was like an inebriated dragon, attempting to burn down our village with liquid fire. He even flapped his arms uncontrollably like little drunk-dragon wings. Then he staggered [took flight majestically] toward the bathroom, shooting his whiskey-fire-vomit across the floor and wall along the way.

The music stopped and everyone collectively gasped. We all jumped up and ran into the bathroom where Aaron was already sitting on the toilet with his head in his hands. Corey and I grabbed a hold of him.

"Dude, are you gonna be okay?!" I said.

"Wooo …" he held up one of his hands as he attempted to keep his little party going.

"Get him some water," Corey said to me. He had his hand on Aaron's back as Aaron leaned forward.

I sprinted to one of the beds and grabbed a bottle of water off of it, then ran back to the bathroom. Aaron was on the floor, covered and surrounded by vomit, and Corey was standing in the corner with a look of pure confusion and horror on his face.

"How the fuck? What just happened?" I asked. "I was gone maybe three seconds!"

"Dude … he just tipped over, and … I don't know—I really don't know."

"We must get him into the shower," Sajeer said.

He and Corey picked Aaron up by the arms and carried him into a big gym-room-style shower next to the toilet room. They gently laid him on the floor, and Praeful Matthew began rinsing the vomit from his shirtless body with a detachable shower hose. Aaron stirred.

"Ugghhh …"

We weren't sure what to do. Eventually we were standing in the bathroom, calmly carrying on a conversation about the various remedies for excessive drunkenness within our separate cultures, while Praeful Matthew ran the hose over Aaron from head to toe. Aaron groaned periodically.

Then suddenly, he sat up. More vomit erupted from his mouth like a fire hose and shot past Praeful Matthew, still holding the hose in bewilderment. "Ugggh! Ahhh!" he was shouting as he spun and crawled on the shower floor. Everyone was shouting and attempting to avoid the vomit-sprinkler as he flung himself around the floor like a grounded fish. Finally he sank down and passed out again. We all resumed conversation and Praeful Matthew held the hose over him again.

"You need culture cream, and crackers," Jam suggested in his thick Indian accent. "Make him not drunk anymore."

"What the fuck is culture cream?" Corey asked. "Are you guys gonna jizz on a cracker and make him eat it?"

"What is ... 'jizz?'" Jam asked. Corey and I laughed.

"Really, what is culture cream?" I asked.

"Cream ... with bacteria," he clarified.

"So ... jizz," Corey laughed.

"Culture of milk ... Matthew will show you if you go to store with him. You can tell me about 'jizz' later."

I volunteered to run to the 7-Eleven with Praeful Matthew, who handed the sprayer to Corey before leaving. We dodged traffic across the street and sped through the alleyways to reach the store as quickly as we could. When we entered, Praeful Matthew walked over to the cooler and pulled out a cup of yogurt.

"Ohhhhh." I realized what Jam was talking about. "Really, yogurt and crackers for a drunk-cure? That's a new one for me."

We hurried back to the hostel. Corey was still spraying Aaron with the cold water in attempt to sober him up and clean him off.

"Okay, we must get him into bed," Sajeer said.

He and Corey grabbed Aaron under the arms and lifted him again. As they did this, Aaron woke up and shouted, "No!—I can do it—I can do it." He stood there for approximately one and a half seconds. Then he fell. I use the term "fell" loosely here, for it was more of a violent flop. It looked like he attempted to backflip *through* the floor. His body made a loud smacking noise on the wet floor and his head thumped against the tiles.

We gasped in horror.

"Umm ... why did we just let him do that?" Corey said. This time when Aaron claimed he could do it by himself, he was ignored. We got him to his bed and fed him the yogurt and crackers.

Soon after this, the IndiAnimals went back to their room, and Corey and I were left to babysit Aaron, who didn't want any part of going to sleep. The puking continued, a dozen times it seemed, and soon he was back on the bathroom floor, rolling around and moaning. Corey and I were exhausted from taking care of him all night; we finally gave up and left him on the bathroom floor, assured that he was sufficiently hydrated and not showing serious signs of alcohol poisoning.

At nine in the morning, I was awakened the squeaky wheels of a rusty mop bucket rolling through the hallway toward our room for its weekly cleaning. Aaron sat up on his bed, blinked and yawned, and then reached for a water bottle. The little old Thai cleaning lady rounded the corner and her eyes widened in terror. The mop handle clattered to the floor along with her jaw. The entire floor was blanketed in a lake of vomit. The fan lay on its side in the middle of it. Bottles and cans were strewn about, and a container of fried rice had exploded on the wall. She made uncomfortable high-pitched gasps as she shuffled around the vomit and went into the bathroom. She screamed as if she'd seen a spider. But it was not a spider. It was the toilet room. Puke was on the walls, all over the floor, even on the back of the toilet. It was on the door and door handle. Loose toilet paper was strewn among the slop. A trail of vomit led to the shower room where there was more puke. It was unbelievable that such a volume of liquid could come out of one human being. About one-tenth of it had made it into the trash can or toilet.

"No, no, no ..." she walked out of the bathroom, past the lake of vomit, past the mop and cleaning supplies she had dropped, and exited the room. She returned a few seconds later, stopped and stared at the mess, and slowly picked up her mop, resigning herself to her fate. Aaron walked over to her:

"I'll clean this," he said, waving a hand over his vile creation, "don't worry about it."

I was expecting some type of conversation to happen, but the woman just handed him the mop and turned around and left before he would change his mind.

"So Aaron," Corey said, "remember when you bitched at us for staying up all night drinking in Italy at the campground hostel? I never want to hear you bitch about us drinking again."

He smiled as he ran the mop through the mess. "Yeah … that's fair enough."

. . .

A couple of days later, as I was typing away on a freelancing skills test and Aaron was watching a movie on his laptop, Corey said something that neither Aaron nor I were prepared to hear. He cleared his throat, breaking the usual evening silence while we all did our own thing. "Guys, I have something to tell you. I don't really know how to say this, so I'm just gonna come right out with it. I've been doing a lot of thinking lately, and I think it's best for me to go home early. Katie is buying me a plane ticket tonight, and I'm leaving tomorrow."

18

FAREWELL
BANGKOK, THAILAND

September 20th

Corey's delivery of the news left Aaron and I speechless for several moments. Of course we'd known all along that he was planning to leave early, when we would leave Australia. The real shocker was that he would want to go home to her at all. You see, it was only a few days prior when he told us she'd cheated on him while we were away.

Hearing of the affair, the thought of my own heartbreak came crashing back. He began delivering the all-too-familiar excusive pining while my own sad song replayed in a flash of gut-twisting vignettes. Our stories were eerily similar, down to the ages of the children caught in the crossfire.

"Man, I'm gonna give you some advice," I said. "As you know, I've been right where you're sitting. And I can tell you she's not going to change. I wish I would have stayed broken up with Samantha after the first time she cheated on me. Don't make it any harder on you, or more importantly, the kids."

But, of course, he wouldn't listen to reason. He somehow found a way to blame himself. It was his fault because he'd left. It was his fault for not giving her enough attention. And on and on and so it goes. We would later find out that she had basically started seeing the guy right after we left: dates, dinners, shopping trips, all within two weeks of our departure. Unfortunately though, the worst part of Corey's saga is yet to come.

Before we get to that though, I'll explain the events leading up to his departure. After he found this news out, he spent long hours video chatting with her as well as several friends back home who attempted to console him on the matter. An overwhelming majority, as any rational-thinking person would assume, told him to forget her and enjoy the trip of a lifetime as a newly single man. He wouldn't listen to logic or reason though. We talked about it at length, but I could tell his mind was made from the start: he wanted to go home and be with her. I would bring up the things she had done to him since we'd left, from downright disrespect right on up to, oh, letting another dude put his dick inside her. Or letting a *different* guy sleep in her bed with her. He continually stuck up for her and made excuses on how it was his fault and how he thought she was innocent. I wanted to slap him and say, "WAKE UP! PULL THE LABIA FROM YOUR EYES!" but I knew it was no use. I had been there before. It wasn't just her he was considering. It was the children, who he had raised as his own. It was the idea of being part of a family, of being a father. I knew in my core how it would all end. But what could I say? I'd been in his shoes.

Still, the thought of losing him as a traveling companion was crushing. I felt like my best friend had stabbed me in the back. After all we had gone through, he was going to abandon us and leave me with Aaron, who I couldn't seem to find a way to get along with no matter how hard I tried. We had just spent over a hundred dollars on a new camera for him. Aaron had paid for a majority of his plane tickets to even come on the trip. And this was how he was repaying us for everything? Leaving us high and dry to go home to some girl who obviously didn't give two shits about his well being?

My throat tightened with sadness when I dwelled on these thoughts. I knew I had to be a good friend and try to understand, though. So the next night we headed to the night market, got some souvenirs for him to take home to our friends and family and called the IndiAnimals over for a going-away party. It was bittersweet.

Another comical attempt to quit smoking had been scheduled to start the next day and Aaron and I forfeited one of our nicotine patches so he could use it on the long plane flight home. He was set to travel through South Korea and across the west coast of the US back to Ohio. We hugged him one last time and posed for a picture, which the Indian-Animals took for us. They called a taxi for him and we gathered outside the hostel to wait for it.

"I can't believe you're really leaving right now, before we finally get to enjoy the trip." I attempted a last-ditch plead to get him to stay.

"I just have to do what I think is right, man," he answered. He was going—there was no question about it. "I'll do my best to try and help you guys out when I get back home. Be careful and take care of yourselves … and don't kill each other."

We laughed nervously. Aaron and I glanced at each other with equal worry. Then the taxi pulled up, and we tossed Corey's bag in the back. We had divvied up group items that he'd been carrying, so mine and Aaron's packs both gained weight. We hugged again and he slid into the back seat of the taxi. We watched the cab rocket into the chaotic bustle of tuk-tuks, speeding buses, and scooters. After the cab slipped out of sight, we turned and walked back to the hostel.

My thoughts were twisting and turning: Were Aaron and I going to be able to get along? Things had gotten easier with the lower cost of living in Southeast Asia. But would we have enough money to make it through the rest of the trip? I knew Australia and New Zealand would be expensive—possibly even more expensive than Europe.

More than anything, I was just sad. Sad because my friend had abandoned me with this guy who I barely got along with and sad that he wasn't going to be around to talk to anymore. Corey and I had the same sense of humor and almost the same personality. One of my only sources of joy during the shittier times in Europe had been when I'd found a way to laugh at it with him. Was I going to be able to do that now?

I went back to my bunk and opened my laptop. I started typing away on freelancing sites, continuing the never-ending search for more money.

. . .

Corey's return home to Katie had turned out even worse than I could ever have expected. Shortly after his arrival home, she dropped a bombshell on him: She was pregnant. You wanna take a guess who the father was? SPOILER ALERT: It certainly wasn't Corey. What was worse, though, was the ultimatum she gave him: If he *stayed* with her and helped her out, she would keep the baby. But if he broke up with her, she was going to get an abortion. Yes, you read that correctly. Not being able to live with himself for causing an abortion (in his mind) he stayed with her. I suspect that she knew she was pregnant before he came home, but she chose not to tell him just so he would return. The crazy thing is that he stayed with her during the whole pregnancy, taking care of her kids (nobody saw much of him during this period) and it wasn't until the baby was born that he realized he just couldn't bring himself to do it. He told her he needed some time to think about things. What did she do when this guy, who had done all of this selfless shit for her, told her he needed some time to think about how he was going to help her raise the baby she cheated on him to conceive? She texted him the next day and broke up with him. Thus, poor big-hearted Corey was thrown out into the world as a single man again, having wasted the rest of his trip and probably the only chance he would have to see Australia and New Zealand. All of that for trying to, for a lack of better words, *turn a ho into a housewife.*

I wish I could say I was there to help talk him through all of this, but that's not what happened. It wasn't until I got home that I learned of most of this. Once Corey left, he seemed to forget that Aaron and I even existed. I only heard from him maybe three or four times during the rest of our trip. In fact, it took him over two months to even drop off the belongings that Aaron had sent home to his parents' house, which was only about a ten minute drive from where Corey spent a majority of his days.

The case with Corey wasn't unique. As the loneliness of isolation and poverty in a foreign land hugged me in its dark, strangely comforting embrace, I made the terrible conclusion that maybe all the people I'd considered so close may not have been close at all. Maybe my view of them was from the far side of the prism. When you leave, I discovered, life just goes on without you. Sure, they don't write you off in anger or anything like that, but you're not around to do the same old things with your friends every weekend and thus aren't considered much in daily thought. Out of all of my friends back home, only two or three of them regularly messaged me to ask how things were going.

Fortunately for us, even if some were too busy to message us on a regular basis, they still showed their care and support by donating money through the website. In the end, that's what made the entire trip possible. If not for the donations rolling in, we'd have run out of money soon after Europe. I always felt bad having a donations system set up, but we tried to even out this feeling by offering things in return, such as a souvenir, postcard, or a video of a song dedicated to specific supporters.

So just as life returned to normalcy at home once we'd left our friends and family months earlier, life on the other side of the world eventually became normal without Corey. Normal as it may be by our standards, that is. However, the rest of the trip carried an unmistakable offbeat feeling in the absence of our optimistic, bearded friend.

19

ISLAND LIFE: MARIJUANA AND MONKEY BUSINESS

KOH PHANGAN, THAILAND

September 24th

A day or two before Corey left I'd decided to shoot my shot with a pretty young woman who worked at one of the food stands nearby. We texted back and forth about a potential meetup. After Corey left, I invited Aaron to join us for a tour of nearby temples.

If I had any hopes of romance with Looktal they were dashed the moment she laid eyes on Aaron. Back home he could be considered the Clint Eastwood of the local creek, floating in his kayak with his tanned, muscled torso and deftly flinging fish from their hideouts. He was mysterious. Quiet. Capable. Thus, the women in our hometown swooned after him. After traveling together for several months, my perception of him had grown more akin to Mr. Magoo than anything else. Looktal, however, saw no bumbling bafoonery with an upside down map or salt-encrusted McDonald's burgers. She saw the beautiful six-foot-something bronzed Greek statue standing before her. Aaron, for his part, remained aloof, which made her infatuation downright terminal.

As the day wore on, I felt myself fusing into the wallpaper.

At the end of the day we bade farewell to Looktal and returned to our hostel for a going-away party with The IndiAnimals. Early the next morning we took a twelve-hour bus ride south to the port city of Surat-Thani, then boarded a ferry to the island of Koh Samui. Two days and two long ferry rides later we were unloading on the shore of Koh Phangan, an island which, when translated to English, exotically means *Island Phangan*. I honestly have no clue what *Phangan* means. Probably booze. Booze Island. I noticed during our last ferry ride that the island was a party place for backpackers. This was a change from Bangkok, where I don't think I saw a single tourist during the entire three weeks we were there. Strangely contrasted to my desires back in Europe, I felt no pull toward joining the island party.

We stepped off the pier and were hounded by a mob of taxi cab drivers. *"Hey guy! Taxi ride to hostel! Cheap, cheap, cheap!"* They jumped in our faces and patted our shoulders and reached for our bags.

This not being our first rodeo, we shouldered past the slick salesmen who were grabbing naïve backpackers by the dozen. Farther down the road we found a smaller group of taxi drivers lounging under a grove of coconut trees.

"Taxi?" Aaron asked.

"Yee, taxi! You come, come."

I asked him how much: it was about half what the guys on the pier were quoting. *Take that, amateurs.* He threw our backpacks onto the roof rack of a rickety Toyota pickup (a Songthaew) and motioned for us to sit on some metal benches that had been welded to the inside of the bed. I noticed he didn't tie our bags down. Instead of leaving, he kept inviting more people over until the entire pickup was filled to the gills with backpackers.

Then, at last, the truck sprang to life as the driver popped the clutch and screeched onto the road. I grabbed onto a metal bar next to me. The truck squealed again as we jetted into the main roadway. The driver was a fucking maniac. The only two speeds he knew were *"NASCAR"* and "ballistic cruise missile" and the only braking technique he knew was "your asshole is now in your esophagus." The young kid sitting across from me clenched the metal seat below him. I stared downward at nothing in particular, stuck in a terrified trance as if we were in a landing craft about to hit Omaha Beach on D-Day.

We hauled ass up the steep mountain road, banking and breaking and praying. Once we'd reached the top, we could see the entire south side of the island. We had little time to enjoy the view however, before we were barreling down the other side, skidding around corners.

"How in the hell are all of our bags staying up there?" a British backpacker wondered aloud to his girlfriend.

After our rusted rocket ship came to a sliding halt in the gravel, we were ushered off the taxi while our driver threw (quite literally) all of our bags into a pile on the ground.

We spent considerable time walking around the island in search of our hostel, during which I realized that I was going to like this place *a lot* more than Bangkok. I saw nothing but smiles, coconut and banana trees, and delicious Thai food. And everything was dirt, dirt cheap. *Paradise,* I thought. We lucked out on our hostel as well; for a measly $2.36 per night we were in a private, clean room with air conditioning and access to a warm shower. I know, a warm shower on a tropical island seems unnecessary or even undesirable. But in Bangkok our shower held a steady temperature equivalent to deep space. No matter how hot it was outside, that freezing shower was torture.

We befriended the British hostel manager named Paul, who told us during our first conversation with him that, "You can get a joint or a bag of weed up there at the Reggae Bar if that's ya fancy. I like to smoke quite a bit me-self, and I'll be glad to share a spliff with ya late-uh."

He later hooked us up by comp'ing the rest of our stay in exchange for a review on a hostel-booking website. On that note, Koh Phangan turned out to be a period of blissful relief for our bank account—not only because things were cheaper but also because I started to make some real money doing graphic design work. The travel blogger groups on Facebook had landed me a few jobs, and those people had referred other people, so on and so forth until I was working steadily. Now understand that I was charging insanely low rates in order to attract more clients. That being said, given our cheap cost of living, it was decent money to us. Forty dollars went a long way when we were only spending about eight or ten bucks a day total on living expenses.

We were unwilling to spend any more precious dollars on partying. After our many Bangkok bashes with the IndiAnimals, we figured we'd gotten that out of our system for a while anyway.

With the exception of a few days where we hung out and swam at the beach and one day where we made a music video, I spent most of the daytime working. In the evenings, I downloaded movies and watched them on my laptop.

One evening Aaron asked if I would mind if he messaged Looktal.

"Ahhh, moving in on my girl, eh?" I said jokingly.

His face reddened. "Well dude you've gotten all the girls so far—I should at least get *one*."

"First of all I was kidding. Did you see the way she looked at you? I stood no chance. Second, we'll never see her again. Third, what do you mean I've 'gotten' all the girls? Like they're fuckin Pokémon cards? The only sex I've had on this trip has been with myself, typically in a hammock."

"Well maybe not sex, but you've hung out with more girls than any of us."

"You mean I *talked* to them? I mean that's basically it dude, I've hung out with more girls because usually you have to talk to them in order to hang out with them." And then, somewhat bemusedly to myself, "Unless you look like *you*, apparently."

"Well I never know what to say when you guys are all sitting around talking. Every time I want to say something, I don't know how to get a word in."

This last line struck me to a bemused realization. "Dude, really, it's fine. You should talk to her. I don't know if you noticed, but she couldn't stop staring at you. I didn't stand a chance."

I put on my headphones and laid back on my bunk, staring at the ceiling. I thought back to all the times Corey and I had sat around with groups of people, drinking and laughing, while Aaron sat in the background, quietly sipping on his drink. I thought about all the conversations we'd had in the nature preserve, where Corey and I would reminisce about funny things we'd done with our friends over the years while Aaron only brought up stories involving his cousins or brothers. The poor kid had never been allowed to do anything. He parents kept him so sheltered that he had never had a chance to interact with other kids growing up like I had. They sent him to that damn Catholic school (where they apparently taught him that red meat and salt is, like, super good for you) and told him his whole life that their opinions about the world were irrefutable facts. I had been handling our differences all wrong. I'd been *angry* at him for being raised differently, which was, of course, entirely out of his control. And who was I to define what's "normal" and what's "different" anyway? Here I was several months into a journey where the diversity of human experience smacked me on the nose at every turn. My holier-than-thou notion that I'd become empathetic to the individual beliefs and struggles of humans all around the world didn't stretch to my own neighbors. My supposed Confucianism was more like disguised condescension.

Under all of the backwardness that drove me up the wall, I saw glimpses of a guy who wanted to experience more of life. He just didn't know how. Not only that, but he'd been programmed to feel guilty about it, per the standard religious norm: *if it feels good, then God will probably punish you eternally for it.*

Suddenly I felt ashamed. Clearly he wanted to come out of his shell a bit more and I'd been bruising his confidence at every turn. I thought maybe I should try to help instead of hinder his efforts. I could show him that there's more to life than money in a box under your bed. That it's good to let out your emotions now and then rather than bottle them up until you explode, as he'd done in the Tiber Creek Campground Hostel, besieging my linen fort. He was no longer under the control of his parents and could do whatever he wanted.

Later that evening I apologized to him for how I'd handled everything thus far and told him that I was going to try harder to accept our differences. He confessed that he'd felt fault on his end too, and we talked openly of our realizations. Finding that we had come to mostly the same conclusions, we shook hands and decided maybe we could get along after all. That night when I went to bed I felt like a huge weight had lifted off my shoulders. I hoped our truce would last and that we'd both come out of the whole thing as better men for having learned to accept each other.

• • •

We spent a little over a week on the paradise island that was Koh Phangan. The time passed by quickly as we settled into a routine. We tried a different Thai dish every night, every one of them as delicious as the last.

One day we rented a scooter to explore the island. Yes, one scooter. We were still poor, after all, so instead of opting for a pair of scooters to tour the island on, we paired up like a happy couple and I held onto the back of the scooter while Aaron drove. We planned to visit some of the island's waterfalls, but were disappointed to find that they had all been reduced to trickles during a recent dry spell.

We were able to stop and play around with an elephant for a bit and get some pictures with it. I saw that it was chained to a stake on the ground and could wander only a few feet in any direction. It made me sad, and got me thinking about some of the other things I'd seen in Asia. I hoped they at least enjoyed their jungle walks with the tourists, but I decided I wouldn't be patronizing any more businesses that involved animal tourism.

Then I thought back on the women at the pussy show and wondered how they ended up there. I decided I wouldn't patronize any more businesses that involved sex tourism either. Anything that could cause a living being to suffer, I would try to avoid.

. . .

We'd been cigarette-free for a couple of days before leaving Bangkok. I quit cold turkey, but Aaron again insisted on weening himself off slowly, only smoking a few a day. I pleaded with him not to do this as it had failed miserably in the past (see: picking up old dirty butts and rolling them into cigarettes in the nature preserve) but he insisted he could do it this time. I at least got him to agree not to buy any more packs and just smoke the rest of what he had left. Of course, as had happened before in Europe, he always seemed to have just a teensy bit of tobacco left, tucked away in his pack somewhere. It made it hard not to give into temptation and smoke when I had to watch him light up every so often, but this time I stuck to my guns. Eventually, after a couple days on Koh Phangan, he ran out of his hoarded stash of stale tobacco. We had finally quit smoking.

After we spent several days getting to know our new surroundings, we decided we should start planning our next moves. There were several options to consider. One thing was becoming clear: online income aside, we couldn't make it much longer without either a boost in finances or a decrease in living expenses. Given how low our expenses already were, it didn't seem like we could get much lower. Aaron researched islands in Indonesia on which we could stay in a beach hut for a couple of months and save a ton of money. The only problem was that a lot of them didn't have any Internet connection, which would prevent me from continuing to work online. There was also the added complication of actually getting to a tiny island in the South Pacific which looked to be no small task, usually performed by small boat or airplane. I thought back to the rusty Toyota pickup that brought us to our hostel, then to the rusty boat that ferried us to the island. I imagined a small airplane in Indonesia. My mind's eye painted the image of a lawn mower blade strapped to an old rowboat with huge palm fronds for wings. Then I watched in my imagination as a small Indonesian man would throw our bags into a basket on the top and motion for us to sit in lawn chairs bungee-strapped to the contraption.

"We should take a boat if we're going to do that," I said.

We knew we were headed to Malaysia within a few days when our Thai visas ran out, so we sent Couchsurfing requests to hosts in the country and researched hostels and guesthouses. Aaron spotted a killer deal at a small travel agency on our current island, which would take us from our hostel (they would pick us up in a van at the front door) to a guesthouse in Malaysia.

Then there was Katie's one good deed. When Corey had left, she paid for his plane ticket, leaving an unused ticket from Australia to Los Angeles. (We hadn't booked anything between Thailand and Australia, planning instead to figure out a way there as we went). I realized we might be entitled to some cash for the unused ticket, so I contacted our travel agent. Surprisingly—given the ridiculous effort it had taken to try to change our tickets in Europe—she quickly canceled Corey's last ticket and refunded the ticket price to my account. We were elated. Since Aaron had paid for the majority of that ticket, we got almost all of it—close to a thousand dollars.

We counted up our total assets: Aaron's cash, still in his hidden compartment in his belt, and my PayPal account and bank account, the latter of which now holding Corey's refunded ticket money. We were doing better than we thought, although it also caused us to realize that there was definitely no fucking way we were going to make it another six or eight months.

After much deliberation, we decided to cut the whole trip short. Instead of going to Indonesia and living out a couple months as coconut-cracking tribesmen, we'd fly out of Malaysia from Kuala Lumpur in a few weeks and head straight to Perth, Australia, where we'd spend a month. Then we'd fly to New Zealand for a short two-week stay, arriving in the states by mid-November and returning home in Ohio by Christmas. We'd have more than enough to live comfortably for the rest of the trip, provided we could find free places to stay in Australia and New Zealand. Before we had a chance to change our minds, we booked our plane tickets from Kuala Lumpur to Perth.

Then Aaron suggested a dangerous game: "We should buy a few cigarettes to celebrate!"

Now ... hear him out at least. The local convenience store sold little miniature packs holding only five cigarettes instead of the usual twenty. Aaron reasoned that, on this joyous occasion, we could treat ourselves to one. After all, it was only a measly ... paltry ... inconsequential five cigarettes.

I paused for a moment and thought about it. I knew it was a bad idea, given that we'd pretty much made it through the rough patch of quitting smoking. But this was just five cigarettes. Not twenty, which would certainly leave us addicted once again, but a mere five, which should be *totally fine.*

"I'll go grab em!"

The door slammed open as I erupted from its frame, careening toward the convenience store with reckless abandon. I shucked off my sandals at the entrance mat and scampered toward the forbidden nicotine, rubbing my hands together like a mischievous raccoon. Upon reaching the counter, I noticed that the shelf which usually held the smaller packs was empty. "Where are the little packs?" I asked the Thai clerk.

"No small pack, only big pack left," he answered.

I considered my options. On one hand, I knew that if I bought a full pack of twenty cigarettes, we'd soon be smokers again. On the other hand, I already had my mind set on smoking a cigarette. My mouth salivated. My racoon-claws steepled together like a comic book villain plotting a caper. "Okay, give me a big pack."

Now ... hear me out. I figured I could just take out five cigarettes and then throw the rest of the pack away without telling Aaron. I knew if he saw the whole pack we'd end up smoking them and it would all be over for our nicotine cessation. After all, it was only one US dollar for the whole pack. Better to throw them away and not have to worry about it. I removed the five cigarettes and held them in one hand, with the rest of the pack in the other hand as I walked back toward the hostel. I saw a lone trash can next to the road. I stopped in front of it, holding the pack over the opening. I tried to release my grip on them, but my brain wouldn't let me do it. I stared at the pack. It was just a flimsy rectangle of thin cardboard holding fifteen paper tubes filled with dried plants. *That's it,* I thought. *That's all it is.* Then I imagined that moment when the smoke would enter my lungs. Heavenly, calming, blissful mist. This was my moment. This was where I was either a man of mental fortitude who stuck to his convictions, or where I caved and gave into temptation like a careless child. You've read this story long enough to know what I did.

After stashing the almost-full pack on top of an air conditioning unit that was mounted next to our second-story porch, I entered the hostel room with the other five cigarettes.

Aaron's face lit up with joy like a kid on Christmas morning. "DID YOU GET THEM?!"

"I GOT EM … COME ON!" we skipped outside to light the cigarettes. Shortly thereafter, we both sat on the railing to keep from falling over with dizziness. Fantastic, wonderful, majestic nicotine.

That night before I went to sleep, I innocently mentioned to Aaron that I was going out to the bathroom to "poop." This was actually just an excuse to grab my secret pack of cigarettes off of the air conditioning unit and smoke half of one. The next day, I repeated the act while Aaron was watching a movie on his laptop. We had been rationing our five cigarettes, but with my sneaking off to "poop" in between those shared with Aaron, I had become addicted again.

After a day or two of this I'd still only smoked four cigarettes from the pack, considering I had only been smoking a bit of each one. I decided that was it. I couldn't go the rest of the trip sneaking cigarettes behind Aaron's back. He would think I had some kind of intestinal parasite causing me to shit sixteen times a day. I fought the urge from then on and let the pack sit untouched on the air conditioning unit. In retrospect, I don't know why I didn't just throw them away. I did well with it, though, and didn't touch them even once for a full day. On that second day however, things got interesting.

"Dude!" Aaron shouted into the hostel room door while I was

working on my laptop.

"What?"

"You're not gonna believe this. Someone threw a full pack of cigarettes off the balcony. It's laying on that big scrap pile by the bathroom!"

My eyes widened. *Surely not.* "Are you sure it's not just an empty pack?" I asked.

"NOPE. I can see right into it where it landed. It's almost full!"

"But—I mean—how are you going to get over there? It's behind a fence."

"I'm about to go down and hop it!"

Well, shit. I followed him out to the balcony where he excitedly pointed to my forlorn pack of cigarettes, which had apparently fallen from the top of the air conditioning unit during the night. Sure enough, the top was wide open and several cigarettes were poking out. I had no choice but to play dumb with him. "No way! Why would somebody leave a full pack of cigarettes down there?"

"I know, right! And they're even our brand! Someone must have left them sitting on this balcony ledge right here and they fell off."

"Yep—I bet that's exactly what happened."

Aaron wasted no time in hopping the fence and grabbing the pack. We each lit up a cigarette. "So," I said, "we're pretty much smoking again then, right?"

"Nah man, we'll quit after this pack is done."

Before leaving Koh Phangan we were back up to a pack a day each. The funniest thing about this incident is that I never told Aaron what had really happened. To this day he still thinks that pack just somehow ended up on the scrap pile. So Aaron, as you're reading this for the first time, possibly already planning my demise for printing our various disagreements in Europe along with all the Catholic jokes … I'm sorry, I couldn't help myself.

20

CHEESEBURGERS, POOP–DITCHES, AND BUDDHIST MONKS FROM SPAIN

PENANG, MALAYSIA

October 3rd

The trek from Koh Phangan was comprised of ferries between islands, then a long, shaky bus ride from Surat Thani to a small town on the Malaysian border. There we stayed in a hostel that looked like it was abandoned fifty years earlier. The bathroom was … interesting. What was weird to me was the "shitting system." I call it this because I wouldn't quite call it a toilet, while at the same time it wasn't one of those holes in the floor that you see a lot in Southeast Asia. It was a set of pink tiled steps, which led up to a platform about three feet off the ground. The thing looked like a Mayan temple or something. There was a hole at the top, and the person was expected to hover on the slippery tile over the hole while gripping a handle on the wall.

After finishing their business, the person would spray his or her asshole clean with a salvaged sink-sprayer hanging on the wall from a rusty coathanger. With the slippery tile already presenting an opportunity to fall into the poophole, the water-spraying part only added to the adventure. There was no stall or anything like that. Just the sprayer, a sink, and the poop-fortress towering over everything in the corner of the room. I refrained from taking a number two during our stay there.

After staying in the Pink Palace of Poopy for one night, we were ushered onto a crammed bus with a bunch of local Thai and Malay travelers. We spent most of the day bouncing around on the road south. At one point the bus stopped and we were herded on foot over the border into Malaysia. Our passports were stamped, and then we re-boarded the bus on the other side. Hours later we were plopped into the middle of a busy street on the island of Penang.

Aaron stayed to guard the packs while I left to find the hostel we'd booked online. When I found it, I was disappointed. It looked totally different than the website, with the rooms encrusted in a thin layer of grime and the A/C on the fritz. In Europe we were used to such disappointments. In Italy, for example, we'd sprung on an air-conditioned hostel only to find that the "air-conditioning" was actually just an oscillating fan in the middle of the room. We laughed it off and moved on. But now? We'd been in Southeast Asia for a month and had been living like aristocrats. This hostel would simply not do. When I rejoined Aaron we decided to stay the night and then find something better the next day.

On the way over, I made an earth-shattering discovery. For the past month or two, I had been desperately craving something from back home. Something that, coupled with beers and some buddies, could be beset upon an American flag with eagles soaring overhead. Something just as American as the Fourth of July and apple pie. A cheeseburger. Not a shitty McDonald's one, but a thick, juicy, cholesterol packed heart-stopper.

But alas, as far as I could tell these Western patties of salty splendor were not available to the poor, cheeseburger-deprived Asians. Don't get me wrong, I absolutely loved the Thai food. But after you eat rice and chicken or some variation of that for weeks on end, you start craving something different. Or in my case, something familiar. So you can imagine my overwhelming joy when

I rounded a corner in Penang, Malaysia, and saw a small stand with a sign that read: "American Cheeseburgers & Hot Dogs."

My legs became wobbly and I held onto the side of a building for support.

"Aaron, oh my god … I can't … there's a … I don't …"

"Huh? Are you okay?"

"Cheeseburgers … fucking cheeseburgers dude."

"Where?"

"Is it—oh my god, is it real? Is it a mirage?" I gasped.

I pointed out the stand and we approached it. A line of younger locals were waiting for their taste and we filed into place behind them. After a couple minutes, it started to rain. Tropical, Malaysian rain, pouring buckets of water on you in a matter of milliseconds. Aaron retreated to the hostel and I volunteered to grab his food. I didn't care about the rain. You could have stabbed me in the face right there and I would have waited to get my cheeseburger before I let the ambulance cart me away to a hospital. The Earth could have been ending by meteor strike and a small spaceship could have swooped down to save a handful of Earth's inhabitants and I wouldn't have moved from the line. "Give me a minute, almost have my burger," I would have said.

After finally arriving at the front of the line, soaking wet and just as happy as I'd been the first time I received a blowjob, I ordered a double cheeseburger with bacon, lettuce, and onion, along with some french fries.

The man slapped together my precious burger and heaped a pile of fries into a small bag. I snatched it and scurried to the hostel. If people came too close to me, I hissed and growled at them like an angry opposum. I ran upstairs and sat the bag down on a table in the common room.

"AAAAARON. BURRRRRGERS ARE HERE."

He walked out balancing his laptop on a single palm and typing with the other, clearly only half-interested.

I unwrapped my beautiful treasure and stared at it for a moment. "For weeks, I have waited for this." I bit into the burger. My hopes dropped through the floor and into the depths of fiery, torturous hell. I grimaced. "This thing tastes like a fucking hot dog. Exactly like a hot dog. How is that even possible?"

Aaron took a bite of his. "Yep—hot dog."

I thought about calling our embassy and telling them that American dignity had been attacked here on Penang Island. Send in the fucking Apache helicopters and tanks. I wanted to walk back to the burger stand and impale the sorry excuse for a cook in the chest with an American flag.

Instead, I scarfed down the rest of the burger along with the fries without a further word of complaint and then ate there again for the next two nights.

• • •

Just after I'd finished the hotdogburger, a young guy with a short and bushy beard walked up the stairs. "Hey guys, is it back that way to the rooms?" he asked as he pointed down the hallway behind Aaron and me. He had a Spanish accent.

"Yeah man, just down there and on your right," I answered.

He paused for a moment. "Is this a good place? I was just walking down the street and saw that it was cheap so I said 'what the hell!' But I'm not so sure."

"Well to be honest, it's uhhh ... pretty bad, man. We're going to try and find a nicer place tomorrow," I said.

We talked to the guy—Marc—for a moment and learned that he was from Spain and had just arrived in Malaysia from neighboring Myanmar. I'm not one of those types of people that talk about "energy" or whatever, but this guy put off some kind of really good, laid-back vibe with me. Which was why, when he asked within only a couple of minutes after meeting him if "we would mind if he traveled with us for a while" that I consented without hesitation. Aaron agreed, and we offered to share a private room with him at the next spot. All of us liked the idea of having a cleaner room with actual beds and privacy for cheaper than we were paying for a dorm room full of people, so it was a no-brainer.

The three of us walked down to a nearby guesthouse to set up our room for the next couple nights. The short, probably four-foot-ten girl running the counter seemed friendly, as did a small man running around who appeared to be the manager. She showed us the room, along with clean-looking showers.

Marc spoke up after seeing the room. "What do you guys think about just coming here tonight even though we have already paid for the room at the other hostel?"

"You read my mind," I said. Aaron was on the same page as well. We set everything up and returned with all of our bags.

We got to know Marc well over the next few days. Out of all the people I met during my months traveling that year, he was the person I connected with the most. He was just a cool, level-headed dude. We always seemed to be on the same page about everything. The story of his journey before meeting us was crazy.

He had gone to Thailand on vacation and decided to make a visa run to Myanmar with a friend. It was there that he learned he could live in Buddhist monasteries for free, as long as he practiced meditation. He figured he would give it a try, so he stayed at one. All said and done, he ended up living in several different monasteries for a total of six months. He'd spend hours and hours every day, just meditating. The rules of the monasteries were strict: no talking, no eating other than at meal times, no cigarettes, and even no masturbating. Upwards of ten hours each day was spent in silent meditation, with a few breaks in between.

Marc led us in several group meditations to teach us what it was all about. I loved it. I felt like I had a natural high afterward, like I was floating or something. Each session was about thirty minutes or so. Marc would direct us to focus our thoughts on a particular body part for several moments: *forehead ... nose ... lips ... chin ... neck, etc.* until we had worked down our entire bodies and back up. The result would sometimes be tingling sensations in these body parts as we followed along with the exercise.

We met an Australian couple named Jenny and Tom who were also staying in the guesthouse. Marc started talking to them originally, as they had been practicing meditation at workshops in the area. They had just been married and were starting six years of uninterrupted travel. We got along famously with them and the five of us frequented the guesthouse restaurant downstairs to sit and chat. No one drank or partied. We all just sat around eating food and talking about our previous travels and our views on life. Marc taught Aaron how to make bracelets out of string, as the monks had taught him in one of the monasteries during his free time. Later I had Aaron teach it to me as well. It was a relaxing way to pass the time when I wasn't working.

One such freelance gig was perfectly timed. I got a little creative after a while and shifted from strictly graphic design work to doing just about anything that earn get a paycheck. A friend—who for the sake of her college degree will remain nameless—asked me if I could write an essay for her college class. The topic was Buddhism. I laughed and looked to my right, where Marc—a man who had just spent six months living and learning Buddhism in real, traditional monasteries—was sitting and watching a movie on his cell phone. I waved my hand to get his attention.

He removed his headphones—"What's up?"

"Can you tell me enough about Buddhism, like, the history of it and stuff, to write a paper for someone?"

"My friend, I can tell you enough about Buddhism to write a book. Where would you like to start?"

Thus, my first college essay received an "A"—even though I've never paid for, nor attended a university of any kind. I ended up doing a few more on different subjects before returning home.

We had planned to travel together to some islands southwest of Penang before Marc returned to Thailand. That never happened. We loved the guesthouse so much, and the friends we had made there, that every time we came up with a departure date, it got scrubbed.

"I'm thinking maybe we should just stay another couple nights here, what do you guys think?" Marc would suggest.

"Yup, that's cool with me." Then a few days later, the same conversation would recur.

The owner and the girl working there both became friends of

ours during our stay. We'd get free fruit, free sodas, and even got discounted laundry service.

The great cheeseburger blunder was avenged by the discovery of a different obsession: Milo. For those of you poor, poor souls who've never had a taste of Milo, let me fill you in:

Milo is made by Nestle. In fact, it's almost identical to Nesquik, except for one significant difference: the crunchies. Imagine Nesquik with little crunchy bits of chocolate in it. The Malays made it with warm milk and served it over ice—a *hot Milo* is what you would order. Tom introduced me to this powdered miracle-substance.

"You've never fucking heard of Milo, mate?!" he'd exclaimed with astonishment. He called over the short manager girl and she brought me a glass of the mystery liquid.

My eyes widened upon my first taste. It was gone in approximately three seconds.

He went on to tell me that they made Milo cereal, candy bars, ice cream, milkshakes, just about anything else I could imagine. Later that evening I made a trip to the store and tried one of just about all of them. The ice cream. The fucking Milo ice cream. Amazing.

Aaron didn't catch onto the Milo craze that Tom and I were on. He and Marc both had a food obsession of their own: Indian cuisine. Aaron could eat the hottest shit on the fucking planet and it wouldn't bother the guy one bit. You could fill a bowl with fresh lava, top it off with some of Satan's pubes, and then a dragon could come by and fart on it and he would scarf the thing down. He'd be as red as a fire hydrant and sweating his ass off, but he'd finish it. Then he'd say something like, "It really wasn't as bad as they said it was gonna be."

I never did see a single place that offered Malay food. In fact, I still have no idea what Malay food even is, or if it's even a thing.

Many times I just ate at the guesthouse restaurant. I spent every morning sitting at a table overlooking the street, sipping on a coffee or an iced Milo and eating a ham and cheese omelet he most American thing I'd had in months. Outside, in the morning hustle and bustle, Malay and Indian locals would pass on bicycles, small cars, and big, lumbering buses. To enter the shops and restaurants, people would walk on wooden planks over the canals of feces. Oh wait, did I forget to mention that? Yes, in lieu of traditional cement sidewalks, the Malay (or more likely British) builders of yesteryear felt it more convenient to put two or three foot ditches along the roads. Then they said, "Hey those ditches look okay, but what should we fill them with?"

"Rainwater!" somebody shouted.

"Every city has rainwater. Something more original."

Someone else offered, "How about a 'lazy river' of shit, piss, and dead animal carcasses?" Everyone collectively gasped, clapped, and gathered outside to begin shitting in the ditches.

In reality, I'm not sure what those canals of slime were really filled with. All I know is they were brown, stinky, and I saw more than one bloated animal carcass floating in them along with scores of wrappers and beer bottles. The astonishing thing was that they were just *right there* with nothing over them. You would think they'd put a grate on them or something. No, they were just wide open ditches where some unsuspecting person could slip and fall right into the cholera factory below. Storefronts had thin wooden boards lain over the ditch upon which you could walk.

This is, no doubt, the origin story for the ubiquitous mosquito hordes. Luckily, our new guesthouse was far enough away from the street that we didn't seem to have any mosquitos bugging us.

• • •

After ten days in Penang, we finally made plans to leave. Marc was headed north to Koh Phangan, and Aaron and I were headed to Kuala Lumpur for a few days before catching our flight to Australia. We spent our last night in the guesthouse hanging with Marc and the hostel staff. Jenny and Tom had left the previous night, but the owner of the guesthouse joined in on our party and supplied us with a few free drinks, some watermelon, and plenty of Durham cigarettes. It was a bittersweet gathering. I was sad to part ways with Marc. I had grown to feel like he'd been one of my best friends for years. I wished Corey had stuck around long enough to meet him, because they would have loved each other. We tried our best to convince Marc to come with us to Australia, but he said he'd never have enough money to make it. I laughed at that, because neither did Aaron and I. Even with free places to stay, we'd be cutting it a little too close for comfort.

As happens all too often when traveling, we said farewell to new friends having only just met them, and set forth on our next adventure. It's a strange feeling, going to a new place. On one hand, you're somewhat reluctant to give up the comfort that you've found where you're at. On the other hand, you never know what the next place will offer. Just another of long term travel's complicated peculiarities.

21

KUALA LUMPUR
KUALA LUMPUR, MALAYSIA

October 13th

It was a long, quiet bus ride from Penang to Kuala Lumpur. Upon our arrival there, we were ushered off the bus and into a central transportation depot of sorts. We spotted a hostel across the roadway, so we saddled our packs, sauntered over, and paid our two bits for a room. After showing us our digs, the attendant told us to "turn off the lights and air conditioning unit" when we left the room. I still have no idea where the air conditioning unit was, but it sure as fuck wasn't anywhere near our room. The beds were covered in cigarette burns and admittedly I added a few more to their collection before leaving. You could hear the television blaring a foreign soap opera in the front room. Our little ceiling fan squeaked and rocked back and forth. We sat down our packs and sat on our beds.

"Well," Aaron said. "At least the mosquitos can't get us in here."

I laughed.

A cockroach scurried across the floor between our feet. I lifted my feet onto the bed and lit up a cigarette.

. . .

It wasn't until the last thirty years or so that Malaysia became Malaysia as we know it today. The result of hundreds of years of influence and rule by different religions, countries, and ideals has left the country a confusing potpourri of culture. First the northern Asians of the steppe, then the Dutch East India company, then the British—who colonized the country up until the first sight of a Japanese Zero—until the country finally gained independence after the war.

Taxis are called "taksi" which I'll assume blindly, is simply how the locals heard the British word being pronounced. You'll find a modernized supermarket sitting right next to a fish shop whose workers threw guts and scrap meat into the poop-ditches out front. Somehow no one had correlated the hordes of tenacious mosquitos with stagnant water, so the poop-ditches remained as a remnant of earlier years. It was as if the inhabitants couldn't figure out whether they wanted to catch up with modernized countries or remain in simplicity. For us—being budget travelers—simplicity was what we found. Aside from the wonderful guesthouse we'd stayed in with Marc in Penang, I'd found nothing but grime, slime, and sweat in the other places we stayed.

Normally I'd have no qualm with these, considering we'd been ensconced in street-living thus far. But at this point in our journey, I was just so … fucking … tired. I wanted to go home, honestly. I had come to the conclusion that maybe long-term travel wasn't my cup of tea. At least not this kind of long-term travel. I missed home and its comforts and I was tired of being dirty all the time. I hoped Australia would bring some familiarities of my former life. People will inevitably read his and say the negative things they will, but the reader should be reminded that at this point, money was such an issue that we weren't exactly going out and enjoying these places. The vast majority of my days were spent sitting in front of a computer trying to bring in more money.

• • •

Aaron and I only had a few days in Kuala Lumpur to prepare for our flight to Australia. One of the main tasks to accomplish was buying winter clothes. At some point during our stay in Penang, it had dawned on me that maybe we should do *some kind* of research on New Zealand. It sounds ridiculous—even to me—that when we'd booked a two-week stay there while planning our trip back at home, we had no idea what we were going to do during our stay. I didn't know shit about New Zealand. I just thought, *Hey, if I go to New Zealand, I'll be able to tell people that I've been to New Zealand!* I had assumed that we'd be sweating our balls off during our stay there and in Australia just like everywhere else.

Anyway, now I figured I'd see just what there was to do while we were there. So I messaged one of my graphic design clients who happened to live in Christchurch. She sent me the names of some places to check out, so I Googled them. The first image I saw was a huge, turquoise-colored lake. "Wow," I said to Aaron. "You should see how cool this lake loo—wait, is that fucking *snow?!*"

"Snow?" Aaron asked.

"There's snow in this picture—that can't be right. New Zealand is like, pretty far south, right?"

It was lost on me at the moment—rather ironically, considering my obsession with polar exploration novels—that if you were to just keep on heading south, you'd end up in Antarctica.

"I'm gonna look up the temperature there," Aaron said. A few moments later … "Forty-five degrees there right now. It's forty-five fuckin degrees!"

"Oh—my—god."

I'd given all the cold-weather gear I had to Corey to take home when he'd left. I didn't want the extra weight. I mean everything: the pants I'd bought in Switzerland; my hooded sweatshirt; even my sleeping bag. Suddenly we found ourselves trying to find winter clothing in a country that had never even seen snow.

You can probably guess how that went. It took several explorations before finding some discount rags to bring with us.

• • •

The rest of our time in KL was spent eating, researching, and—if we're being one hundred percent honest here—laying around watching movies on our computers and smoking enough cigarettes to supply the cast of *Mad Men* for an entire season. I had contacted a Couchsurfing host in Perth, Australia who had agreed to put us up for a week. That situation had been a debacle all in its own:

Australia—or, Oz—had been ignored during our planning stage because we already had a free place to stay there. Back in high school, we'd had a foreign exchange student named Ryan who came to our tiny town all the way from the Land Down Under. He made a lot of friends there, myself and Corey included. In fact, Corey and I had made plans years prior to go and visit him at his home in Perth, but they fell through when we realized that A.) We were too poor to afford plane tickets without saving up for quite a while, and B.) We were too unmotivated to save up for quite a while. So the plans were scrapped.

In the planning of our journey around the world, we knew Oz would be on our list of must-see countries, so we contacted Ryan, who gladly agreed to put us up.

However, as usual, things went tits-up. Back in Bangkok I received a message from Ryan saying that he had "moved way out in the middle of the Outback for a new job" and could no longer host us in Perth. This was bad news for us, considering that Oz was the most expensive country on our list. He offered to put us up in his new place, but warned that there wouldn't be much to do and it would cost a couple hundred dollars to board a train there from Perth, where our plane was set to land. We couldn't afford it. We were bummed. I had really looked forward to seeing him and it seemed crazy that here I was going to actually be *in* Oz and not even get a chance to grab a beer with my friend. There wasn't much that could be done though, so our planning efforts went toward finding places to stay. Damo, the Aussie from INOUT hostel in Barcelona, offered to put us up in Melbourne and get me some shows booked if I could make it there. Again, travel-fare was too costly to justify. Our departure flight was from Perth, so we would have had to find a way back across the continent before leaving. I sent messages to Bella and Naomi, two Aussie girls we had met at Hostel Happy Days in Rome, but neither was of much use for us either. So, we were left with Couchsurfing.

Luckily, we had pretty good luck in finding our first host, Anna. She not only accepted our request and offered to put us up for a week, but also offered to pick us up from the airport when we arrived. She told us there would be two other Couchsurfers staying there as well—a British couple—but since we had sent her a request first, we'd get a spare room all to ourselves.

We didn't know what we'd do beyond that first week, but this was a great start. We had about a month in Oz before flying on to New Zealand. We figured we could just hop around between Couchsurfing hosts in Perth or find a place where we could camp for free, similar to what we'd done in Rome at the nature preserve.

With our housing taken care of, we enjoyed our last couple of days in Asia by gorging ourselves on delicious food. We knew we'd soon be back to a diet of rice, tuna, and peanut butter.

Getting to the places without being killed was the tricky part. One thing I've neglected to mention about Southeast Asia—which played an immense part in our daily lives (or continuance thereof)—was the dodging of traffic every day in order to go anywhere. It was insane. There were no crosswalks, at least as far as I could tell. Huge buses catapulted down the streets in a destructive manner, ignorant of any pedestrians who may be so unfortunate to find themselves on the road at the wrong time. Taksis and other cars and small trucks filled spaces between the big buses and an infinite number of scooters, tuk-tuks, and motorcycles did a slalom through the whole busy parade. Crossing a street was done like so:

1. Approach street. Look both ways.
2. Wait for a small gap in between the vehicles speeding past in the lane directly in front of you.

3. Pray to whatever deity you call God.
4. Sprint forward through the gap and stop in the middle of the street between the lanes to avoid being hit by traffic in the next lane. Traffic is rushing past you from one or two feet away on both sides now.
5. Repeat steps 2-4.
6. Once you've reached the middle lane, pause and catch your breath/make sure your asshole hasn't imploded from excessive puckering.
7. Repeat steps 2-4. You're close to being across now. A bus whizzes past, a foot away from your face.
8. Pee your pants just a little.
9. RUN! Last lane.
10. Try not to remind yourself that you'll have to repeat this process two to ten times to get where-ever you're going.

Somehow we made it through our two-month stay in Asia without becoming hood ornaments, although there were countless close calls.

With the purchase of whatever cold weather garments we could find (not a sufficient amount), a place to stay in Perth secured, and just enough money to make it home without starving to death; our adventure in Thailand and Malaysia came to a close.

I had one last rinse in the slime-pit of a shower in our hostel and looked through a window in the stall at the rooftop between buildings directly outside, which was covered in decaying food waste, dead rats, and other trash. The flap that was supposed to cover the window opening was torn and visibly moldy, hanging on by a couple threads and a prayer. The water was, of course, ice cold, and I felt decidedly more dirty afterward. I went back to my bed, smoked a cigarette, and then rolled back and forth for several hours until my alarm went off at five, approximately twenty minutes after I'd eventually fallen asleep. I cursed everything that had caused me to be awake at that hour and lit up another cigarette as I threw my things into my pack to leave.

We took a taksi to the airport, which helpfully dropped us off at the wrong terminal. We were then stopped by police as we attempted to run across the busy airport streets to find another ride. From there we were directed four floors down to a parking garage where *taksis* awaited riders. This one took us to the correct airport where we shuffled through a maze of shuttles before finding our terminal. I smoked approximately one entire pack of cigarettes during this two-hour ordeal. We were shown the path to our plane at the very last minute and ran through the rain across the tarmac. We boarded just as the stairs were about to be pulled away.

I remember distinctly thinking as the plane taxied onto the runway the same thing I had thought two months earlier around the time we were leaving Europe: *Finally, some food other than—oh wait, we'll still be eating rice every day.*

22

DOWN UNDER
PERTH, AUSTRALIA

October 17th

Anna was a short-haired woman with an athletic build. When she met us in front of the Perth International Airport, she was wearing Oakley sunglasses. After a round of introductions, we threw our bags into her white sedan and hopped in. She explained on the way to her house that we'd have a room all to ourselves and could pretty much do what we pleased during our stay there. She worked during the day, but we'd be given a key to the house to come and go as we desired. Her house was in the suburbs, but we could take a bus nearby into downtown Perth. Her only rule was that we not smoke inside. Coincidentally, guess what Aaron and I planned to do when we arrived in Oz? You guessed it—quit smoking. In fact, we'd been so confident, even despite our pathetic failures in the past (see: smoking cigarette butts found on the ground or my fever-dream-like shenanigans on Koh Phangan) that we'd listed on our Couchsurfing request that we were non-smokers. Obviously neither of us actually *wanted* to quit, but we'd heard rumors of cigarettes costing $20 USD a pack in The Land Down Under. So we really didn't have a choice. We entered Australia with little more than a handful of smokes and the drive to quit once and for all. No, seriously, we were seriously serious this time. We were really quitting. I know you're already expecting us to fail, but, I even wrote it in big letters in my journal this time, so I would know how serious I was. That drive to quit didn't stop us from carefully rationing the last of our Marlboros, though. They became the equivalent of fresh water to shipwreck survivors; just a drag here and there to tide us over from killing and eating each other.

On that note, as could probably be expected, complications arose from our nicotine deprivation. We started to get on each other's nerves again. Well, to Aaron's credit, I think he handled it pretty well. I was less successful. Every single thing that Aaron did ate away at me: The fact that he went to sleep at like nine and woke up at eight in the morning for no reason whatsoever. The fact that, because of this, he was always coming into the room early as shit in the evening and saying, "You care if I turn this light off, man?" and then a half hour later, quietly whispering in the darkness, "How much longer you think you're gonna be up?"

"I don't know man—whenever I get tired, I guess? I didn't plan out what time I'd fall asleep tonight; it's not like we have anything to do tomorrow. Is the light from my computer keeping you up or something?"

"No," he would always say, "I was just wondering," and then roll back over. Those little exchanges nipped at me like parasites burrowed under skin. I snapped at him here and there, but for the most part willed myself to indifference.

The second day in Perth, the other two Couchsurfers Anna had mentioned arrived. She gave them a spot in the living room. The nice thing to do would have been to offer them our room, but that wasn't happening. We were alternating nights of sleeping on the bed or the floor, and neither Aaron nor I were ready to give that up.

Ashley and Sarah were a British couple who were planning to move semi-permanently to Oz. Their relationship was fueled by a mutual thirst for adventure and the comical bantering of an elderly couple. Ash said the most ridiculous shit to that woman, and she just rolled her eyes and smiled. She'd drop something, or forget something, and he'd say, in his British accent, "You're so fucking stupid, I don't even know why I let you keep being my girlfriend." She'd respond, "Ash, I love you, you'd give the shirt off your back to anyone. But I'm not entirely sure you could even spell 'shirt.'" They were staying with Anna for a few days while they shopped around for an Outback-capable vehicle. They planned to drive it through the desert to a farm where they'd been hired to work for the coming season.

Anna took the four of us on a grand tour of Perth while we were there. We checked out the beach, a park where we searched in vain for kangaroos, and she even cooked us dinner and bought beers on quite a few occasions.

The kangaroo thing was a big deal. All four of the foreigners were obsessed with seeing one. Anna had hoped we'd spot one in the nearby park, but alas, we were left "roo-less" during our visit. We did however, go to a children's festival in the park with Anna's niece, whereupon stopping for hot dogs, Ash told Sarah she was "probably the fattest person ever in the history of human beings." Fat jokes seemed to be among his favorite, despite Sarah weighing maybe a hundred pounds soaking wet.

• • •

One day when Aaron and I were in downtown Perth searching for additional winter clothing, I spotted a stage being set up and several food vendors lined up along a community center of sorts. I walked up and asked one of the food vendors what was going on.

"It's a festival we have every month where local bands play. You should stick around and check it out!"

"What do you think?" I asked Aaron. "We could check out some local music."

"Ehh. I'd rather just head back to the house," he replied.

"Really? And do what, sit on Facebook?"

"I'm just not really into that kind of thing like you are. I kind of just wanna head back and relax."

I figured he probably wanted to go back to chat with Looktaal. "Well, I'm staying. You can do whatever you want, dude."

He was surprised. "Oh. That's cool I guess. So you want me to just ride the bus back alone then?"

"Yeah. If that's okay?"

"Well do you think you can walk with me to the bus station?"

"Huh?"

"I'm just not sure I can find it. Could you walk me there?"

"Dude. I'll give you the map and draw a line to the bus station. It's like five blocks, I really don't want to walk all the way there and then all the way back."

He stared at me with desperation.

"For fuck's sake—fine." I later commented that it seemed like I was his dad and he was my mom at the same time. What I mean by that is, he was always nagging like a mother would (*"I think you should go to bed soon if we're going to be waking up early tomorrow, etc."*), but at the same time I'd had to hold his hand through practically everything he did for the entire duration of the trip. I mean, he couldn't even walk to the bus station by himself? It was driving me crazy.

I barely said a word the whole way. I could tell he was expecting me to walk all the way there and then decide not to walk the distance back to the festival, thus cajoling me into heading back to Anna's with him. When we arrived across the street from the bus station, I blatantly patronized him by asking in a sarcastic and motherly tone, "Okay Aaron, that's the bus station across the street there. Do you need me to cross the walk with you or do you think you can do that by yourself?"

He didn't catch, or at least didn't acknowledge my patronizing attitude—"No, that's okay."

"Do you need me to help you get to your bus? It's bus number twenty-six. You'll have to look on the platform listings to see where it will be at."

"No, I should uh … I should be able to handle it."

"All right, well I'm going back to the park to hear some music."

"You're not spending money on food or anything down there, right?" he asked in a thinly-veiled condescending tone.

"No man, I'm just going to go watch some bands play."

"Okay, just making sure."

I gave him the map with the bus schedules on it to lie to rest all worries of him accidentally boarding a bus to Darwin or something. Then I watched as he made his way across the crosswalk, stopped at the sidewalk on the other side to look in all directions for a moment, and then made his way to the bus station.

"Jesus Christ," I muttered to myself before turning around, walking to the first fast-food joint I saw, and stuffing my face with greasy fries just to spite him. Then I enjoyed the music and afterwards opted for the longer bus route home to see part of the city and have some time alone while I listened to music.

. . .

"Do you want to go on a road trip with us?" Ash asked while we were eating dinner a couple nights later. "We're going to buy that jeep tomorrow and we're thinking about driving around for a while. You two are more than welcome to join if you're keen."

"For how long?"

"Just a couple weeks. Didn't you say you have a friend that moved to the Outback?"

"Yeah, Ryan. He's in Kalgoorlie."

"Well we could drop you off with him and then head to the farm we're working on, and you guys could just catch the train back to Perth for your flight from there."

Aaron and I were both elated. I contacted Ryan, who was just as excited to hear the news. I told him it would be a week or two until we made it there, which he said was fine.

The next day we went with Ash and Sarah to pick up their new vehicle, a Mitsubishi Pajero. We stopped off at an outdoors store we spotted on the way, where I searched for a sleeping bag and Aaron searched for a liner.

The cheapest one I could find was $60 USD, but there was little choice. We would be camping the entire time during the road trip with Ash and Sarah, so I would freeze if I didn't have one. This, of course, prompted more bickering between Aaron and me:

"You're going to spend *sixty dollars* on a sleeping bag?"

"I don't really have a choice," I said.

"We could ask Ash and Sarah to take us to a Goodwill or something and try to find one."

"I mean maybe, but I doubt we'd even find something and then we'd just have to turn around and ask them to drive back here."

"You know what, just do whatever the hell you want. If you want to spend all our money on dumb shit, just go for it!"

I grabbed the sleeping bag and walked up to the counter where I paid for it, walked back outside, and smoked one of the last remaining cigarettes. Ash and Sarah had witnessed our exchange and quietly slipped off to another part of the store where they focused on buying supplies for our road trip. I scribbled in my journal the usual rants and ravings about my travel partner and tried to calm myself down before walking back into the store to help Sarah and Ash with their stuff. My mood was lightened a bit watching Ash hilariously petition Sarah for permission to buy a $190 spear gun. The thing was massive; it looked like the type of weapon you'd use to land a prize-winning tuna. He claimed it would pay for itself when he killed all of our food with it. Their thick British accents for some reason seemed to make everything even funnier than it already was:

"Ashley, you're not spending two hundred quid on a fucking spear gun."

"But it would be fucking epic, imagine all the animals I could kill with this thing: dolphins, kangaroos, snakes ..."

"You aren't going to kill any animals you dolt, you wouldn't even know how to operate that contraption."

"How about I buy it anyway, and just shoot you. And then we'll see how much your opinion fucking matters, Sarah."

"If I wasn't around to keep you from doing stupid shit like this on a daily basis, you'd wind up dead within a week."

Ashley lost the battle, but vowed to return and buy the spear gun at some point. He brought it up every day for a week afterward—*"If you would have let me buy my spear gun ..."*

Aaron and I didn't speak to each other during the whole ride home. We had gotten along so well in Asia, and now here we were only a week into Oz and already back to square one. I was nearing my breaking point and I didn't know what was going to happen when I finally reached it.

Just one more month, I thought to myself. Only five weeks remained until our return flight to the United States. Once arriving in Los Angeles, I'd be staying with an aunt for about a month, and Aaron would be flying to his grandparents' house in Phoenix. The journey to Ohio from California hadn't been figured out in the least bit and it was something that would be difficult to organize. By the time we hit US soil we knew we'd be broke. We thought about hitchhiking back or possibly trying to scrounge enough money to get a bus ticket. All I knew was that once we made it to California, I was going to be away from Aaron. I don't care if you like someone or not, if you spend every single waking moment together for months on end, you are going to want some time apart. Now imagine that you don't get along with that person. That's taking it lightly ... imagine you have grown almost to *hate* that person. Now imagine that *everything you do* is decided by them in some fashion because you share all your money, of which there is very little. You can't even go and buy a goddamned apple without asking their permission.

Don't misunderstand me; I know it wasn't all Aaron. I know I'm hard to get along with sometimes. I did all kinds of shit that annoyed him to no end. To his credit, he did a better job handling it than me while we were in Australia. As I browsed the outdoors store with Ash and Sarah, I noticed a display of lightweight foldable shovels and found myself wondering, *I wonder how long it would take to dig a grave in the Outback with one of those things?* There was a moment where I glanced back at Aaron and our eyes met. I think he knew what I was thinking. He was probably wondering the same thing.

23

ROAD TRIP
PERTH TO ALBANY, AUSTRALIA

October 21st

Upon leaving Perth to take a "walkabout"—or more appropriately, "driveabout"—through Western Australia, we had two goals. One, we wanted to see a kangaroo. Two, we needed to save enough money to make it back from Ryan's to Perth so we could catch our flight to New Zealand.

It didn't take long to achieve the first goal. Shortly after leaving Perth, Ash shouted to Sarah as we were driving down the highway, "Babe, get your camera! I see a kangaroo!"

Sarah excitedly rummaged through the middle console and pulled out her camera. "Where is it?! I don't see it!"

"Right there!" he pointed with a huge smile to a dead and decomposing pile of fur next to the road that we were passing. Our first kangaroo was road kill.

She shot him an angry stare and set the camera back down with an annoyed sigh. He just kept smiling. "Should I turn around so you can get a photo?"

"You're such a dick, Ashley."

We spent most of the first day after leaving Anna's rigging the Pajero with a platform in the back so Sarah and Ashley could sleep in it, so our first campsite was only about an hour south of Perth. It was in a huge national park. Upon entering the inner trails of the park, we noticed signs that said *"DANGER: POISON"* and *"Please keep all pets leashed to avoid accidental death."*

"Well that can't be good," I noted.

"I thought this was a fucking park or something," Ashley said. "How can they just dump a bunch of poison in a public park?"

No one had an answer for that. We circled around the area for a while, looking for a spot that wasn't going to silently kill us in our sleep. At one point, we came across a guy riding a dirt bike on one of the trails.

"Hey man," Ashley asked as he pulled up next to him, "do you know if we're allowed to camp here?"

"Ahhh no worries," the guy had the thickest backwoods Australian accent I've ever heard—"ya just find yee a spot wheh-evah ya want … an if a rangah comes and gives ya a propah botha, just tell eem bugger off and wait for a tick uh two then come back."

"Oh, okay, cool—but uhh, what about all these signs about poison?"

"Ahh fackkk, that's ten-eighty poison, yeah. They're tryin'a bait an kill all the foxes runnin crazy through hee. Just wash ya hands before ya eat and you'll be right off, eh."

That was enough for us, so we drove around for a few more minutes before finding a spot and calling it "home" for the night. Aaron and I pitched our hammocks while Ashley and Sarah tried out their new truck digs. I stayed surprisingly warm, given how cold it had been getting at night. The new sleeping bag was deemed a worthy purchase.

The next day we continued driving down the coast. We ended up at Cape Leeuwin, the furthest southwestern point in Australia. From there, you see the Indian Ocean and Southern (Antarctic) Ocean collide. Conflicting currents of the two oceans caused a tent-like line of waves extending away from the peninsula. Behind our watch point stood a picturesque white lighthouse.

We spent almost an hour staring at the oceans and taking pictures. Aaron mostly kept his distance from me and I from him. Every word he spoke caused an irritated tic within me that I labored to keep contained. On a very much related note, we had finally made it a few days without so much as a puff on a cigarette after we'd finished the last of our rationed tobacco.

After leaving the lighthouse, we aimed the GPS (or "sat-nav," as it was referred to by Ash and Sarah) toward a national park nearby. Having traveled over three hundred kilometers from Perth to the Cape, we were now headed east toward a town called Esperance. Nearby was Cape le Grand National Park, hosting a beach where Kangaroos allegedly hung out.

The drive to Esperance was to be spread out over a few days, with several stops along the way. The first stop was in another park. In an attempt to save money, we opted to try something new: Most parks required campers to fill out a card, post it on a stake outside of their spot, and pay in the morning when the ranger came around, or drop it in a box. As much as I'd love to be an honest contributor to the Australian National Park system, I was not a man of means. Thus, nefarious practices were adopted. We simply took the card, set it out on the post, and hoped we could leave before a ranger came around. This time we all slept in a family-sized tent that had come free with the jeep when Ash and Sarah bought it. In the morning, we hastily packed everything up and looked around. With no ranger in sight, we hopped in the vehicle and took off.

. . .

That afternoon Ashley and Sarah went to check out some skywalk thing through the tree canopy in another national park. Aaron and I couldn't afford it, obviously, so we opted to wait in the jeep for them. We figured we would use the time to calculate our current finances.

Despite the scrimping and saving, money was already an issue again. I had not accounted for the gas and food needed for a road trip when I was budgeting the rest of the trip back in Malaysia.

I had budgeted a minimum of $650 to make it through New Zealand. This included plane tickets from Auckland to Christchurch on the South Island. My graphic design client, Abbi, had basically said the North Island was a waste of time. I had calculated expenses down to the last apple and jar of peanut butter. $650 did not include hostel or hotel stays other than one night upon our arrival in Auckland to recuperate after the flight from Oz.

The main problem with that figure was that by this point in our cruise across Oz, we only had about $600 left, total. So not only were we $50 short of our New Zealand budget, but we still had another two weeks or so in Oz to cover gas and food, not to mention $120 for train tickets from Kalgoorlie to Perth after our intended visit with Ryan.

I calculated that we needed at least another $500 on top of our current $600 to make it through the trip without starving to death or being stranded somewhere. I desperately hoped some graphic design work would be waiting for me when would regain Internet access at Ryan's.

On top of these woes, there was still the lingering question of our return to the US: How were we getting home to Ohio from Los Angeles?

We were both floored upon coming to these realizations. I sat down the notebook and rested my head in my hand. And that's when Aaron said it. That statement he'd uttered so many fucking times, that served no purpose other than his own self-aggrandizement: "I just wish we all could have brought the same amount of money."

"Aaron, I told you before; I don't ever want to hear that again, man. You're like a broken record. What does it matter now?"

"I'm just saying. You wouldn't feel the same if you had put in more money than me; if it was the other way around."

If the reader will remember, chapters and chapters ago, all the way back to a mountainside in Switzerland after Wilson the drug dealer had dropped the three of us off. This was the first time (of so many) that Aaron had spoken those words. It was the time he claimed that it was "his" money, and essentially made me and Corey feel like a couple of assholes who were bumming off him or something. I had told him, "Aaron, I promise you, throughout the course of this trip I will make more money than you brought."

He had laughed in my face and continued to go on about how he had "broke his back" to get that money, etcetera, etcetera. I had drastically altered my lifestyle to create our website, sold almost all of my worldly possessions, and would be returning to a world of bills with no money left whatsoever. It had made me so angry that he'd been so arrogant about it, that I actually started keeping track of the money I made from that point forward. *Meticulously ... tediously ...* every single fucking cent.

I didn't say shit about it, though. I personally wouldn't have cared if I brought more money in than he had. But he had been so obnoxious about it that I was set to prove him wrong. For those months when I busked, worked on the website, or found freelance gigs, I penciled each penny earned into my journal.

Around the time we made it to Kuala Lumpur in Malayasia, I calculated that I had officially brought more money to the table than Aaron had. Now, to be completely honest with the reader, crossing that threshold filled me with a malevolent, evil jubliance. But I didn't say a single word to Aaron. So why, you are asking yourself, did I take the time to carefully record all of this information? For one, I honestly wanted to know how much money I would end up making from the different things I was doing for future trip planning. But yes, I also did it because I knew, at some point, Aaron would bring it up and throw it in my face again. It was his favorite arguing point and he had used it to put me down over and over again. He didn't bring it up when we were getting along, but I knew he'd spin his greatest hits again at some point. And now, here it was…

"You wouldn't feel the same if you had put in more money than me; if it was the other way around."

"Actually, Aaron … I have put in more money than you. I told you that I would, and I did. A little under a month ago I surpassed what you brought overall. And no, it actually doesn't bother me that I've put in more money than you."

He scoffed. "Yeah, whatever. You haven't made more money than I brought. There's no way."

"Well …" I cleared my throat as I opened my journal and flipped to the pages upon which I'd been writing everything down. "You'll see here … that's all the money Corey and I made busking in Europe … there's all the money that's come in from the website …" His gaze turned to serious concern as he saw all of my detailed financial notes. I continued, "There's all the graphic design money I've brought in … and there's the money I brought with me when we left. If you'll see here, this number—" I pointed to the total sum of all my earnings—"*This* number is higher than *that* number. *That* number is the amount that you brought with you. Now, you haven't—as far as I know—made any money since we left have you? While I was working, and you were sitting around watching Steven Seagal movies on your laptop?"

His face darkened to a deep crimson. He drew in a sharp breath as if he was going to say something and then cut himself off. There were a few beats of suspenseful silence before he finally spoke.

"You seriously took all the time to write that down?"

"After you rubbed it in my face in Europe over and over again? You bet your ass I did. But really, I don't mind that I've put in more money than you, dude. I won't ever rub it in your face—well, other than right now, because—I'll be honest—I'm really enjoying this."

"That's bullshit dude. It's not like you actually *made* the money from donations … that's all of our money."

"Ask yourself, how many of these donations have come from one of *your* friends or family members? None. Also ask yourself, exactly how many hours or even minutes you've spent building or maintaining the website that brought in the donations in the first place? Zero."

"It's not like you really *did* anything, though. I worked my ass off for my money."

That was it … after all he had said to me throughout this journey that had busted my spirit, hurt my pride, or angered me ... that was the straw that broke the camel's back. That he trivialized all the work I had done while he was sitting around. That he hadn't really done any different work than he'd always done since he'd been working with his father, but acted like he'd somehow worked like a slave during the three months before we left. I had worked much too hard while he sat around during the trip to listen to that kind of shit.

"I want to punch you in the goddamn face right now. You should just shut your fucking mouth."

He scoffed. "Oh, is that right?"

"Yeah, that's right." About this time Ashley and Sarah returned to view and walked toward the jeep, unaware of the argument that was taking place. I looked back at Aaron. "You should shut up now before I clock you upside your ignorant, arrogant head."

"Maybe you should just do it then, huh?"

"Maybe I fucking will."

"Yeah, okay."

I wanted to. My fists were clenched and my face was probably just as red as his. I wanted nothing more than to bury my knuckles right square on his nose with every ounce of force I could muster. Two things stopped me from doing so. One, Aaron would kick my ass. He would annihilate me. I'm not a large person, nor am I a fighter. I would have punched him and then he would have made me his bitch. Two, I had already decided, in a fraction of a second after his infuriating statement, that I was finally done with him. That was it—no more. Thus, neither getting my ass kicked nor continuing to argue with him would be worth it.

Ashley and Sarah sat down and continued their own conversation as if World War Three was not about to start in the seats behind them. It was clear they sense the tension, however. Aaron and I stared in opposite directions, silently stewing.

That night, we stayed at what would ironically end up being my favorite campsite of the whole road trip. It was in a cove near Albany, WA, where the Southern Ocean crashed upon rocky shores and a cold wind swept the coast. It made me think of arctic landscapes, and I thought of the explorers I loved reading so much about: Peary, Mawson, Scott, Amundsen. Fearless wanderers of the extremities of the world.

After we set up our tent amidst a shantytown of shacks and other campers, I sat on an outcropping of rock overlooking the sea. The ocean was violent there, waves crashing on the rocks with the sound of thunder, spray emitting from the collision. The foamy water would wash up across the rocks and snake its way back, to be recycled into the chaos once more. I looked at nature's might and pondered my own situation. Aaron and I's relationship seemed similar in a way: clashing against each other with dramatic grandeur, bickering back and forth as we made our way through the obstacles along our path. There would be a pause or moment of serenity where the bickering stopped, and the water hung in the balance for a moment. Then, it would slip backward slowly, where it was doomed to repeat the process all over again.

This is it, I thought, staying true to my decision earlier in the day. *Why keep this going. It will never change.*

I walked back to the tent and asked Aaron to step outside with me for a moment. It was the first time we'd even acknowledged each other since the explosive argument hours earlier. We both had a seat in the back of the jeep where we could have some conversational privacy from Ash and Sarah, who had been avoiding even acknowledging our battle.

"Man. I've been thinking a lot about this all day," I said. "We're just two totally different people. I don't hate you or anything, I want you to know that. We're just … different. We have personalities that clash and I don't think we'll ever truly find a way to get along. I don't really know how else to lead up to this, so I'm just going to say it: I've decided that after we leave Ryan's in Kalgoorlie, I'm going on alone."

24

KANGAROO BEACH
ALBANY TO KALGOORLIE, AUSTRALIA

October 24th

"But … what would I do?"

Aaron's face faded from anger to concern.

"We'll have a week with Ryan in Kalgoorlie. That should give you plenty of time to figure out what you want to do. You have a little more money than I do right now, but I'll split what I've earned from the website fifty-fifty with you and then we'll go our separate ways."

"Wow, you've put a lot of thought into this. You must really want to get rid of me."

"I'm not going to turn this into another argument. We're just different people. You do a lot of things that drive me crazy, and I'm sure I do the same to you. We just can't get along. I'd rather enjoy the last part of this trip than spend it arguing with you over and over."

"I just … I wouldn't know what to do …"

"Well, you'll have time to figure that out. In Kalgoorlie you can research everything. I'll give you all of my notes for New Zealand too."

"There's nothing I can do to make this better? To keep you from doing this?"

It felt like I was going through a breakup or something.

"Aaron, we're just different people," I repeated. "I'll never ask you to change, because you are who you are and I'm sure there are millions of people in this world who would get along great with you. Unfortunately, I'm not one of those people."

"Like, what do I do that makes you so angry?"

"I'm not going to go into specifics, Aaron. It's not important. There are just quirks you have that I can't stand, man. That's it."

"Like—like what though, specifically? Maybe it's something I could work on, to try to help us get along better. I don't think it's a good idea for us to split up. I mean we don't have much longer to go …"

"There are just things that irk me. Little things that aren't worth mentioning. We're just different. That's all it is. No need to hurt anyone's feelings more than we already have. Let's just call it what it is and move forward. I think it's what's best for both of us to be happy."

"I really don't know what I'll do though."

"I'm sorry man. You'll have plenty of time to figure that stuff out."

"I don't see how we can't work all of this out. I mean, what is it that I do that makes you so mad?"

"Aaron, seriously, I'm not going to do this. It's only going to hurt feelings and it will accomplish nothing."

"Specifically, though, like I just want to know what I'm doing to piss you off."

"Oh my god, dude …"

"I think you can at least tell me."

"You really want to know?"

"Yeah I do."

"Okay, fine," I exploded. "You go to sleep at fucking eight pm and wake up at dawn for no reason like an eighty-year old man. You're constantly nagging me over every single little thing I do and tell me off every time I want to spend even the tiniest bit of money. And that's while *I know for a fact* you have at least two grand in a box at home that you left to keep for when you get back, even though you have no fucking bills because you live with mommy and daddy at twenty-six fucking years old—"

"I don't have two grand at home!"

He was lying. Before we'd left he'd told me and Corey how he had sold a couple of his possessions last-minute, gaining an extra three grand. He put $1,000 into the trip fund and said we wouldn't need the rest of it anyway, so he was leaving it at home. Later in the trip when we realized how dire our situation was, he denied the entire conversation had ever happened.

"Yes, you do. So you sit and do nothing while you watch me freelancing or busking. You bitch and moan about money all the time, but wouldn't get off your ass and find a job in Italy to make any more. Do you want me to go on?"

"No. I think that's enough." He was silent for a moment. "Well … do you want me to tell you all the stuff that you do that drives me crazy?"

"No."

"Oh—well—I don't really know what to say then."

I sat there catching my breath. Two emotions hit me concurrently. The first was guilt. I had just said some really hurtful, mean things to him. I realized that, and regretted it almost immediately. I could tell I had really hurt his feelings. Which is why the second emotion is the one that surprised me: relief. Getting all of that off my chest was cathartic. I had bottled most of it up for months, letting it fester and build up inside me. We were both silent for a long time while we thought about what to say or do next. Finally Aaron broke the silence.

"Do you think maybe a lot of this has to do with the fact that we haven't had any cigarettes in like four days?"

I mulled on the thought for a moment. I let out a bemused puff of air.

"Man … Yes. I think probably ninety percent of it is that. Oh my god."

"I feel like if we smoked a cigarette right now we would probably be perfectly fine."

We both laughed—the first shared moment of humor we'd had in as long as I could remember.

"I think you're right."

"Should we just say fuck it and buy a bag of tobacco tomorrow? I don't think it's worth us killing each other over."

"Fuck it. We only have a month or so left, we might as well try to enjoy it."

"Does that mean you're not leaving me then?"

I wasn't. Just like that, in the matter of about two minutes—between my explosion of anger and then the subsequent realization that nicotine withdrawal was probably causing a lot of our current bickering, I changed my mind.

That night I slept like a baby. A gigantic weight had lifted off of my shoulders. I apologized to Aaron for everything I had said. The next day we bought one pack of cigarettes (for $22 USD), broke one of them apart and rolled it into two smaller cigarettes and then smoked them. I felt like a completely different person. Damn you tobacco and your evil bullshit mind games. Nicotine addiction is one crooked nasty bitch.

That was the last time we attempted to quit smoking during our travels together. I couldn't even begin to count how many times we'd tried. There were the very first attempts before we even left home, when I bought probably six different packs of nicotine patches, only to start smoking again as soon as the steps were finished. Then there was our first flight, to Spain—we had resolved to smoke the three or four cigarettes we had left and call it quits once we arrived in Europe, but Blake had bought us each a new pack right before he and Ali dropped us off at the airport. Then there were separate attempts in Germany, Switzerland, Italy (multiple times there), two or three attempts in Thailand, another one in Malaysia … I really don't know how many total. I think back to picking up cigarette butts from the ground at bus stations in Italy. When I'm diagnosed with lung cancer, which is inevitable given all of the strange things I did to my respiratory system during that period of my life, I'll reminisce and think, *Yup, that's where I got it. No doubts there.*

. . .

Our wagon train rolled through Oz with renewed spirit. We finally saw our first group of kangaroos—a bunch of them actually—and before we knew it they became like deer back home in Ohio. We avoided hitting them on the road constantly.

We made it to Esperance, where we photographed kangaroos lounging on the beach. There were even some with joeys in their pouch. I sipped my morning coffee with my cigarette and watched the 'roos hop around the beach as the calm ocean lapped waves behind them. I had expected to spend a full day there at least, since this had actually been the principle destination of our road trip. Instead, the tent was packed up, and we were quickly on our way after being hassled by a park ranger and forced to hand over the money for our camping spot.

We made it to Kalgoorlie that evening and spent one last night camping together. We cooked dinner, swapped stories, and joked about our cultural differences. There'd been a noticeable language barrier during our time together, which was surprising considering we all spoke English as a first language. There were different terms for certain items that led to confusion. One time, Sarah was searching through the food bin, asking if we had any pudding.

I was confused. "Pudding? Yeah I'm pretty sure I haven't seen any pudding in there. When the hell did we buy pudding?"

"I thought we had some cakes," she replied.

"Yeah cakes; we never got any pudding."

"Ohhh. In the UK, pudding is just what you would call dessert."

Chips are *crisps.* Trucks are *lorries.* Getting drunk is getting "pissed." Everything is *proper. "I'm about to give you a proper beating." "I was proper pissed (drunk)."*

As we waited for Ryan to pick us up the next morning, Ash and Sarah treated us to a "proper" English breakfast of beans on toast with cheese. We all stood around the jeep we'd lived in for the past week or two and snapped a picture together. Once again, as had been consistent throughout our journey, groups of people came and went. New friends, hosts, rides, whatever they may have been each time. That was the constant: They were only there for a short period and then it was back to just Aaron and me. Even Corey, in the grand scale of things, had only been with us for two months before he'd had enough of vagabond life. For better or worse, Aaron and I were stuck together until our feet hit American soil. The good news was that we had been getting along famously after reintroducing nicotine into our bloodstream. I wondered if it would continue to last, but at the same time made up my mind that either way I would stick it out. We were in the home stretch. So far, we hadn't been stuck living under bridges or in nature preserves. I knew New Zealand was going to hold untold misadventures, there was no denying that, given our thin wallets. I just hoped we'd be able to make it the rest of the way through Oz under roofs instead of bridges.

25
OUTBACK
KALGOORLIE, AUSTRALIA

October 28th

Ryan was the first familiar face I'd seen since leaving home. Although we were never close friends when he was living in the US, we seemed to share the same ideals on life in general—from religion, to science, to environmental concerns and politics.

He met us at the campground shortly after Sarah and Ashley puttered away in the Pajero. After a round of hugs and introductions we tossed our gear into his car and climbed inside.

"So..." Ryan said, "What the hell happened to Corey?"

When I explained, he was flabbergasted. "Oh my god, what the hell is he doing?!"

"I really can't answer that question, because I have no fucking clue."

"Well …. anyway … So you guys are staying for about a week then?" he asked, steering the car onto the main road.

"Yeah, that's the game plan. We'll take a train back to Perth the day before our flight."

"Cool. I've got some fun stuff planned. I figure we can drive in and do some camping in the outback one night. You guys gotta see the stars out here, for sure. And if you want, we can go check out some bars and stuff."

"Camping sounds awesome! We don't really have the cash flow to go to any bars, though."

"Ahh man, no worries there. I got you guys. Just let me show you a good time."

We arrived at his house after a short drive and he gave us a run-down of the place.

"There's a small store just up the street there if you need to buy ciggies or food or anything. I have a dog that I'm watching for a year or two for a friend who's out traveling. His name's Mango. If you guys could take him on a walk to the park a couple streets over about once a day, that would be great. He's an Australian Shepherd; they have a lot of energy."

"Definitely man, that's no problem at all."

"Other than that, just chill guys. Make yourselves at home and do whatever."

•   •   •

A few days into our stay, we loaded Ryan's car with camping equipment and a cooler full of kangaroo steaks and plenty of beer. For hours the little car crackled over dusty gravel roads until the last scattered remnants of civilization disappeared and we were surrounded with Martian red desert and clear blue skies. When we arrived at the campsite, there was absolute silence and tranquility.

We set up lawn chairs on a small rise overlooking a dry lakebed to watch the sunset. It was one of the most captivating scenes I saw during our entire journey around the world. Everything glowed different shades of red, orange, or brown. The massive Australian sun loomed like a neighboring planet, peeking over the trees onto the lakebed as we bade it goodbye from our lawn chairs.

We clicked on our headlamps and started a fire to cook our 'roo steaks. They were a little tough, but the flavor was excellent. Afterward, we drove a few hundred yards away from the campsite and lay down on the sand to watch the stars.

It felt as if we were in a giant snow-globe. With nothing but flatness all around us and no light pollution for an easy hundred miles in any direction, you could see stars in a giant half sphere all around you. It was the first time in my life I can recall looking straight forward and seeing a sky full of stars—as if I was standing on a huge sand-covered Frisbee in the middle of space and looking out over its edge. The Milky Way struck an ethereal hazy line through the panorama.

As always happens when a group of people stare at a night sky filled with stars, philosophical thoughts and discussion emerge. I'm sure as ancient humans lay on the ground looking upward, their conversations weren't too different from our own today. Just as us, they likely marveled at the mysterious and infinite darkness, gazed at the stars and pondered life's infinite questions: *Where did we come from? Why are we here? Is there anyone else out there?*

We spent several hours discussing all various matters of life, death, and the worlds beyond before meandering back to the campsite. I slept soundly in the cool desert, soothed by the strangely liberating ponderance of life's existential insignificance.

• • •

I wasn't able to get much graphic design work done while I was in Kalgoorlie. It wasn't for a lack of time; there was plenty of that. I just didn't have any work coming in. I spent some time pitching jobs and planning the next stages of the trip instead. I contacted two Aussie girls, Bella and Naomi, whom we'd met at Hostel Happy Days Roma, and asked if we could stay with either of them for a night before heading to the airport in a couple days. They were kind of weird about it. Both seemed somewhat hesitant to offer a bed or couch, but eventually Bella told us we could pitch our sleeping bags in her back yard. This was more than enough for us anyway, so we happily accepted. She would pick us up from the train station when we made it back to Perth.

As for New Zealand, things weren't looking great. A few invoices had been paid by the time I arrived in Kalgoorlie, but they didn't improve our situation by much. We booked a flight from Auckland to Christchurch for about $300. That, coupled with the $167 train ride back to Perth, left a paltry sum to make it through our two weeks there, but the flight seemed cheaper than trying to make our way to the southern coast of the North Island, hopping a boat over, and then making our way to Christchurch and Tekapo, where my client Abbi said we could camp.

We went out with Ryan on several occasions, once to the bars and a couple of other times to parties. Again, I felt alienated around my peers when we visited the bars. I hadn't gotten tipsy since sometime around Bangkok. I enjoyed parties where I could actually sit and chat with people, though. This was something that has stuck with me since returning home. Gone are the days when I enjoyed crowded bars, screaming over the music, and waiting thirty minutes to be served a drink.

Aaron didn't join Ryan and me for the last get-together during our stay in Kalgoorlie. Instead, he stayed at Ryan's to video chat with Looktaal back in Bangkok. Things had gotten pretty serious between the two of them. Given his inexperience in romantic affairs and what he'd told me of their conversations I felt a pang of concern that he was quickly falling for her despite what to me sounded like a one-sided infatuation. But he seemed to be happy when he was talking to her, so I supposed that was all that really mattered. We didn't talk about it much.

When I got home from the party with Ryan that night he was acting all depressed and moping around, so I asked him if everything was okay. We stepped out for a cigarette.

"Looktaal told me she doesn't want to talk to me anymore." He bent over his cigarette and his face glowed orange for a moment.

"Oh man … How did that come about?"

"I don't know. She just said that it wouldn't work out between us right now and stuff … she didn't really tell me why. She just said that and then logged off of Skype."

"Damn dude, that really sucks. Do you think there's another guy or something?"

"Well she has a boyfriend, but she's supposed to break up with him."

"Wait … what? She's had a boyfriend this whole time?"

He puffed on his cigarette, staring into the yard. I moved on without an answer. "You think she decided to stay with him?"

"I don't know man. She wouldn't really tell me anything."

We sat on the porch for another hour, chain smoking cigarettes and talking through his situation. I measured his woes against parallels in my own life and tried to extract any nuggets of wisdom for him to utilize.

I got my first lesson early in life, when I developed a crush on the prettiest girl in third grade: Jillian Jacobs. On the way to school one morning I penned a romantic letter, delivering poetic endearments like, "my daddy is a fire man" and "I like to wach *Chip and Dale's Rescue Rangers*, it is probly my favrite show" and most importantly, "u r the most prettiest girl in the whole third grade and maybe even the whole world." Then I went on, like a blundering fool, to ask if she would "be my girl frind?"

I carefully folded my love letter and sealed it with a rather well-drawn heart. I handed it to her at lunchtime along with my favorite Beanie-Baby toy, Freckles the Giraffe. It was a tough choice, Freckles being the best of my Beanie-Baby collection, but I deemed it a worthy sacrifice to court the girl of my dreams—the one-and-only magnificent Jillian Jacobs. After handing her the note and my prized giraffe, I scurried back to my table and awaited to hear from my perfect, stunning, hopefully soon-to-be new girlfriend.

But alas, it was not meant to be. After only a few short minutes, beautiful Jillian came over and threw Freckles the Giraffe at my lap. "I already have this one," she proclaimed before tearing up my letter, tossing it into a cloud of confetti, and then turning around and walking away in a huff. My little heart crunched up like a paper ball. A whisper of giggles circled me. I slid Freckles the Giraffe onto my lap and turned my watery eyes toward my salisbury steak. In that moment, Third Grade Tom learned that women could do more damage to a human being than anything else on this earth. I decided right then and there that they did, in fact, have kooties, just like Jeffy Thompson said they did; although they were kooties of the *soul*, rather than kooties on your "peepee" like he'd told me. (It turns out you can get those as well though, if you meet the right girl.) I told myself, "Forget her. No more girls, *ever*. You'll have more time now to focus on your Super Mario 3 and Lego-building skills."

Looking back, it's good that it failed in a plume of smoke and fire the way it did. Say if she'd felt sorry for me, accepted my letter, and we'd made a real go of it. Holding hands in the playground, scribbling love notes, the works. Then, months down the line, the true feelings came to the surface and we had a nasty split. Would she have gotten shared custody of Freckles the Giraffe? Or worse, would Freckles go to live with her outright? After all, I was only a third grader. I couldn't support Freckles on a measly chores allowance. No judge in their right mind would have given me custody. Would I have ever made it to that final level of Super Mario 3 where those wooden ship cannons made me want to smash my goddamned Nintendo controller against my television screen? It's good that life works out the way it does, for better or worse, because that's the way it must happen in order for us to be where we are and who we are in the present.

So when I saw Aaron in his situation, I couldn't help but feel both sorrow and jealousy toward him. Jealousy that he was feeling the warm, sweet jangle of emotions called "love"—of which there is no similar feeling in the world; and sorrow that this girl was taking that love and squashing it like a bug. He was many years behind in the school-of-hard-knocks romance curriculum and probably had many hard lessons to come. But famously these lessons can only be learned, not taught. So I did my best to console him without shaking him by the shoulders and shouting, "She had a boyfriend this whole time! Run, Aaron! Run!"

It was fortunate I took this approach, because the next day I noticed him chatting with Looktaal. Later, when he came into the kitchen to make a coffee, I asked him about it. "I thought Looktal broke it off? What happened there?"

"Oh … yeah. I think we're fine. She messaged me this morning and said she didn't mean anything she said last night."

I winced, but held my tongue. Obviously she tried to work it out with the boyfriend and it didn't pan out, so she came back to Aaron with some lame excuse and he'd eaten it right up.

"That's great man," I said.

. . .

A couple days later we said our goodbyes to Ryan and boarded a train toward Perth. We pulled into the train station that evening. I went to a pay phone and called the number Bella had given me. No answer. She was supposed to pick us up from the train station upon our arrival, but she was nowhere in sight. We waited and waited. I called again an hour later. No answer. By the time the sun began to set, the train station was closing. We walked outside and set our bags near the entranceway, unsure what to do. We started looking for potential sleeping spots, but there didn't seem to be any winners. We were in a populated residential area. A couple of cigarettes later, a security guard came outside and asked if we were Aaron and Tom.

"Yeah," Aaron said.

"Someone is on the phone for you in here," he told us.

We both breathed a sigh of relief. Aaron went inside to talk to Bella while I waited with the gear. He returned outside a few moments later.

"She's not coming."

"Huh?!" I asked.

"She said she went to the wrong train station earlier and ended up driving around for a half hour, so she just went home instead of coming here. She said she's already in her PJs now, so she doesn't want to leave again. She said we could take a taxi to her house, but I told her we didn't have money."

"Are you serious? Did you tell her we'd have to sleep on the streets?"

"Yeah. She said she was sorry."

"Sorry? You've gotta be kidding me."

I assumed she had her reasons and tried to think nothing more of it. We now had to find a place to sleep for the night. The train to the airport wouldn't be leaving until late afternoon the next day, but we couldn't wander too far from the train station, just in case.

We walked around the area, finding a children's park and quickly abandoning that idea; a group of trees that we eventually decided was too close to the roadway; and finally a little opening between three brick walls about a hundred yards from the station. The opening to the "cove" was facing the train station. Since it was abandoned at nighttime, this would give us visual cover from the road as well as houses in the area. We wouldn't have to worry about people spotting us until the next morning when cars would start pulling into the train station.

As we a pot of rice bubbled over our backpacking stove, I laid my sleeping bag out over the sand and bunched up my clothes as a pillow. My inflatable backpacking pillow had been punctured and abandoned long ago under a bridge somewhere in Europe. I wolfed down the meal, smoked a cigarette, and pulled the bag up over my head to avoid the cold night air.

Sleep eluded me. I rolled around and around. It felt as if no sooner than I'd finally closed my eyes, they were open again as light and heat filled the air around my head. I groggily threw my sleeping bag open to escape the heat of the sun and pulled my bandanna over my eyes to try to fall back asleep. It was to no avail. I sat up and saw that the train station parking lot was filled with cars. I made some coffee over our stove as Aaron stirred to consciousness, and then I packed up my gear.

"You wanna get packed up so we can head into the train station and get Wi-Fi?" I asked.

"I'd kind of like to stay out here a while longer," Aaron replied.

"Why? I mean what is there to do out here?"

"I don't know. I just don't wanna head in there just yet."

"Uhh … okay. Well, see you later then."

"You're gonna head in now?"

"Yeah, I'm not sitting out here in the sun and staring at the ground."

"Oh ... well, I'll be in in a while."

"All right then."

I was confused, but had long ago stopped trying to make sense of the things he said or did. So I went inside and watched movies on my laptop while I counted the hours until our bus came to take us to the airport. They dragged on and on. I estimated I had slept only about two hours total. Now I was about to board a flight to New Zealand which would take about six and a half hours, landing us in Auckland at around six in the morning. The next day we would take a flight south to Christchurch and from there make our way to Lake Tekapo where we would camp for a week or more before returning to the city.

I opened my journal to a page where I had tallied up our financial situation before leaving Kalgoorlie, titled as, *Just how fucked are we?*

- *$240.00 - Bank Account*
- *$137.00 - Cash on Aaron*
- *$110.00 - Cash in Australian dollars*
- *$65.00 - PayPal*
- *$25 Odesk (freelancing website)*
- *$125 - Unpaid invoices*
= *$702.00 total*
Minus $266.00 for plane tickets in NZ
Minus $167.00 for the train ride from Kalgoorlie to Perth
Leaves us a total of $269 to make it through New Zealand.

If the reader will remember, I had calculated around $650 to be the minimum cost to survive two weeks there. Things did not look promising, but there was nothing left to do on our part but hope for the best and dive in headfirst, as we always did.

26

NO SLEEP TiL AUCKLAND
AUCKLAND. NEW ZEALAND

November 6th

We shuffled into Auckland like a pair of zombies. Even after the sleepless night outside the train station in Perth, I hadn't dozed at all on the flight. The all-too-familiar feeling of uncertainty made sure of that. I was still clueless how we were going to make it through New Zealand with the small amount of money we had remaining. All I knew was this: I was tired as fuck and I would figure it out later—as usual.

Customs was quite an interesting adventure in and of itself. First, we were approached by a drug-sniffing dog. A drug-sniffing beagle, to be specific. It wagged its tail and lightly sniffed the air next to us as we passed. The next thing we knew we were being stopped by security. "Do you have any drugs?"

Here we go again. "No, no drugs."

"Have you done drugs recently?"

"I smoked a joint a few days ago," Aaron said, referring to one of the Australians we'd met at Kalgoorlie who had shared some with him.

I looked at Aaron with incredulity. *Why in the fuck would you tell him that?!*

"The dog doesn't care about that; he's trained to find *white stuff.*"

I let out a quiet sigh.

"Oh, well—I haven't done any of that," Aaron said.

I looked down at the dog. He was staring at me with his tongue out, wagging his tail ever so slightly. "I think he just wants to be petted," I said.

"No, he doesn't want to be petted. He's a highly trained canine officer. He only shows interest in someone if he smells drugs," the security guard asserted. The dog walked toward me.

"Yeah, seriously though, I think he just wants to be petted. I promise you we don't have any drugs."

"Sir, the dog is highly—"

"Hey there little fella, awww yes you're just a friendly puppy aren't you?" I petted the beagle as it licked my hand and continued its happy wagging.

I looked up at the guard. He lowered his eyes embarrassingly. "Sorry for bothering you."

"Are you kidding? This was the highlight of my day."

We left the fierce, drug-decimating Snoopy crew, and approached some kind of Orwellian machine that took our photo. There were large signs, which read "*NO HATS OR SUNGLASSES*" placed along both sides of the line.

It's important that I stop here and paint a picture for the reader. I haven't mentioned so far, for lack of necessity, that Aaron wore an army green special-forces-style boonie hat everywhere we went. New York, Spain, Germany, Italy, Thailand … everywhere. In Bangkok he wore it along with an army green rain poncho, which made him look like an American soldier.

Before we'd even entered the airport, I'd said something to him about the hat: "Dude take that thing off, you look like you're here to bomb the fuckin place or something."

"Huh? What's wrong with my hat?"

Here we were in line, with all the "*NO HATS*" signs around.

I didn't even think of it until it was too late—"Take your hat off, Aaron."

"Huh?" he asked innocently as he approached the front of the line.

"Sir!" a voice called from behind us. I looked around and saw a security guard. "Come with me please."

"Me?" Aaron asked.

"Yes, you. NOW."

Aaron glanced back at me as they grabbed him and led him away from the line and on to god-knows-where. I quickly diverted my stare forward and acted like I didn't even know him. I turned to the person behind me—"That guy was creepy … wonder if he's a terrorist or something?" Then I shrugged and walked through the line and out of the airport.

Aaron caught up to me as I was smoking a cigarette by the entrance. "Dude, that was crazy. They were asking me all kinds of questions and shit."

"That's because you were dressed like fucking *Rambo* with that hat, man."

• • •

We found a place called Kiwi Backpackers Hostel near to the airport, which offered a free shuttle. We had one night to kill before taking our plane to the South Island, so we opted to spend the cash for a real bed. It was $30 apiece each night for a room. Compare that to the $1-3 we had been paying in Southeast Asia for a room all to ourselves. This was why we were only allowing ourselves one night in a hostel during our entire stay in New Zealand. And really, I'm not sure what the hell we were thinking to pay for even the one.

After a quick phone call, the shuttle showed up at the airport and took us to the hostel. At the airport, I came up with the idea to try to get the hostel to lock up the majority of my possessions during our foray on the South Island. I knew we were going to spend our time hitchhiking around down there and camping in random areas, so I saw no point of dragging around all of my electronic equipment. We had to come back to the same place to catch a ride to the airport anyway, so it would all be waiting here when we returned north. My pack weighed close to seventy pounds now after taking on some of Corey's gear when he left. That didn't include my guitar, which I still carried slung over my shoulder alongside my pack. After we booked a room and were ready to settle in, I asked the receptionist whether this was possible.

"Yeah, sure no problem," she said with a smile. So far I was loving the locals. Everyone whom we'd encountered thus far was overly friendly.

I left just about everything. My laptop, the audio interface and microphone, tripods—anything that wasn't directly related to camping. My pack dropped from seventy pounds all the way down to about thirty-five. It felt like a feather.

Aaron, on the other hand, wanted to hang on to just about everything he had. He handed me a small plastic bag with some rocks and a few odds and ends.

"Is this really all you want to drop? You're not going to need your computer or any of that stuff, you know."

"Yeah, I think everything else in here is stuff I need. I'd like to keep the computer just in case."

"All right, suit yourself."

While settling into our room we met a young Alaskan named Brian, who was bicycling around New Zealand. We decided to jump a bus into downtown Auckland with him and check out the city. The lack of sleep was catching up with me, so I figured this would be a way to wake myself back up. I had adopted a system for fighting jet lag which basically consisted of forcing myself to stay awake until a reasonable hour in the new time zone. Whenever I arrived there, I planned to stay awake until at least nine the same night, so I could fall asleep and wake up at a normal time. So far I was doing good, but I could feel twenty-four hours of no sleep catching up with me, especially after having to sleep outside of the train station for my last rest, really making it feel closer to thirty-six hours.

We followed our new friend to the bus stop and headed toward the city. Brian had worked for the National Park System in Alaska, at Denali Nat'l Park. If you're unfamiliar, this is the park in which Christopher McCandless (*Into The Wild*) met his untimely end in an abandoned school bus. Brian had hiked to the bus, some twenty miles into the wilderness, on several occasions.

Auckland was a fairly large city; I saw busking potential if we had been planning to stay there. We strolled around for an hour before finding an outdoors store so Brian could buy fuel for his backpacking stove. While Aaron and I sat on a bench outside the store I felt myself dozing off. Brian returned and we began making our way to the bus station. I checked my phone and my eyes widened when I noticed the date. "OH MY GOD."

"What?!" they both spun around.

"The International Date Line. I got it backwards. I thought we would land on the same day, but it skipped ahead one. Our flight to Christchurch was *today*—almost four hours ago!"

"No way, that can't be right," Aaron said.

"Look at my phone—it's the sixth."

"Mother ... fucker. Well what the hell are we gonna do?"

Brian offered a possible solution: "Sometimes when that happens the airline will let you catch a ride on an open seat of a later flight. It's worth a try."

So we had to make it back to the Kiwi Backpackers Hostel to use their phone and hopefully catch the shuttle to the airport. Unfortunately for us, it didn't turn out to be so simple. The bus system in Auckland was confusing, and we ended up hopping on the wrong bus (a couple of the wrong buses actually) before finally making it back to the Backpackers Hostel two hours later. The sleep deprivation was starting to destroy me both physically and emotionally. I was nearing thirty hours without rest.

I ran up to the counter at our hostel—"Can I please use your phone?! We missed a plane flight!"

"I thought you were staying here tonight?"

"It's a long story ... we might be."

She handed me the phone, and I called JetStar, our airline. After navigating a web of phone prompts and hold music, I was finally connected with a cheerful male voice on the other side and met with the usual customer-service routine. *"I'm so sorry that happened, sir. I'll do my best to resolve this issue."* I explained what had happened, and his reply was encouraging. "This shouldn't be too much of a problem, have you heard of 'standby?'"

"I think that's what our friend here told us about, but we're not sure how it works exactly."

"Well basically you'd wait at the airport, and when a seat opens up, you can hop on it. They should be able to do that, but you'll have to go down there and talk to them."

"That would be incredible. So we can do that today?"

"Yes. Just head to the airport, and go to the JetStar counter. They will be able to put you on the standby list, as long as you're okay with waiting for an available flight. It could be minutes or hours, we really don't know when it comes to this type of thing."

"We don't care. That's perfect. Thanks so much, man."

I was so relieved. I told the girl at reception that we'd have to cancel our stay for the night since we needed to head back to the airport right away. She quickly took care of everything. I handed her the pack that was to be stored there during our two weeks on the South Island and we hopped on the bus after saying goodbye to Brian.

By the time the shuttle van rolled into the departures curb at the airport, a dull headache thudded behind my eyes. We dodged rolling suitcases and slalomed through groups of people, rushing toward the JetStar counter. I approached the woman behind the desk. "Hi, I just spoke to one of your phone representatives. We missed a flight earlier due to a misunderstanding with the International Date Line. He told me you could put us on standby to catch a flight to Christchurch."

"Sorry, we don't do standby."

"What do you mean? I just got off the phone with one of your reps. He told me to come in here."

"I'm sorry, but I don't know why he told you that. We've never done standby."

"So what are you saying? That we've just lost all the money we paid for our flights?"

"I'm sorry, but, yes. Tickets are non-refundable."

"Are you kidding me? We just lost $300 and you're not going to do *anything* to try and fix this? I mean I get it —it's our fault, but come on you can't *try* to help?"

She shook her head. "Unfortunately we—"

"FUCK IT. JESUS FUCKING TAPDANCING CHRIST."

I wheeled around and marched the other way; Aaron sprinted behind to catch up. "What are we gonna do now?" he asked.

My face was tingling with anger. "I guess take the shuttle back to the hostel. We obviously can't afford another ticket. We're going to have to hitchhike south or something."

We made it outside and each smoked a cigarette to calm down. I was so tired that I couldn't even comprehend most of what was happening. I was taking everything exactly as it happened and dealing with it retroactively. After the cigarette, I walked back into the airport to use the pay phone while Aaron waited outside with the bags. I called the number for the Kiwi Backpackers Hostel and promptly heard a couple of clicks as the digital payphone reset and ate my dollar. Yes, a whole dollar to make a goddamned phone call. That was it. That was the final straw. I came unhinged.

I staggered through the airport toward the customer service desk, far on the other side. I cursed loudly to myself the entire way—"FUCKING PIECE OF SHIT. OF COURSE THAT GOD-DAMN PHONE WOULD EAT MY MONEY. STUPID COCK-SUCKING FUCKING AIRPORT. THIS IS THE DUMBEST COUNTRY IN EXISTENCE. '*SORRRY SIR, WE CAN'T RE-FUND YOUR TICKET.*' Yeah, FUCK YOU BITCH … FUCKING BULLSHIT STUPID GODDAMN PLACE …"

Faces glared back at me. Flashes of sympathy, of disinterest, of fear. I approached the customer service desk still raving.

"I NEED TO USE A PHONE."

"Well hey there sir!" the cheerful fellow behind the desk said with a blinding smile. "You can use the phones over there along that wall by the accommodation listings."

"THE PAY PHONE ATE MY DOLLAR."

"Well sir, I'm sorry to hear that. Those phones over there by the accommodation listings are free!"

"YOU MEAN I DIDN'T EVEN HAVE TO USE THE PAY PHONE IN THE FIRST PLACE? I CAN USE THOSE FOR FREE?"

"That's exactly right! They're there for people to call hotels and taxis and such."

"OH ... I ... uh ... thanks."

I called the Kiwi Backpackers Hostel and got the receptionist girl I'd been working with all day. "It's me ... they screwed us ... I need a ride please."

"Oh, are you kidding me? I thought the guy on the phone said you could get a standby ticket?"

"Correct."

"I'll send the van over. Don't worry about paying."

After making it back to the Kiwi Backpacker's Hostel, we were pretty much decimated. We could only afford one night's stay there, so we had to form a game plan for the next day. In the end, there was only one option: to hitchhike to the southern coast and then hop a boat down to the South Island. We had to buy some stove fuel in the city, as well as food, and then find a way to the edge of town where we could catch a ride south.

Surprisingly, after close to thirty-six hours since my fitful rest outside of the train station in Perth, I had a lot of trouble falling asleep that night. I tossed and turned while feelings of worry, anger, and despair rattled around my brain.

27

KiWi LOVE ON THE NAKED BUS
AUCKLAND TO CHRISTCHURCH, NEW ZEALAND

November 7th

The next morning we headed into downtown Auckland and bought fuel for our stove. Afterwards we planned to start hitch-hiking south, however we couldn't find a bus route that would take us to the edge of town. We talked to a few locals and received the same advice from all of them: *"Why don't you just use Naked Bus?"*

My first thought was that we were being coerced into a Kiwi-style orgy. *Well,* I thought, *I can think of worse ways to pass the time.* But, it turns out that Naked Bus isn't an orgy. It also turns out that Kiwis look at you strangely if you ask them if they're inviting you to an orgy. In actuality, Naked Bus is a private transit line offering rides around New Zealand on the cheap. It was only about $8-15 for some rides through the South Island. The North Island was a tad more expensive, costing us about $30 each to reach the ferry ports in Wellington. We figured that this would end up being cheaper than hitchhiking there anyway—it would have taken several days to make our way to the port, costing us more money in food and tobacco. Both of those were expensive—tobacco cost even more in New Zealand than it had in Oz.

So, we booked the tickets. The only problem was that our bus didn't leave until the next morning. So we were faced with the task of finding a place to sleep for free in a large city. This was no easy endeavor. We had walked around a pier earlier in the day and decided that we could duck behind one of the buildings there for the night. It was still afternoon at this point, so I was in no hurry to leave the comfort and Internet connection that the transit station was offering. But Aaron insisted that we head toward the pier.

"Why? It won't be dark for a few more hours. We'll be twiddling our thumbs down there with nothing to do."

"Well it's not like there's much to do here either. I think we should just get a move-on and head that way."

"It's like a ten-minute walk. I don't think it's a good idea to go there without the cover of darkness anyway. Everyone will see us setting up to sleep there."

We bickered for a minute and I finally told him he could go down there if he wanted, but I wasn't leaving until I was ready to go to sleep. Unwilling to walk there by himself, he relented and sat alongside me until evening. I thought back and remembered how he had done the same thing at the train station in Perth when we had camped outside. Why the hell was he insistent on preferring to sit and stare at the ground?

After darkness descended upon Auckland, we walked down to the pier and laid our sleeping bags between the wall of a building and some benches, out of sight.

We cooked up some rice and were well into scarfing it down when we were approached by a large Kiwi security guard who was making his rounds on the pier.

"Hey, whatcha boys doin back hee?"

"Uhh … well … to be honest we were hoping to sleep here. We don't have any money for a place to stay," Aaron told him.

"Ahh man. I can't let ya stay hee, sorry. It'd get me in some shit with my boss. But I can tell ya a good place to set up where the cops won't botha ya."

He told us about a park a few blocks away where we could hopefully slip into the bushes unnoticed.

"Just try to sneak in theeh. If the cops find ya, they'll prolly fine ya or take you in, but as long as you're quiet and keep in the shadows up theya, I think you'll do all roight."

"Thanks man, we appreciate the advice. Is it okay if we finish eating before we head up there?"

"No worries. An good luck to ya both."

The Kiwis were certainly not swaying in their friendliness. I had yet to encounter a local who wasn't cheerful or helpful to us in some manner. I mean, where else are you going to find a security guard who would kick you out and then turn around and give you advice for illegal camping?

We finished our dinner and then walked to the park. We found a dark area and slipped into it to set up camp for the night. We used leaves and branches to cover our bags and then we both got in our sleeping bags and passed out. I slept like a baby.

The morning after waking, we made our way to the bus station and hopped onboard the bus to Wellington. I passed the twelve-hour cruise listening to music or watching downloaded movies on my phone.

Once arriving in Wellington, we had to search to find a place to sleep in yet another large city. After arriving in the bus station, I wandered around for an hour or so while Aaron watched the gear. I couldn't find a single place where I thought we'd be able to sleep undetected. I came back defeated.

Aaron offered to go look himself, coming back about twenty minutes later. "Dude, I found us the perfect spot!" he exclaimed.

"Thank god," I muttered as I threw my pack onto my shoulders and picked up my guitar.

I followed him across the main intersection near the bus station and behind a few buildings. We walked down an alley and emerged in a parking garage.

"Right back in there," he motioned to a dark corner of the parking garage.

"Are you serious?" I answered. "We're going to get run over by a fucking car."

"Nah man, we'll be fine. Nobody's gonna come in here."

I was skeptical, but Aaron was right—it was probably the best place we'd find in the area. I was even less enthused when the smell of urine crept into my nostrils and I saw shards of broken beer bottles littering the asphalt upon which we were to be sleeping. I swept the area with my foot and tried my best to spot the piss puddle that was causing the unpleasant odor. I did not sleep well.

The next morning we woke up and started making a cup of coffee when a security guard pulled up. "Hey, you guys need to move it along. Can't sleep hee."

"Uhh, okay," Aaron said. "Is it cool if we finish making this cup of coffee before we leave?"

"Yeah, that's fine."

"Okay, thanks."

The guard drove away.

"I mean obviously we've already slept—that was kind of pointless wasn't it?" I said with a chuckle.

"Yeah, well, just be glad he showed up now and not in the middle of the night I guess."

We finished our coffee and walked to the ferry station. Here we would board a boat to Picton, a port on the South Island. From there it would be another ride the following day to Christchurch and then yet another to Lake Tekapo. I sat outside of the ferry station to play some guitar while we were waiting. Before long, I was approached by a security guard (the number of security guards everywhere seemed to be overwhelming). I thought he was going to tell me to stop playing, but he walked up with a big smile. "Hey man! Nice guitar! Is it smaller for traveling or something?"

"Yeah man. It's called a 'Little Martin' traveler guitar."

"You mind if I play it?"

"Sure, go for it." I handed him the guitar.

He started strumming a reggae rhythm and sang in an upbeat,

soft tone.

"Damn dude, you're pretty good!" I said.

"Ahhh no brotha man, I suck!" he laughed. He was being modest; the guy had the voice of a reggae angel. "What kind of music do you like?"

"A bunch of stuff really, but mainly some newer folk rock and a ton of classic rock and oldies."

I named a couple of bands and he told me he hadn't heard of them.

"What kind of music do you listen to?" I asked.

"I listen to a lot of roots reggae and such."

"How about Sublime?"

"Yeah man, I love Sublime! Dude, you gotta check out these local blokes …"

Before I knew it, we were each scribbling down lists for one another to look up later and exchanging tunes on the guitar.

"Well, I better get back to my post, man," he finally said as he stood up. "You take care, eh?"

I said my goodbye and walked back into the ferry station to prepare for boarding. The ferry we booked was comically luxurious considering what our living situation had been over the past few days. We had comfortable leather seats with power outlets and the ship even had Wi-Fi.

After arriving in Picton, we made our way to the bus station from which we'd be leaving for Christchurch the next day. We had to find somewhere to sleep that night. An argument erupted as, once again, Aaron wanted to go to find a spot early and sit there for hours and hours until it got dark.

"Why don't we just go into the bus station and hang out on their Wi-Fi for a while?" I argued.

"I mean, I don't have anything to do on Wi-Fi."

"There are countless ways to kill time if you have an Internet connection, man. I mean what are you going to do when you get to this place, wherever it might be?"

"I think we should just get a move-on, get things set up. We need to get some groceries too."

"We have like six hours before it gets dark. We have plenty of time to sit around on Wi-Fi, go get groceries, and then go to find a sleeping spot after dark. People are going to see us, plain as day, walking into a sleeping spot. Plus I want to charge my phone and stuff before we get on the bus tomorrow."

"God, we always have to do whatever you want. I don't get why it's so important to play on your phone all the time."

"Aaron, I don't understand why you're insistent on going somewhere and staring at the fucking grass for hours! How about this: I'll let you sit with the stuff while the phones charge and I'll go to the supermarket myself and get the groceries and shit. Or vice versa."

"Splitting up would be stupid. We should just both go there together and then head to the park to find a sleeping spot."

I finally had enough. "Aaron, you can do whatever the fuck you want. If you want to go to the grocery store, go. If not, don't. I'm going into this bus station to charge my phone. I'll be at that fucking park over there when it gets dark. If you're there, cool. If not, whatever."

He exploded back. "You're such a fucking asshole. I guess I'll go get the groceries then and you can sit with the stuff if that's what you want to do *so* bad."

"Whatever."

Our mood didn't improve the rest of the evening, and after we went to the park much earlier than I'd wanted (mainly because I was tired of hearing him continue to complain) I left him to sit and stare at the ground like he'd wanted while I went to the bay to play guitar and watch the sunset.

A cute Chinese woman came up and sat next to me on the bench after I'd been there for about an hour. She attempted to communicate with me, but didn't speak any English, so nothing really came of it. I sat and played songs and she listened. Soon some younger teenage Kiwi kids came and sat near me as well. The Chinese girl left, and they started asking me all kinds of questions: *"Where ya from?" "Are you with the guy in the bushes over there?"*

"United States. Yes, I'll assume that's my friend Aaron you saw in the bushes."

After answering enough pointless questions, I walked back over to Aaron. He had found a spot behind some trees where he was sitting and heating up rice. I didn't mention to him the fact that, exactly like I said would happen, people had spotted us before darkness had been able to conceal our campsite. We decided we should move spots. Once darkness had completely fallen and we'd eaten our dinner, we moved to an escarpment of young trees a short distance away. We were just setting out our sleeping bags when we saw some kids walking through the middle of the park.

"Homeless guys? Hey homeless guys, where are you?"

Aaron and I both remained silent. We were unsure of their intentions.

"We should just throw some rocks into the bushes until we hear them," one of the kids said.

Aaron reached for his sheath knife and I grabbed a stick nearby, both of us worried that the group of teenagers were up to something insidious. Eventually they circled around to a concrete platform behind and above us, and looked down into our makeshift campsite.

"Hey there they are!"

"What do you want?" Aaron asked.

"Hey, can you guys buy us a box?" one of the kids asked.

"A what?" I asked.

"Of vodka," another kid answered.

"Uhh … how old are you guys?"

"Sixteen."

"I don't know …"

"We wanna party with these girls and we told them we can get vodka."

I thought back to my high school years. I shrugged my shoulders at Aaron.

"Give us five bucks and we will," Aaron said.

"Tell ya what mate, we'll give you ten."

"Okay, meet me back down here and show me where the liquor store is."

I woke up periodically throughout the night itching like crazy from ants that were crawling into my sleeping bag. Once again, just after we'd woken up and started making our instant coffee, a security officer approached us.

"Hey, sorry, but you guys can't sleep here."

And again, "Can we finish making our coffee?"

"Sure thing, mate."

We both laughed after the exchange. "Well, hopefully they keep kicking us out *after* we spend the night," Aaron said.

On the bus ride to Christchurch we passed through rolling hills of wildflowers and snow-capped mountains. Winding roads led us through the most wonderful views I'd seen so far on our journey; even more captivating than the landscapes in Switzerland. I wrote a passage in my journal:

That feeling of absolute awe when you see something so beautiful as these New Zealand mountains and countryside. Easily comparable to the first time I set eyes on the Grand Canyon in Arizona, the Rocky Mountains in Colorado, or the Badlands in South Dakota.

That feeling of breathlessness and inspiration, your pupils growing wide in an attempt to capture all of its beauty.

Your mind goes numb. All other thoughts drift into your subconscious and you find yourself thinking of big-picture things such as the origins and purpose of life.

You take a picture, but you know it's useless. It's too big, no, too emotional to capture. It can't be caught at all, and its captivating spell can only be experienced by those who drive, fly, or walk to get there themselves.

Misty-hazy wonderful blues and puffy white clouds meet snow and rock covered peaks which then fall to a never-ending landscape of the most perfect green rolling hills; and you think to yourself: Not everyone will make the journey to see this. And for that, I'm saddened.

28
ESCAPE FROM MOUNT TEKAPO
TEKAPO, NEW ZEALAND

November 10th

We pulled our bags off the bus in Christchurch and snagged a folded paper map from a tourism display. On it we spotted a nearby park, which we figured would be our "hotel" for the night. There were also icons which showed Wi-Fi locations. We set our sights on one right next to the park, called "Pallet-Pavilion."

A terrible earthquake hit Christchurch in 2011 that left much of the city covered in rubble. Afterward, the community came together to rebuild. Anything that could be recycled, was. Any bare lot was used for community projects. There was a mini-golf course throughout the entire city that was constructed from materials recycled from earthquake rubble. An entire shopping mall made from old shipping containers. Pallet Pavilion was one of these projects. It was an open forum built of recycled wood pallets and anything else they could find in the wreckage of the city: tables made out of road signs, old crates as chairs ... there were flowers planted throughout the pavilion and a stage was set up in the corner for bands. Coffee and snacks were sold in a little shack off to one side. It was open-air, kind of like an old-style fort built out of colorful pallets and flowers. Each pallet that made up the walls had a name written on it; of a volunteer who had helped during its construction. The community projects organization was called "Gap Filler."

We were grateful for free Internet, considering, ironically, how hard it is to come by in a lot of developed areas of the world. I posted something on our Facebook page about how we had made it to Christchurch and would be trying to find a place to sleep in a nearby park.

As I was going through emails, I saw a comment on the post from Abbi, my New Zealand graphic design client who'd told us which spots to check out during our stay. "Hey, I live in Christchurch! You guys can stay at my place if you want."

She offered to meet us at a bus station near her house. In less than an hour we went from planning to sleep in the bushes in a city park to drinking beers on her back porch while her roommate grilled steaks, chicken, and shrimp. Our trail-sodden clothes were spinning in her laundry room.

Abbi was a slender Irishwoman who had moved to New Zealand a year prior. She was a travel blogger, which was how I connected with her for design work. Her roommates were Juanita (pronounced Juh-neeta), a Kiwi, and Jimbo, who was a Brit.

"What are your plans for the next week or so?" Juanita asked as we sipped beer and waited on the food to cook.

"Well we're headed to Lake Tekapo to camp for the next week, then we'll be back here to catch a flight back to Auckland." (Even though we'd missed our first flight, our return flight was still valid.)

"What the fuck are you gonna do in Tekapo for six days?" Jimbo asked with a laugh.

We didn't know more than what we'd seen in pictures, but it looked as if Tekapo was a small town nestled alongside a blue lake and surrounded by mountains.

"We're going to find a place around there to camp. We don't really have enough money to do anything else."

"You're gonna be bored off your fucking asses, mate!"

There wasn't much we could do about it, so we didn't really address the issue. Boredom was something with which we were all too familiar.

After dinner, we all sat around drinking and chatting. They asked me to get out the guitar and I happily obliged, drinking and playing late into the night. We had to be up early in the morning to catch another bus to the University Plaza, where we would catch our second bus on to Tekapo, but that didn't put much of a hindrance on the partying for the night.

Jimbo continued to tease us about Tekapo. "We'll be here all cozy this week and these two stupid fuckers are going to be sitting in the mountains jackin off for five fuckin days."

I blurted out, "So far on this trip I've masturbated on a train; a plane; a hammock; and now after the ferry to Picton, even a fuckin boat."

Aaron practically spit out his beer—"HUH?!"

Everyone laughed. "Are you fuckin kiddin me mate?!" Jimbo asked.

"All I need is a bus and I'll have my masturbation bucket-list completed."

"You really did that in all those places?" Aaron asked, astonished and disgusted.

"Don't act like you're not impressed." The masturbation bucket-list idea arose from, as you could probably guess, a drunken joke between Corey and me before leaving.

"My question is," Jimbo jumped in again, "is crankin it on a fuckin bicycle on that list of yours? Cause that could get tricky."

"Okay, so *two* more items on the bucket list."

I woke up the next morning with a raging hangover. Juanita prepared containers of food for us to take to Tekapo. I offered to put them in my pack since I had more room than Aaron and they wouldn't fit in our grocery bags.

Several hours later our bus wound the mountain roads into Tekapo. The narrow passageways of the climb into the mountain range opened to a wide, clear vista. Lake Tekapo shone a brilliant robin's egg blue. Glacial mountains pounded minerals into dust and filtered it into the water that fed the lake, providing its deeply saturated turquoise hue. We were mesmerized by the thing. We couldn't stop staring at it. Surrounding the lake were steep hills, dotted with areas of forest, yellow-green grass, and rocky outcrops. At the top of one peak was a group of buildings, the Tekapo Observatory. Tekapo itself was more of a station than a town, with a couple of restaurants, a grocery store, and a hotel. There were scattered guesthouses and cabins throughout the surrounding area.

After we'd exited the bus and loosed a cannonade of photos, we threw our packs on and started hiking around the lake. We saw a copse of trees on the mountainside at one end of the lake. We figured we'd head up there, set up camp and come down to the lake periodically for water.

As we rounded the lake and started up the mountain, Aaron began to lag behind. The extra weight of his pack was taking its toll. I, on the other hand, had no problems after dropping all my extra weight, and practically skipped up the trail.

"Come on, dude!" I hopped forward with a smile as he labored onward, leaning forward to relieve his shoulders periodically.

My skipping stopped as we climbed higher up the mountain and the grade and altitude increased. Our lungs were groping for oxygen in the thin air by the time we finally discovered a suitable campsite. The spot was a couple hundred yards to the left of the trail, up a steep grade. It was underneath a huge pine tree. There was an open spot in the thick lower branches, which provided somewhat of a natural cove. We draped our rain fly over one of the branches to create a canopy. Looking at the extreme incline of our campsite, I knew I would sled down the mountain in my sleeping bag if I didn't rig something up. So I came up with an idea to "anchor" myself: I took a rock about the size of a tennis ball and placed it in the top of my sleeping bag's hood. I pulled the bag tight around the rock and then tied a rope around the bag below the rock. The rope then led up to the tree, where it was tied to one of the roots, anchoring my bag firmly to the tree. Aaron didn't think the incline would pose too much of a problem, so he didn't do anything.

Turns out we were both wrong. Aaron woke up halfway down the mountain in the middle of the night and had to climb back up several times. I ended up forced into a ball in the bottom of my sleeping bag every hour or so. We would have to try something different the next night.

The following day we did nothing. I mean absolutely nothing. I played guitar for a while, wrote in my journal, sat and looked at the lake, and ended up laying under the canopy bouncing tiny pinecones off of the back of my guitar and trying to land them into a cup. We made a slingshot out of my guitar strap and used it to try to launch rocks all the way down to the lake, hundreds of feet below. We watched episodes of a TV show on my phone before it finally died. We drank a lot of coffee and smoked a lot of cigarettes. We sat and stared at the lake, mesmerized by its color. I was laughing already at what Jimbo had said. *What the fuck were we going to do there for a week?* We spent hours and hours as a counter in our heads ticked and tocked, bleeding the minutes until a week would pass. That night, Aaron came up with a plan to relieve our involuntary nighttime adventures on the apline slide. We could tie one end of our hammocks to the trunk of the tree, and the other end to one of the outlying branches. This would make the top part of the hammock pretty much on the ground, while the other end would be lifted away from the grade, essentially making a level platform. We already knew that hammocks were bad for cold weather because of the lack of insulation underneath, but we figured since most of our bodies would be on the ground it wouldn't be too bad.

I rigged mine up, but Aaron couldn't get his to work correctly due to a lack of sufficient branches on his side. Instead, he took a thick piece of bark and used it as a shovel, digging a ditch into the mountain at a somewhat level grade. We settled into our sleeping positions for the night and I felt surprisingly comfortable. I fell asleep quickly.

About three hours later, I woke up in a fit of trembling. My entire body convulsed with cold shivers. It felt like even my insides were trembling. I couldn't catch my breath. I could feel the cold air sliding below me as it blew up the side of the mountain. I labored to unzip my hammock so I could get onto solid ground. My hand was shaking so badly I could hardly grip the zipper. I couldn't think clearly and my motor functions were off-kilter. I wondered if I was experiencing the beginning stages of hypothermia. Finally I was able to grasp the hammock zipper and open it. I rolled out of the hammock and onto the ground, where I immediately assumed the fetal position and sunk deep into my sleeping bag. I was still shaking uncontrollably and felt dizzy even though I was lying down.

What the hell is wrong with me? I wondered as I blew into my cupped hands. After twenty minutes or so, my situation hadn't improved. I couldn't concentrate on anything and I felt my thoughts skipping around sporadically. I had an idea during one of these fleeting moments and finally sprung to action to try to get myself back to normal. I reached for the backpacking stove and coffee cup. The pots clanged as my hands shakily rummaged through the cooking gear. Aaron stirred, but didn't wake. I filled the cup with water and set it over the backpacking stove after it was lit. As soon as I saw steam coming from the cup, I grabbed it from the stove and gulped it down. I felt the warm water enter my stomach and begin to heat up my body. I filled it again and put it back on the stove. I sipped the next one and wrapped my hands around the warm cup. I finally stopped shaking.

That episode scared me. It was a moment of clarity when I suddenly realized that this wasn't sleeping under a bridge next to a town like we'd done in Europe. We were stranded high up in the mountains, pretty far away from any kind of help if something were to happen. We were unprepared for the colder mountain air, even after the purchases we'd made in Perth. We had to get down to lower ground the next day, I was sure of that.

The next morning Aaron woke up and stretched. "Man, did you think it got kinda cold last night? I was freezing my balls off."

"You don't even want to know."

Before heading to flat ground, we decided to hike the rest of the way up the mountain to Mt. Johns Observatory. It didn't look like it was much farther from our spot to the peak. We made sure most of our gear was tucked under the green canopy and started climbing. We decided the best way up would be through a vein of granite boulders, just beyond a brush area next to our campsite. However, we'd only made it a dozen yards or so before becoming snagged and tangled in thick briar patches. We retreated back to camp and cut sideways across the mountain until we saw a clear path to the rocks. Here we were able to force our way through the brush and start climbing up the granite. A short while later we were gasping for air and lying on the rocks.

"Why the fuck are we doing this?" I asked between gasps.

"Because we're stupid assholes," Aaron replied.

"You're a … you're a stupid asshole for … making me do this …"

"This was *your* damn idea …"

"Ah fuck. Just throw me off of this goddamn mountain … it would be a sweet release from this pain."

"You ready to … uh … [gasp] keep movin?"

"Let me … let me just … finish this cigarette first."

It turned out that the hike was much longer than we thought, and it took several more cigarette/asthma attack stops before making it to the summit. We visited the cafe at the Observatory and watched with salivation as tourists drank expensive coffee and ate pastries. I went into the bathroom and filled up our water bottles from the sink.

After taking in the views, we headed back down to camp. There we rested for a moment, packed up our gear, and then climbed the rest of the way down the mountain. Once we reached the trail at the bottom, we hiked around the lake toward a potential new campsite on the opposite side. We had spotted a low-lying wood-ed area that looked secluded.

The hike that day totaled something like four or five miles around the lake, not including the brilliant idea to trek up to the mountaintop like we were goddamn Krakauer. The trail around the lake led to a dog walking park and then an expanse of pine trees threaded with trails. We walked around until Aaron spotted a suitable location. There either fallen trees or small hills on all sides of us, creating somewhat of a natural vagabond "nest," if you will.

We had no view this time; the boredom was even worse than before. My thoughts spun and twisted in my head and turned dark. In my opinion, there is such a thing as too much time to think. Typically, people spend most of their day doing something that occupies their thoughts. Whether it's work, family, friends, hobbies, even watching TV. Usually the only time a person is just sitting and thinking about things is right before they go to sleep or in the shower. Even then, it's usually thoughts about the next day, problems in your relationship, something like that.

Imagine you have none of that to occupy your time. No friends to talk to, no family to take care of, no job to go to. Imagine you're so secluded that there is absolutely *nothing* on your to-do list either. There's only one thing you can do to pass the time—*think*.

"About what?" you might ask. Well, I'll tell you: everything. *What does life mean? Why the fuck am I here? Am I wasting my life? Am I going to die out here? If I did, what would my funeral be like? Who would be there? Would my friends say nice things about me?*

I grew depressed, anxious, and downright paranoid. Morbid thoughts plagued over me and I was sure that I would somehow die before returning home. Maybe Aaron would die … *what would I tell his parents?* I thought I was going crazy. All I did all day was think, think, think.

I began to wonder if this was human nature, that after all the distracting thoughts which fill a persons mind—family, relationships, work, etc.—are gone, is the meaning of life and death all that are left to ponder?

I thought of Christopher McCandless, who I mentioned a couple of chapters back. When he died in an abandoned bus in the Alaskan wilderness, he hadn't had any human contact in months. He died slowly, of starvation, and had nothing but time with which to think about life. One of his last journal entries was scribbled between the lines of a book:

"Happiness only real when shared."

That can be taken a number of ways. I think what he meant by it is what I felt out on that mountainside: if you don't have someone to share your happiness with, is it really even there? What's the point of life without other humans to share it with? Without things to distract us from our fates, all we're left with is our fates to contemplate.

I wondered if I was alone in this typhoon of emotions and the subsequent epiphany I was having. I asked Aaron at one point, "Hey man. Have you been having real weird thoughts since we've been out here?"

"Like …?"

"Like … I don't know, about life and death and shit … I just keep having morbid, weird thoughts floating through my head."

"Dude, I kinda thought I was going crazy … I can't stop thinking about all kinds of shit … it's fuckin weird."

"We need to get the fuck off of his mountain."

"Yeah. Definitely."

• • •

That evening we stashed all of our gear in the bushes and covered it with pine needles. We walked a couple of miles to a cafe and bought a cup of coffee each, in exchange for Wi-Fi use. Abbi and her roommates had agreed to let us stay in their house again before our flight back to Auckland left in a few days. I sent her a message asking if we could come back early. I was sure it wouldn't be a problem. Then I sent an email to Naked Bus asking if we could change our return ticket to the next day. I received an email back within the hour that notified us that the change had been made.

"They're letting us do it," I told Aaron. "We can leave tomorrow afternoon."

"Oh thank god," he replied.

We were almost completely out of money, so buying new tickets would have been out of the question. We had enough for food and tobacco to make it until our flight to LA in a week, and our return flight to Auckland was already paid for. We had roughly $80 left to our names after the cup of coffee we'd just bought. That was the grand total of everything, bank accounts and wallets included. I hoped that would get us back without trouble.

Another moment of good news arrived when I checked my Facebook and saw a message from Blake:

"Ali and I are coming to pick you up in LA. We're leaving the day after Thanksgiving, so we'll see you about three days after that!"

Aaron and I were toasting our coffee cups again. They had come through—it was a huge weight off of our shoulders.

After we finished our coffee and lounged around on Wi-Fi for a while, we walked back to our camp. After a dinner of—you guessed it—rice and tuna, we sat and talked about plans for when we returned home, plans for future traveling, and laughed about all the shitty things we had been through together.

That evening I started to feel sick and ended up lying down earlier than usual. I had a splitting headache and chills, but didn't have a fever. As I lay in my sleeping bag, my head once again spinning, I longed for a warm shower and a real bed.

My only solace was that I would finally be leaving this goddamned mountain the next day and off to a real bed. Then, in a few more short days, I would be on a plane to LA where I'd be welcomed to a room and a bed at my Aunt Donna's house. I imagined the coffee. *Real coffee* whenever I wanted it. Cheeseburgers. *Real cheeseburgers.* Food, and cigarettes, and beer—and did I mention coffee?—and a real bed and toilet. Was there really much more to life than that? Then another thought hit me: Aaron would be flying on to his Grandpa's house in Phoenix only a few days after our arrival in LA. For the first time in five months, I would be alone. No one to answer to, no one to share the money I had earned with, no one to ask me, *"When are you shutting that light off?"* or, *"Do you really think you should spend money on that?"*

I fantasized further, another month ahead, when I would be home. I imagined walking into a store with a wallet full of money. I'd buy a six-pack of beer and a pack of Camels. I wouldn't feel bad about spending money at all. I'd put gas into my car and drive home. Not walk, not hitchhike, not have to figure out a train system ... I'd fucking *drive* myself there. The easiest shit in the world compared to what I had now become used to. One month. Just one month, and I'd be free to do as I pleased again.

29
ONE LAST TIME
AUCKLAND, NEW ZEALAND

November 15th

We arrived in Christchurch sometime the next afternoon. The first thing we did was walk to the Pallet Pavilion to jump on Wi-Fi and see if Abbi had messaged me. Our spirits were elated at the thought of a shower that night. Such was our discussion during our walk to the Pavilion.

Once we arrived there, I connected to the Wi-Fi and checked my messages. I saw one from Abbi:

"So sorry! My flatmate has people here tonight, so Saturday and Sunday night would be better. I hope you find somewhere warm to sleep."

We'd have to sleep on the streets again.

"I swear, somebody cursed this fucking trip, man." I said.

"No shit. Nothing but bad luck since the beginning."

I knew it wasn't Abbi's fault, or even her roommates, so we weren't angry with them. They were doing us a huge favor by letting us stay there, and feeding us, and doing our laundry. It was our fault for once again doing things last minute and for being so broke in the first place.

Pallet Pavilion was shutting down for the day so we set out hiking across the city in search of a place to sleep for the night. We ended up at a strip mall at first. We were in search of Wi-Fi more than anything else—it was still hours until dark. We connected outside of the place and spent the next few hours writing in our journals, playing around on social media, and eating peanut butter sandwiches. The hours dragged on.

When darkness fell, we set out to find a place to bed down for the night. We checked out a few places—an abandoned lot, a small bridge near a park, the park itself—before settling on a weeded area next to a public garden. The ruins of a crumbled stone building lay next to us. The weeds rose high around us, providing natural cover. We cooked up some rice on the corner of the old building's foundation and then laid down in our sleeping bags for the night. I slept poorly because of heavy traffic nearby and woke around eight to see Aaron already up and making coffee.

"Traffic?" I asked him.

"Fuckin light, man. Been up for an hour or so."

"Traffic got me. All night with that shit."

"Yeah it was bugging me too. Three more days."

"Three more days."

Afterward, Aaron once again wanted to sit there and stare at the grass, while I opted to go to Pallet Pavilion and get on Wi-Fi. That little patch of grass was miserable; I had no idea why he wanted to sit there. I had long since stopped waiting around for him when it came to stuff like that, though. I just did my own thing and he caught up later. In retrospect, much like me, he probably just wanted a single goddamn minute to himself.

Abbi met us at the bus stop around two in the afternoon and wanted to show us around the city. We were both exhausted after sleeping so poorly the night before, coupled with our ordeal in Tekapo, and told her we'd rather do it the following day if possible. She said that would be fine.

Back at her house, Jimbo greeted us with a shit-eating grin.

"How'd ya enjoy all the exiting fun in Tekapo, boys?"

"Oh fuck off, man," I laughed. "We didn't realize there was nothing but the lake there!"

"I was wondering. I thought, *what in the hell are these kids gonna do down there for a week? They'll snap their own fucking heads off in boredom!*"

"Yeah, that's basically what happened."

We downed brews and chatted into the evening and went to sleep early. The next day Abbi showed us around Christchurch. It really was incredible what the community did in that city after the earthquake. There were still spray-paint marks on many buildings from rescue teams who had marked them as cleared of any trapped survivors. Recycled materials were used everywhere.

On our final morning, Juanita gave us a ride to the airport. We were sad to say goodbye to our new friends, but we were more than excited to be heading home the next day. This flight would take us back to Auckland, where we planned to pick up the stuff we had left at the Kiwi Backpackers Hostel. We would find a place to spend the night around the area (hint: it wouldn't be in a hotel or hostel) and then catch the shuttle back to the airport and fly thirteen hours to Los Angeles.

Juanita bade us goodbye and took off, and then Aaron and I smoked a quick cigarette before entering the airport. We were right on time, with about forty-five minutes left until our flight.

We walked into the airport and approached the woman at the counter. I gave her our confirmation number and she looked up our tickets. We set our bags on the scale and she looked at us confusedly. "Uhh, you don't have any checked bags on this ticket …"

"Huh? We don't get checked bags?" Aaron asked.

"No, if you want to check any bags it's $70 for each one."

My heart sank. "Wait, what? What if we don't have the money for that?"

"Ahh, geez. You'd either have to miss your flight or leave one of your bags."

"Well, we're obviously not doing that."

My thoughts started racing. Suddenly the half hour we had

remaining until our plane departed seemed like thirty seconds. There was no time to call someone and have money wired or transferred to my bank account. We had $80 total. That was it. No emergency reserves, nothing.

"There has to be something we can do," Aaron pleaded.

"Well, if you can somehow fit those bags in the carry-on compartment you'll be okay. It can't weigh more than sixteen kilos [thirty-five pounds], though."

I shot a look at Aaron and wanted to remind him how it would have been a good idea to leave his useless heavy shit back at the hostel in Auckland as I'd asked. We both knew his was easily double that. But there was no time for bickering. Problem number two was that his bag actually weighed too much even as a checked bag. I told him he better go through and find whatever he can afford to throw away. I ran over to the test carry-on compartment and crammed my pack into it by literally stomping it with my foot to make it fit. "Is this cool?"

"Yep, you're good. Just have to get his bag weight down."

"There's not really anything I can throw away," Aaron stammered.

"The food," I finally offered. "We have to dump the food."

There was no time to argue. We started chucking everything into the trash can: apples, cans of tuna, a bag of rice, everything except for one half-empty jar of peanut butter.

"I hate to do this to you," the woman at the counter winced as she spoke, "but you can't take the guitar as carry-on. You'll have to buy a seat for it."

"What?!"

"Hold on though, I might be able to help you out." She typed on the computer.

"Anything you can do, I'll love you for it."

"If I use my employee discount, I can buy a spare ticket in my name for five dollars. Will that work?"

"We have exactly eighty dollars. So seventy for the checked bag and five for the guitar? Not taxes or other fees?"

"Yes. Seventy-five is the total for all of it."

"Okay … let's do it."

I handed her my debit card and watched as the rest of our money disappeared with a deft swipe. We were broke, just threw away all of our food, and still had over twenty-four hours before our flight departed to Los Angeles.

We boarded the flight with minutes to spare and made the short ride to Auckland. When we arrived in the familiar airport, the Kiwi Backpackers Hostel shuttle picked us up. I grabbed our bag from storage after saying hello to the same girl who was working the counter a couple weeks earlier.

"I need to arrange a shuttle to the airport tomorrow," I told her.

"You need me to give you a room tonight then?"

"No."

"But ... you need a shuttle tomorrow?"

"Yeah ..."

"So where are you staying tonight?"

"Somewhere ... out there ..." I motioned outside. "We don't have any more money."

"Oh man, that's terrible. I'll tell you what: Don't worry about paying for the shuttle tomorrow." (You normally had to pay $10 for the shuttle if you weren't staying at the hostel. I had planned on figuring that out when the time came, probably by straight-up begging for money from people.)

"That would be so, so helpful. Thank you, thank you, thank you. You've been so great to us."

"No worries, really. Just never take me traveling with you. I think you have the worst luck I've ever seen."

I chuckled. "Don't get me started."

After walking out of the hostel, Aaron and I searched for place to spend the night. Out of the fourteen days we'd spent in New Zealand, only four had been under a roof. The rest were spent on the streets or in the mountains. This night would be no different. We still had a bit of time to kill before we could head anywhere to sleep. We spent it sitting at a picnic table in the foyer of an apartment complex. Ryan had given me a book before we'd left Oz, so I was alternating between doing language lessons on my phone and reading it. I'd left the book with my belongings in Auckland

and let me tell you,—I regretted that over and over again when we'd been bored out of our minds in Tekapo. Aaron was sketching in his notebook. At one point he made a trip to the grocery store and used our remaining $5 to buy a loaf of bread. All we had was that and the last bit of peanut butter. It would need to be rationed in order to get us through the next day.

It seemed to take an eternity for darkness to fall over Auckland that evening. We packed up our things and laid them down on the side of an apartment building. There weren't any places better than that, at least that we could see. *This is the last time I'm going to have to do this,* I thought. I pulled my sleeping bag over my eyes and fell asleep.

I awoke around six-thirty with puffy, groggy eyes. I had slept fitfully, worrying about police or someone else finding and bothering us in such an exposed area. Rain was pattering against my face. It had apparently been raining for a while, because my sleeping bag was soaked. The first beams of light were hazing over the apartment buildings.

"Aaron, wake up," I said, nudging his shoulder. "It's raining."

"Motherfucker."

"Yep. Sounds about right, eh?"

He rubbed his eyes and stared at the grass for a moment. "Pretty much."

We headed back to the shelter of the foyer and laid our sleeping bags out on the concrete to dry. Boredom once again reared its head, along with pangs of hunger which seem to always coincide. Unfortunately, we only had about two and a half sandwiches worth of peanut butter left. We each had a slice of bread for breakfast.

One of the apartment doors opened and an older, sharply dressed Filipino man stepped out. "Hey boys, you all right out here?"

"Yeah," Aaron answered. "We had to sleep outside last night and the rain woke us up."

"I see. I am making some coffee—would you like some?"

I turned around and my face lit up. "Coffee?"

"I'll take that as a yes. Give me a moment."

We'd had to throw out the rest of our instant coffee with the food at Christchurch Airport.

The man returned a few moments later with two cups of hot coffee. "Here you go."

"You're a godsend," I told him as I sipped the delicious black brew.

He laughed and then ducked back into his apartment, returning a moment later with two croissants. "Here, take these as well."

"Thank you," Aaron said.

"You're Americans?"

"Yes," I said.

He said with a smile as he sat on one of the other tables in the foyer. "So how did you end up in Auckland, sleeping on the side of my apartment?"

I looked at Aaron and we both smiled.

"Well, where do you want me to start?" I asked.

"At the beginning of course," the man said as he threw up his hand. "Really, tell me your story."

Aaron and I described the bullet points of our journey. I told him how I'd lost my girlfriend and my job. We told him we'd saved up what little money we'd had and left pretty much on a whim. That we'd hitchhiked and train-hopped our way through Europe. We told him about rides with drug dealers in Switzerland and sharing a bridge with an emu in Italy. About me meeting a girl in Germany who I wished I could have stayed with, and Aaron meeting a girl in Thailand who he still talked to and hoped to see again someday. I told him about my friends Adriano and Salvadore from the restaurant near the nature preserve, who did their best to teach me every Italian swear word they could think of. We told him about our friend Corey, who had stayed with us through the toughest part of the trip in Europe, but left after arriving in Asia. He laughed as I told him stories of our Indian friends back in Bangkok, probably still throwing parties for any conceivable occasion; of our buddy Paul who was most likely still smoking joints at his desk in the hostel on Koh Phangan. He asked several questions after we told him of Marc, who'd lived with monks in

Myanmar and taught us how to meditate. Then we described our Australian road trip with an eccentric British couple, and Outback camping trips and a friendly dog named Mango. Finally, we told him how we had missed our flight two weeks ago, and how we'd made it to the South Island only to find despair in Tekapo. Afterward, we told him, we'd spent the last of our money on a flight here to Auckland so we could catch a flight home.

"Basically we've managed to screw up at every conceivable turn. Although, I suppose the trip was probably doomed to begin with," I said.

"If you could go back, what would you change? What is your biggest regret from all of it?" he asked.

That's when it hit me. "Huh. Nothing. I guess I wouldn't change any of it. I mean, it's actually kind of funny, really."

"At the very least, you will make your friends laugh at your stories, no?"

"Oh, they'll definitely laugh, yes."

He chuckled and collected our coffee cups. "Well! I must go to work now. I want you to think about this when you're on your flight home, while I'm sitting in my boring office all day: I will be mad with jealousy. Think about that, my friends. Now, you be careful and have a safe trip home to your families, okay?"

30

EXODUS
LOS ANGELES, CALIFORNIA TO CHILLICOTHE, OHIO

November 19th

In Los Angeles I had unlimited coffee to drink, plenty of food to eat, a comfortable bed, and a hot shower. The first night we were back in the US, Aaron and I walked to a gas station to buy a bag of tobacco. I sat it on the counter and the clerk rang it up. "That'll be seven dollars and twenty-two cents."

"Seven fucking dollars!" I exclaimed to Aaron.

"Hey man, it's eight-something next door," the clerk argued.

I laughed. We had paid $65 USD for our last bag of tobacco in New Zealand.

Returning to our home country, we had so many strange mannerisms that one acquires when vagabonding around the world. I didn't throw food away. I would eat until I was ready to burst and then I would eat some more. As I rode in the car with Donna, I found myself looking out the window for suitable sleeping spots. I would see a small space between two buildings and involuntarily think, *Man, that would be perfect … there's a store to get water at right next door, too ...*

She took us to the opera one night. I tried to explain to her that we'd been living out of a backpack for over five months, and during that time had worn the same three shirts and two pairs of shorts. Attire at the opera is generally suits, tuxedos, and fancy dresses. She insisted, so we joined her as probably the dirtiest, most out-of-place attendees the LA Opera has ever seen. I'm honestly surprised they even let us into the building in our dirt-crusted pants and ragged t-shirts.

Aaron left after a few days and flew to Phoenix. I had the whole spare bedroom and bathroom to myself and I could come and go as I pleased.

Before I knew it, Blake and Ali arrived. We spent a few days gallivanting around LA, then we drove to Phoenix to pick up Aaron, then headed north to Flagstaff where we stayed with a friend of mine. From there we explored the Grand Canyon: one sight that will never grow old. In the winter snow it was more beautiful than ever.

We drove through the Rockies in the middle of a giant blizzard that consumed the entire western half of the United States and stayed near Boulder, Colorado. The next morning we started driving and didn't stop until we made it to Ohio. We crossed the border to our home state on December 9th—169 days since we had crossed its opposite side heading toward New York.

When I finally made it back to my house, I was in a daze. Mostly from a lack of sleep. Blake and Ali dropped me off at my front door. I unloaded my stuff and gave them both a hug. I thanked them for everything they'd done and explained how I didn't know if I'd ever be able to fully repay them.

Then I walked across the yard to my parents' house. Tears were in everyone's eyes as we saw each other for the first time in so many months. I talked to them for a long while, and then walked back over to my own house. Then I did something I had thought about for months and months. A moment I had dreamed of time and time again. A moment I'd longed for ... I pulled back my thick comforter and slid into my own bed. The most comfortable bed in the fucking world. Trust me, I know.

• • •

Aaron and I didn't talk much after arriving home. He was home for a few short months before returning to Thailand to reunite with Looktaal. Any notions I had of her have thus far proven misguided, for they seem happy together. He stayed in Thailand as long as he could before his visa ran out. He's currently in Australia working on a shrimp boat, assumedly until he can enter Thailand again. Many friends who have been "in the loop" on the happenings of this book have asked me the obvious question you're probably thinking right now as well: *"Does Aaron know you're writing this stuff about him?"* usually followed by, *"Oh man, he's going to hate you."*

To answer the first question: yes. He was fully aware before I even sat down to write this book that the book was being written, and, more importantly, that there were going to be embarrassing things about him in it. I was very straightforward with him before asking him to sign a release. I told him the truth, that I was writing a book and would honestly and accurately depict the events as they happened, at least to the best of my recollection. I did my best to try to write objectively about everything, but granted, this is our story written from *my* point of view. I'm sure he has plenty of complaints about me that I don't even know about. After all, he was better at keeping his grievances to himself than I was at most times.

Yes, he may hate me after reading this. But I hope not. I would never have asked him to change, because he is who he is, and a lot of people love him for those qualities. They just don't mesh well with my own personality. Nothing I've said in this book is a lie. Every single detail of this story is true, down to the dates and even the dialogue to the very best of my recollection. I kept track of our adventure in my journal as it was happening. I have not gone out of my way to make him look bad in this book, as some will inevitably say. Trust me, there are *many* things I've excluded for his sake simply because they were either not funny or not relevant enough to the stories at hand. I've portrayed everything exactly as it happened. The truth is that before we left, neither Corey nor I knew Aaron that well. There were many things I did which certainly drove him crazy, just as I complained of him doing to me. After you spend every day for six months with someone, you find which quirks annoy one another and, well, Aaron and I both had a lot of those with which to poke and prod. I still consider Aaron a friend and wish him all the best. He's found love with Looktaal and he deserves every bit of the happiness they have together.

As for my other travel companion, Corey, well ... you've heard of his tale of heartache since returning home. In all he only spent two months with us out of the six months we were gone, but he played a huge role in our story. He's still one of my best friends and joins me at plenty of shows on the cajon drum. He remains a father to this ex-girlfriend's two children—I say father instead of stepfather because their biological dad isn't even a blip on the radar, while Corey attends every ball game and father-daughter dance, helps pay for school supplies and necessities, and shares custody. The guy is a better father to those kids than many dads are to their own children. So far he has stayed separated from Katie. He says to this day that he doesn't regret leaving our trip early. He didn't know whether he was making the right decision at the time, but he did what he thought was best for him and Katie. I only wish that I can someday have a fraction of the heart he has.

As for my own saga, the trip mended my wounds, but the scar would remain for some time after. Shortly after returning home, Samantha actually married the guy she had cheated on me with, which hurt. But when she showed up at one of my shows a few months later, with a *different* guy on her arm while still "happily" married to the first, I truly felt the stinger fall loose. For so long, I had viewed her cheating as a result of my own shortcomings, or even just her being downright cold-hearted. But after seeing her repeat the same behavior with other partners, I began to believe it was the result of deeper issues that she has dealt with during most of her life. We all have our own emotional struggles and sometimes we don't deal with them as well as we should. It took a long time of being angry and hurt, but I eventually found a way to understand and forgive her in my own conscience and move on.

When I returned home, I thought I was done traveling for a while. I loved the comforts of being home—it took me months to get over being able to walk to my fridge and grab food whenever I wanted it. I spent the first four months building an addition onto my house—space for an office and home recording studio. I continued to play music for a living and do a little graphic design on the side. I got a beagle puppy, named Louie. I tried to find love again. I finally quit smoking, for real this time. No, really. Seriously, I did.

The Ohio winter those first few months home was the worst I've seen in my whole life. The older folks were saying it hadn't been that cold and snowy since the big blizzard that hit back in the seventies. As I battled subzero temperatures and built onto my house, I scrolled through my Facebook feed and saw my Australian and Kiwi friends post pictures of beaches and barbecues. Thanks to hostels, Couchsurfing, and hitchhiking, I had friends from all over the world now to inspire me—and make me sick with jealousy. I stood no chance. Before I knew it, I was lost in daydreams again. I tried to quench my thirst for adventure: I went skydiving. I backpacked nearby state or national parks with my dog when I could. I took a random trip to Boston with my brother and slept in my car for a week. But none of those things soothed the addiction I had acquired.

After a mere five months of being home, I started planning my escape. I resurrected *Artists Abroad* under a new name: *Tune Up and Travel*. Something that was all mine. I wrote about my travel stories, tips for traveling musicians, tips for budget or adventure travelers, anything that interested me and related to my readers. I decided I would head to South America and from there ... who knows? Learning from the faults and mistakes on my past trip, I bought new equipment which would bring down my pack weight and provide useful solutions to problems which had plagued me on the road last time.

But some things never change.

I'm set to depart in a couple of months and do you want to guess how much money I've saved up so far?

$11.36

I'll figure it out. I'm not doing donations this time around. I always felt shitty about that, taking charity from people. I'll work my way around wherever I go, whether it's with my computer or my guitar. Maybe one day I'll grow up and get a real job again. I don't know. I have no intentions, however, on traveling the way I did with Aaron and Corey. I have no desire to sleep under bridges or in culverts ever again. I consider the entire trip a gigantic learning experience. I don't regret a single thing and I would do it all again in a heartbeat—puking under a bridge included. Why? Because it makes a great story. But I won't sit here and act like all of that stuff was enjoyable, as I'm sure you could tell while you read it. So, when I leave again, I'll be aiming for keeping a roof over my head and food in my belly. I could have supported myself on the income I was making toward the end of the trip with Aaron. It was supporting two people that wasn't possible. At the very least, now I *somewhat* know what I'm getting myself into when I leave without a lot of money saved. Only time will tell how the next experience will go.

I set off on my journey with Aaron and Corey to see the world and hopefully answer some of life's burning questions. I'm not sure whether my questions were answer but I know I changed for the better—as almost always happens with travel—and that I'll never look at the world the same. At the beginning of this story I asked the question—*Why? Why did I do it?* I think that question has been answered if I were to do so as simply as possible: I was running away. Is that really a bad thing though? When I ran away, I found answers to questions I didn't even know I was asking. I learned that humans are kind by nature. The world is not scary and evil like we're led to believe growing up. It's a beautiful planet filled with beautiful people who want nothing more than to love and be loved.

I probably don't have the answers you're looking for. You'll have to take your own journey to get those. But before I take off on a hike with my pup Louie in a minute, I'll share with you a passage from my journal which I wrote on the mountainside in Tekapo, where I found parts of myself I didn't even know existed. When I had nothing but time to think about life, this is what I found:

All those who travel will change!

They will realize things about themselves and others.

The world-at-large will lift its mystic veil and reveal a glimpse of itself. It's not just you and your little town. It's everyone, in a world filled with little towns.

There is no single secret or purpose of life, because life is different for everyone. What is best for me may not bring you happiness, and vice versa.

True happiness is finding what you're looking for, whatever that may be.

Happiness is never ceasing to dream.

Happiness is family and friends who love and support you.

Happiness is living life with no regrets.

Love completely and travel often. Enjoy the ride.

ACKNOWLEDGEMENTS

First and foremost I'd like to thank my travel companions, Aaron and Corey, for giving me permission to write about them and share our story. I'd like to thank all of our friends and family who donated to us or helped us out in any way. You guys are the reason we made it home without starving to death. Seriously. I want to thank my mom and dad for everything they've done and continue to do for me. For showing me unwavering support and love in all of my foolhardy and spontaneous endeavors. Lastly I want to thank all of the kind strangers, some of them now close friends, who helped us out along the way. Whether it was a ride, a meal, a two-euro coin, a bed, a shower, or just a smile and a nice word—thank you for everything you've given me, both tangible and spiritual.

ABOUT THE AUTHOR

Tom Edwards lives in Los Angeles where he writes and records music, writes books, short stories, and screenplays, and works in marketing for the audio industry.

Info at
tomedwardsmusic.com

Short-form history lessons in a humorous, conversational tone at
historyfuckyeah.com

Two Bucks to Timbuktu reveals the tricks of the trade of impoverished vagabonds and savvy backpackers. You'll learn how to make money while traveling the world—anything from doing freelance work online, writing best-selling Kindle books, performing paid live web shows as a musician, or getting a job on a sled-dog team in Alaska or a luxury yacht in the Mediterranean.

TWO BUCKS TO
TIMBUKTU

A GUIDE TO EXTRAORDINARY ADVENTURES
WITH AN ORDINARY BANK ACCOUNT

TOM EDWARDS

HISTORY, FUCK YEAH:
Canadian Arctic Wreckspedition

A new take on historical storytelling, the HISTORY, FUCK YEAH series showcases the most incredible, little-known tales of human experience told with a dash of millennial humor.

HISTORYFUCKYEAH.COM